REF

BF   Tolor, Alexander.
698.8
.B4   Research and
T64   clinical
             applications of the
             Bender-Gestalt test

DATE			

Research and Clinical Applications of the Bender-Gestalt Test

Research and Clinical Applications of the Bender-Gestalt Test

By

ALEXANDER TOLOR, Ph.D.

Professor of Psychology
Fairfield University
Fairfield, Connecticut

and

GARY G. BRANNIGAN, Ph.D.

Associate Professor of Psychology
Director, Psychological Services Clinic
State University of New York College at Plattsburgh
Plattsburgh, New York

With a Foreword by

Max L. Hutt

Professor of Psychology, Retired
Ann Arbor, Michigan

CHARLES C THOMAS · PUBLISHER
Springfield · Illinois · U.S.A.

Published and Distributed Throughout the World by
CHARLES C THOMAS • PUBLISHER
Bannerstone House
301-327 East Lawrence Avenue, Springfield, Illinois, U.S.A.

© *1980, by* CHARLES C THOMAS • PUBLISHER
ISBN 0-398-04088-5
Library of Congress Catalog Card Number: 80-13563

With THOMAS BOOKS *careful attention is given to all details of
manufacturing and design. It is the Publisher's desire to present books
that are satisfactory as to their physical qualities and artistic possibilities
and appropriate for their particular use.* THOMAS BOOKS *will be true
to those laws of quality that assure a good name and good will.*

Library of Congress Cataloging in Publication Data
Tolor, Alexander.

Research and clinical applications of the
Bender-Gestalt test.

Bibliography: p.
Includes index.
1. Bender gestalt test. I. Brannigan, Gary G.,
joint author. II. Title. [DNLM: 1. Bender-Gestalt
test. WM145 T653r]
BF698.8.B4T64   616.89'075   80-13563
ISBN 0-398-04088-5

Printed in the United States of America
W-2

to the memory of my mother, Josephine—Tolor
and
to my wife Linda and
my sons Marc and Michael—Brannigan

FOREWORD

In this up-dated review of the research literature on the Bender-Gestalt "Test," Tolor and Brannigan have performed a herculean task. They have brought together, summarized, and evaluated the great many studies that have been published over more than fifteen of the past years, and have furnished us with carefully considered judgments concerning the clinical and research status of this instrument. Their organization of the presentation around several basic topics makes it possible to have access to the present and potential uses of this method in terms of the clinician's or researcher's particular interest. Their overall set of conclusions, presented in Chapter 12, provides a balanced status report of some present values and limitations of the method. Taken together with the previous volume on this subject by Tolor and Schulberg (1963) there is provided a compendium of most of the important work on this method that has been published.

I have taken the liberty of using quotation marks in the previous paragraph for the word "test," because unlike many other procedures in which stimuli, administration, and scoring have been standardized and stabilized, the Bender-Gestalt materials and their uses have shown a great proliferation of forms and procedures. Thus, it is not a single test, in the usual sense, but an adaptable procedure with a variety of sets of test materials, methods of administration, methods of scoring, normative data, and methods of interpretation. In short, it is still an evolving approach to methods of clinical assessment for diverse purposes. Although the virtues of this variegation may be extolled, it makes the task of comparing findings obtained under differing conditions difficult indeed. I believe that this is a sufficiently important consideration, that it is well to highlight this fact, and to keep it clearly in focus in evaluating the utility of the "test" for any given purpose.

As illustrative of the above, let us note that there are at

least three distinctly different sets of test materials. In addition to the more conventional sets of test cards furnished respectively by the American Orthopsychiatric Association (Bender) and by Grune and Stratton (Hutt), there is the set of materials developed by Canter (1966) in order to maximize the effects of brain dysfunction on perceptual-motoric performance. Similarly, there are many methods of administration including those originally proposed by Wertheimer (1923), by Bender (1938), by Hutt (1945, 1969, 1977), by Hutt and Briskin (1960), and by Snortum (1965) employing tachistoscopic methods, and by Hanvik and Andersen (1950) employing the recall method. And as to methods of scoring, which employ either or both *lists* of test factors and *scores* based on such factors, the number is almost legion. Thus, comparisons of studies employing these differing approaches cannot be made directly unless careful evaluation is given to the differences in such approaches. It would be wise to remember that there is no single "test" but only a number of differing test methods.

Keeping these considerations in mind, one can examine the findings reported on these differing methods and note several important conclusions. For one thing, as Tolor and Brannigan show, despite the decline in interest in diagnostic methods over the past two decades, or so, the Bender-Gestalt approach has retained (perhaps increased) its popularity among clinicians, is one of the most widely used clinical techniques in this country, and has generated an extensive and growing number of research studies. Moreover, by and large, these studies have demonstrated increasing degrees of sophistication with respect to theoretical underpinnings and appropriate research design. Thus, the values of this approach in clinical practice as well as in research studies can be judged with considerably more confidence than was the case only fifteen years ago.

Tolor and Brannigan demonstrate in their review of the findings that there is a "heightened interest in the projective applications" of this method, considerable evidence for evaluation of anxiety and depression and for evaluation of level of general adjustment, and the method is "a sensitive instrument in monitoring alcoholic recovery and in predicting response to

surgery for patients having significant psychological problems."
Other aspects of the use of the method in personality evaluation
and in projective personality evaluation still remain in question—
partly due to the inherent difficulties in designing effective
research in these areas. They report only one study in which
cultural influences in Bender-Gestalt productions have been
noted (Fanibanda, 1973), but there are several others bearing
on this topic, e.g. Butler, Coursey, and Gatz, 1976; Gilmore,
Chandy, and Anderson, 1975; Greene and Clark, 1973; Segall,
Campbell, and Herskovitz, 1966; Sonoda, 1973; and Taylor and
Thweatt, 1972. In general it has been found that cultural, social,
and ethnic factors play a remarkably small role in performance
of the usual test factors that are utilized in evaluating Bender-
Gestalt protocols. In general, there appears to be considerable
promise in the area of personality assessment, difficult as research
in this area may be.

Perhaps the area of greatest interest in the utilization of the
Bender-Gestalt approaches is that of assessment of organic brain
dysfunction. Once again it is found that (a) Bender-Gestalt
procedures are highly effective in *group differentiation* of organic
brain damaged patients from other groups (as was observed in
Tolor and Schulberg's 1963 publication); and, (b) Bender-
Gestalt procedures provide as good or better *group differentiation* of organics from other neuropsychiatric and non-neuro-
psychiatric cases than other psychological tests or neurological,
clinical methods. Clinical interpretation of test protocols seems
to offer additional advantages to such differentiation. The problem of *individual* diagnosis is another matter, although some
clinicians appear to have unusual skill in this area. The problem
of individual versus group differentiation is so critical that
separate comment will later be offered on this issue.

Other chapters of this work focus on research findings concerning Bender-Gestalt scores and configurations on children's,
retarded individuals' and psychotics' performance. The usefulness of perceptual-motoric performance in assessing problems
in these areas is demonstrated and possible limitations are presented. Unfortunately, no chapter deals with the Bender-Gestalt
performance of psychoneurotics, as was the case in the previous

presentation by Tolor and Schulberg. There are occasional references to work with neurotics scattered throughout the book as these relate to the chapter arrangements for other topics. I have stated elsewhere "The richness of HABGT records is no more evident than in the protocols and associations of neurotic individuals" (Hutt 1977). I concur fully with Paul Schilder (1938) who said: "gestalt patterns are experiences of an individual who has problems and . . . the final configuration of experience is not merely a problem of perception but a problem of personality." There is a rich lode in this area which remains to be explored systematically.

It should be said that in the area of personality assessment, as well as in more delimited areas, such as assessment for organic brain dysfunction, no single test has been shown to be entirely adequate for individual diagnosis. This conclusion is the basis for the admonition that the clinician utilize a battery of tests whose findings can be integrated with observational data and the individual life history. However valuable the Bender-Gestalt method may be in clinical work, individual assessment cannot rest on the findings of a particular Bender-Gestalt test score. Nor can it rest on the findings of several test scores. Instead the clinician will attempt to integrate the findings from several sources and exercise his best judgment in arriving at his conclusions. But the Bender-Gestalt procedures offer a relatively unique opportunity for detailed and verifiable assessment based on experimental-clinical investigation.

As I have indicated elsewhere (Hutt 1977), the experimental-clinical method (also called "testing-the-limits" and "micro-diagnosis") is an attempt to explore systematically: (a) the antecedents of the behavior manifested in test performance; and, (b) the conditions under which the behavior can be modified. I can only suggest briefly what this method entails. Suppose S performs Figure A on the Bender-Gestalt by drawing it rotated 90 degrees on the test paper. Is this performance indicative of perceptual rotation, and if so, is such rotation due to slow perceptual-motoric development, organic dysfunction, or some other factor? The mere performance involving rotation does not answer any of these questions. But experimental-clinical investigation can, in many cases. The first task of the clinician is to interview S, after he/she has completed the performance on the test, and to ascertain whether S realizes that he/she has rotated the figure. E may present the stimulus figure alongside S's drawing of it, and ask, in effect, "Are these two figures exactly alike?" If S does see a difference he/she may be asked what is different about them. It may be determined that S is clearly and easily able to perceive the difference. If so, inquiry may be made as to why S drew it as he/she did. It might be that it seemed simpler that way, or that it was a careless performance, or that S had an unusual "set" for the task. E could then ask S to draw the figure again exactly as it is on the test card. On the other hand, if S cannot perceive the difference (or perceive it clearly), or if S does but still has difficulty in reproducing the design accurately, various procedures can be attempted experimentally to test for the basis of the difficulty and/or for the ease or difficulty with which it can be corrected. For instance, S can be given a simpler figure with two tangential parts (such as either two circles or two squares) and asked to copy it. Or, S's problem may be due, for example, to either attentional or oppositional features of the personality, and S still persists in rotating his drawing. In such an instance, E may attempt to deal with the specific problem and determine whether performance can be altered and under what conditions. If the problem appears to be developmental rather than organic impairment, S should be able to do better with simpler perceptual-developmental tasks. If the problem involves organic impairment which interferes with performance of complex figure-ground tasks, figures which do not involve this complication should not show similar difficulties. In these and related ways, E attempts to tease out whether the difficulty is motivational, perceptual, intellectual, organic, and the like.

The major issue I have attempted to raise is that individual diagnosis is based only in part on research findings with groups, even with groups that have characteristics similar to the individual. This volume by Tolor and Brannigan has provided us with a masterful review of findings based on the Bender-Gestalt methods. The task of the clinician is to utilize these data so as to make more effective use of the instrument in those cases in which it is applicable. Individual diagnosis, whether involving the integration of findings from a number of tests and personal history, or whether based on the experimental-clinical model of study, can then be more effective. Similarly, the researcher can use the findings and reviews of previous studies to evolve more adequate theoretical formulations for his/her research and design more effective studies of underlying issues. Both groups of workers can widen their perspective by assimilating the data presented in this volume and can, hopefully, improve their effectiveness as a consequence. The research that has been reported suggests that these trends are already operative.

Max L. Hutt

REFERENCES

Bender, L.A. *Visual Motor Gestalt Test and Its Clinical Use*. American Orthopsychiatric Association Research Monograph, No. 3, New York: American Orthopsychiatric Association, 1938.

Butler, O.T., Coursey, R.D., & Gatz, M. Comparison for the Bender Gestalt Test for both black and white brain-damaged patients using two scoring systems. *Journal of Consulting and Clinical Psychology*, 1976, 2, 280-285.

Canter, A. A background interference procedure to increase sensitivity of the Bender-Gestalt Test to organic disorder. *Journal of Consulting Psychology*, 1966, 30, 91-97.

Fanibanda, D.K. Cultural influence on Hutt's adaptation of the Bender-Gestalt: A pilot study. *Journal of Personality Assessment*, 1973, 37, 531-536.

Gilmore, G., Chandy, J., & Anderson, T. The Bender-Gestalt and the Mexican-American student: A report. *Psychology in the Schools*, 1975, 12, 172-175.

Greene, R., & Clark, F.K. Predicting reading readiness with the Bender-Gestalt Test in minority students. Unpublished findings, 1973.

Hanvik, L.J., & Andersen, A.L. The effect of focal brain lesions on recall and on the production of rotations in the Bender-Gestalt Test. *Journal of Consulting Psychology*, 1950, 14, 197-198.

Hutt, M.L. *A Tentative Guide for the Administration and Interpretation of the Bender-Gestalt Test*. U.S. Army, Adjutant General's School, (Restricted), 1945.

Hutt, M.L. *The Hutt Adaptation of the Bender-Gestalt Test*, 2nd ed. New York: Grune & Stratton, 1969.

Hutt, M.L. *The Hutt Adaptation of the Bender-Gestalt Test*, 3rd ed. New York: Grune & Stratton, 1977.

Hutt, M.L., & Briskin, G.J. *The Hutt Adaptation of the Bender-Gestalt Test*. New York: Grune & Stratton, 1960.

Schilder, P. Preface. In Bender, L. A. *A Visual Motor Gestalt Test and Its Clinical Use*. American Orthopsychiatric Association Monograph, No. 3, New York: American Orthopsychiatric Association, 1938.

Segall, M.H., Campbell, D.T., & Herskovitz, M.J. *The Influence of Culture on Visual Perception*. Indianapolis: Bobbs Merrill, 1966.

Snortum, J.R. Performance of different diagnostic groups on the tachistoscopic and copy phases of the Bender-Gestalt. *Journal of Consulting Psychology*, 1965, *4*, 345-351.

Sonoda, T. The Bender Gestalt Test for young children: A review of verification studies made on the Koppitz scoring system. *Kumamoto Shodai Ronshu, Shodai Ronshu*, 1973, *37*, 1-9.

Taylor, H.D., & Thweatt, R.C. Cross-cultural developmental performance of Navajo children on the Bender-Gestalt Test. *Perceptual and Motor Skills*, 1972, *35*, 307-309.

Tolor, A., & Schulberg, H. C. *An Evaluation of the Bender-Gestalt Test*. Springfield, Ill.: Charles C Thomas, 1963.

Wertheimer, M. Studies in the theory of Gestalt psychology. *Psychologische Forschung*, 1923, *4*, 301-350.

PREFACE

A GREAT VARIETY OF psychological tests of every description and type, encompassing a wide range of human functions, have been developed in the relatively short history of the science and profession of clinical psychology. Despite the remarkable proliferation of such assessment techniques, only a comparatively small number has withstood the test of time. The more recent general decline in diagnostic training and in research in the area of diagnosis notwithstanding, the Bender-Gestalt Test is still one of the few instruments that continues, along with the Wechsler Scales, the Projective Drawings, and the Rorschach Inkblot Test, to enjoy a high degree of popularity among clinicians. Furthermore, in spite of the criticism and skepticism about testing, the use of tests in clinical and school settings goes on much as it did before.

In view of the facts that (1) the Bender-Gestalt Test retains sufficient vitality to be one of the most commonly employed assessment techniques in the entire spectrum of clinical diagnostic tools, and (2) the last two comprehensive critical reviews of this instrument were published more than fifteen years ago, it seems appropriate now to reassess the scientific status of this instrument with respect to the multitude of uses to which it has been put. Therefore, the most general and broadest objective of this book will be to update the available information on the Bender-Gestalt Test by carefully examining the literature that has appeared since 1962, i.e. the period not covered by the previous reviews.

As is true when anything of value is accomplished, there are many people behind the scenes who help to make it happen. We would first like to express our gratitude to our respective institutions, Fairfield University and the State University of New York, College at Plattsburgh, not only for providing our home bases, so to speak, in a physical sense, but also for fostering scholarly climates. These universities represent traditions of scholarship blended with the applications of knowledge for the good of society.

We would be remiss if we did not publicly recognize the help of a number of students, both undergraduate and graduate, who aided us with the search of the literature and in many other ways. Some of these students, especially our clinical and school psychology graduate students, made contributions to this book in ways in which they were probably unaware, i.e. by raising provocative questions and issues that forced us to organize our thoughts more clearly.

A debt of gratitude is extended to the secretaries who typed different portions of this manuscript. Among these dedicated individuals are Mrs. Judy Dashnaw, Mrs. Olga Yacco, Mrs. Mary Losee, Ms. Theresa Wolf, Ms. Nancy Dodge, Mrs. Kathy Schor, and Ms. Barbara Holl.

Our families were always supportive, understanding, and patient in our pursuit of this project. Appreciation for the sacrifices they made can hardly be conveyed in a few words.

Finally, we wish to pay tribute to Dr. Lauretta Bender, without whose creativity, clinical expertise, and research wisdom this book would never have seen the light of day.

CONTENTS

Research and Clinical Applications of the Bender-Gestalt Test

CHAPTER 1

INTRODUCTION

Over the many years since 1938 when Dr. Lauretta Bender first introduced her method to the professional community, this procedure, which is now commonly known as the *Visual-Motor Gestalt Test,* or, more simply, as the *Bender-Gestalt Test,* has captured the interest of countless psychologists and psychiatrists dealing with various applied and theoretical issues. The method is based on the theory and principles of Gestalt psychology and on the extensive clinical experience of its originator, which can be traced back to the year 1929. This method has found a favorable reception, particularly in the areas of clinical and school psychology.

It is well known that at least in some quarters a general decline in interest has occurred in, and in the role assigned to, the assessment function. Illustrative of this phenomenon is Michel's (1968) position that there is little consistency in personality dimensions across situations and over time; thus, he argues that traditional assessment procedures have limited value. Tolor (1973), in analyzing the content of five major psychological journals that are publication outlets for clinical psychologists, found a definite decline over a twenty-year span in the percentage of diagnostically oriented publications.

Some of the disenchantment with clinical testing in general and projective instruments in particular derived from the accumulation of negative research findings during the forties and fifties. However, as Blatt (1978) indicated, many of these earlier studies suffered from serious methodological limitations, including a disregard for the configurational approach to the interpretation of test data; the study of variables in isolation; the use of imprecise and unreliable criteria, such as diagnostic classifications;

3

and the failure to distinguish levels of discourse, time span, and an open or closed nature of the system in which behavioral predictions were to be made. Within the context of the Rorschach, but equally applicable to other measures, Blatt asserts that slow but steady progress has been made to examine the research findings when these psychological methods are treated less as "tests" and more as techniques or procedures.

In addition to the more technical problems pertaining to the use and abuse of tests, other social and political issues have been raised regarding the desirability of testing. For example, in recent years many tests have been charged with racial, ethnic, or sexual biases. The labeling process, which sometimes follows from testing, has been purported to be damaging to individuals. So, too, tests have been alleged to be irrelevant to the needs of the patient, especially to the therapeutic enterprise.

Despite some serious questions that have been raised about the value of the testing function, the Bender-Gestalt Test continues to enjoy great popularity as evidenced by the large number of published studies that revolve around this instrument and its widespread and persistent use as a diagnostic tool. It has also been ranked highly in a number of surveys.

Turning to some of the surveys that indicate very positive attitudes towards the Bender-Gestalt Test, Korner (1962) compared the relative frequency of various tests used in 1950 and in 1958 by the Division of Psychology in the Department of Psychiatry at the University of Utah College of Medicine. With adults, the Bender-Gestalt Test ranked sixth in order of usage in 1950 and fourth in 1958. With respect to children, the test moved from fourth position in frequency of use in 1950 to third in 1958, following the *Draw-A-Person Test* and the *WISC*, and ahead of the *Rorschach*.

Mills (1965) found the Bender-Gestalt Test to be the fourth most frequently used projective test, among 21 such measures, for research. This finding was based on studies appearing between 1947 and 1964 in the *Journal of Projective Techniques and Personality Assessment*. Extending this type of survey to ten other journals, encompassing the period between 1947 and 1965, Crenshaw, Bohn, Hoffman, Matthews, and Offenbach (1968) found that Bender's test was the fifth most frequently employed projective method for research. They also noted an increased use of the Bender for research over the years.

Patterning a new survey closely after the one conducted previously by Sundberg (1961) of agencies and hospitals throughout the country, Silverstein (1963) inquired as to which psychological tests were most used in clinical work with the mentally retarded. Based on a national survey of state institutions, Silverstein found that the Bender-Gestalt Test ranked fourth among 49 tests, regardless of which of three measures of usage are employed—namely, the *Total Mentions* rank (the number of respondents who mentioned the tests), the *Weighted Score* rank (which takes into account ratings of frequency of use), and the *Frequent Usage Index* (a purer measure of usage which eliminates from consideration those tests used only occasionally). Silverstein's results were very similar to Sundberg's (1961) in that the Bender-Gestalt Test was also the third or fourth most frequently used measure, depending on the specific criterion, in Sundberg's earlier study.

Further support for the contention that the Bender-Gestalt Test enjoys a persistent vitality and durability as a diagnostic tool is based on Lubin, Wallis, and Paine's (1971) survey of psychological test usage in the United States. This study shows that the Bender-Gestalt Test has maintained or increased its popularity over time. We should also mention Lapointe's (1974) survey of the use of psychological tests by psychologists in Ontario, Canada. In response to the question, "Give a list of the five tests you use most frequently in your work," 260 respondents mentioned the Bender-Gestalt Test as the most frequently used projective personality test. Of all the various tests cited, only the two intelligence tests, the WISC and the *WAIS* (or *Wechsler-Bellevue*), exceeded the Bender-Gestalt Test in frequency of reference.

In a 1974 survey, Brown and McGuire (1976) found that in general the ten most used tests had not undergone any major change over the last fifteen years and that the Bender-Gestalt ranked second in order.

In a major survey of 500 clinical psychologists, which inquired of their use and opinions of psychological tests, Wade and Baker (1977) recently found that 72 percent of all respondents reported using test results at some stage of the treatment process. The respondents seemed to rely on clinical judgment very extensively in the testing, both for test interpretation and for use of test results. The psychologists considered testing more characteristically as an insightful diagnostic process than an objective technical skill. When asked which tests they would recommend that clinical psychology students master, the respondents mentioned the *Rorschach, TAT, WAIS, MMPI,* and the *Bender-Gestalt Test,* in that order, as the five most important tests. To be more specific, of those who used projective tests frequently, 57 percent recommended the use of the Bender-Gestalt Test, and of those who used objective tests frequently, 44 percent recommended that students learn the Bender-Gestalt Test (Wade, Baker, Morton, and Baker 1978). Therefore, this survey showed that clinical psychologists generally continue to devote substantial time to psychological testing despite the many criticisms leveled at the assessment function and the rather negative reactions to projective techniques by those at the university level who train graduate students in clinical psychology (Thelen and Ewing 1970; Shemberg and Keeley 1970). Moreover, this survey reaffirmed the importance assigned to the Bender-Gestalt Test by clinical psychologists. It is also noteworthy that Levy and Fox (1975) found that 90 percent of those who employ clinical psychologists expected them to be test proficient, and that 84 percent require them to have skills in using projective tests.

The status of the Bender-Gestalt Test, as it existed around 1962, has been well publicized in two publications, i.e. Billingslea's (1963) and Tolor and Schulberg's (1963). Both of these reviews reached essentially the same general conclusions. In their comprehensive review of the then extant literature, consisting of some 300 publications, Tolor and Schulberg (1963) were especially struck by the low level of conceptualizations and numerous methodological inadequacies of most Bender-Gestalt research, which made generalizations about the instrument extremely difficult. Their book addressed such issues as the relative validity of the test for different purposes, the differential value of the various scoring systems, the evidence for assigning clinical interpretations to specific test signs or constellations of test features, and related aspects of the test. Many of these issues will be critically examined once more, this time focusing on published studies appearing during the past 15-year period.

Each new study was examined with respect to the major issue addressed by the author(s); and the issue so identified, in large part, determined the placement of the study within one of the several organizing categories of our review. To be sure, some of the decisions as to the inclusion of a study within one or another chapter may have been somewhat arbitrary, but in order to avoid unnecessary repetition, such decisions had to be made. Next, the specific study was carefully analyzed in terms of methodological considerations, the specific populations employed, whether the conclusions appeared warranted by the data, the nature of the contributions made, and the degree to which, and the manner in which, the study in question may be integrated with others.

Beyond this, the aim was to specify whether there is now more attention devoted to underlying processes, whether previously identified research deficiencies have been corrected, to determine possible changes in emphases or research thrusts, new uses of the Bender-Gestalt in keeping with changing views of the role of diagnosis, whether certain previous uses have been discontinued, and whether further definitive conclusions concerning the instrument's validity and reliability may be drawn. After all, the validity and reliability of test measures are the two most critical issues facing the diagnostician.

In the assessment area there are three major pitfalls to be avoided. First is the risk of an excessive preoccupation with one instrument as distinguished from the reliance on many modes for assessment. Second is the failure to take into account the complex person-situation interaction, which includes, of course, the role of the examiner. The third is the overlooking of areas of respondent competencies while stressing areas of pathology. This review will endeavor to be sensitive to these pitfalls.

Also, we will strive to keep in mind the comments made by Bender in the Foreword to the Tolor and Schulberg (1963) book. She attributed the limited empirical validation success of the Bender to four major factors: (a) Insufficient attention has been paid to the theory underlying the test; (b) The test has been used in areas other than the developmental when an adequate rationale for such usage was lacking; (c) The test was being fragmented into elements which were then translated into a small number of scores that lacked reference to the test's rationale; and (d) Invalid criteria were sometimes used for validation studies.

The present review, which encompasses the time period between 1962 and 1978, and covers the English language Bender-Gestalt literature only, will assume at least some degree of familiarity with the nature of the test, especially the nine stimulus designs that are to be copied and the most commonly used modes of administration and interpretation. For those readers who are unfamiliar with these basic aspects of the test, it is suggested that you refer to the original source literature.

The Bender-Gestalt Test has been the object of extensive research, providing an accumulated base of knowledge that is quite considerable. In fact, it is probably one of the most researched instruments in general use by psychologists.

The authors, both being practicing clinicians and researchers with a broad range of experience with the Bender-Gestalt Test in both capacities, have found the Bender-Gestalt Test's simplicity in administration to result in unwarranted enthusiasm and in wild interpretive speculations. Its appeal is understandable, and it has indeed been demonstrated that it has validity for certain problems under specified conditions. Our task will be to refine further understanding of the test's usefulness for specific problems, based on current empirical evidence. We will look with interest at whether the test now meets more closely the standards usually required of test instruments in general, and whether studies of the *processes* involved in functioning on this test (a point made by Tuddenham (1965) as quoted in the *Sixth Mental Measurement Yearbook*) have finally been undertaken. These issues will be pursued in the pages that follow.

An additional feature of this volume is the illustration of the interpretive process, based on several Bender-Gestalt Test protocols, which had been specifically selected to portray different kinds of psychodiagnostic problems in both children and adults. It is our hope that clinical and school psychologists will find these case presentations of interest, and that they will provide readers with the opportunity to compare their own interpretive approach with ours.

CHAPTER 2

VARIATIONS IN ADMINISTRATION

Several variants in the Bender-Gestalt Test administration have been reported in the literature during the last 16 years. For example, Spraings (1966) developed a multiple-choice version of the Bender-Gestalt Test to aid the examiner in making diagnostic decisions. *The Spraings Multiple-Choice Bender-Gestalt* (SMCBG) test requires the individual to inspect each Bender card and then to select the one figure from among 12 alternatives that best matches the original design. The S points to the desired choice in each case. The overall score is based on the total number of correct selections made.

Friedman, Wakefield, Sasek, and Schroeder (1977) modified the Spraings' method by using composite ratings reflecting the degree of similarity or dissimilarity of each of the alternatives in relation to the original figures. This mode of administration was applied to 39 retarded adults and yielded a higher correlation ($r = .72$) with the regular administration of the Bender-Gestalt Test, as scored by Koppitz's (1964) method, than did Spraings' dichotomous technique ($r = .53$). However, it is not made clear by the authors what, if anything, constitutes the superiority of this mode of administration over the conventional method.

In an attempt to increase the objectivity in scoring the Bender-Gestalt Test, Labentz, Linkenhoker, and Aaron (1976) developed a multiple-choice recognition format consisting of 12 variations of four attributes for each of the nine figures. The transformations were based on Gibson, Gibson, Pick, and Osser's (1962) developmental research on the discrimination of letter-like forms. The four transformations were: line to curve, rotation, perspective, and topological (close break).

Correlations between the recognition task and Koppitz's *Developmental Bender Score* in seven groups of children, ranging from preschool ($\overline{X}$ age = 3.5 years) to upper primary grades ($\overline{X}$ age = 9.4 years) were moderate to high and statistically significant for all the age-groups except one, the eight-year-olds. Again, however, this procedure does not appear to have any advantage over the conventional method of administering the Bender.

Allen and Frank (1963) reasoned that the differences between the field upon which the S views the Bender designs, and the field upon which the S is asked to reproduce the designs, could in itself represent an important determinant of the accuracy of the productions. In the event that differences in fields influence performance, the psychodynamic and other interpretive factors may tend to be confounded. When Ss, 39 boys and girls (mean age, eight years, five months; mean IQ, 121), were required to copy the designs on paper identical in size, shape, and axial orientation to that of the stimulus material, with each design drawn on separate four by six inch sheets of paper, it was found that all Ss were better able to approximate the model design in size than when the standard mode of administration was used. The authors concluded that the conventional administration tends to introduce a potential for significant size inaccuracy.

Consistent with this finding is the work of Allen (1968a), and Hasazi, Allen, and Wohlford (1971), with mentally retarded Ss. Subjects administered the Bender in the standard fashion made poorer quality reproductions, as judged by the *Keogh and Smith* (1961) *Scoring System* (Allen 1968a), and produced more rotation, perseveration, and fragmentation errors (Hasazi, Allen, and Wohlford 1971) in comparison to those Ss in the experimental mode of administration. The authors concluded that while some information may be lost, e.g. the relationship of the designs to each other on one page, when this procedure is utilized, it may provide a more *valid* estimate of the individual's psychomotor functioning.

Weiss (1971c) also studied the effects of paper position on the reproduction of the Bender designs. Subjects (seventh graders) who were given the paper in the standard vertical position used considerably more space than those given the paper in the horizontal position.

Further support for the contention that some Bender performance variables, which often are assigned clinical significance, may indeed be affected by different modes of administration (i.e. by external cues) derives from the work of Gravitz and Handler (1968). The study involved varying instructions for "specificity," that is, offering directions that either "some cards" or "nine cards" were to be presented, and for the "positional" factor, that is, either leaving the cards on the table at all times or leaving only the one card to be copied on the table. It had been anticipated that eight organizational variables, patterned after those described by Hutt and Briskin (1960), would change with differences in administration whereas four "control" variables, which allegedly are reflective of more severe perceptual distortion or breakdown in reality testing, would not be affected by modifying the external cues. The results supported the hypothesis since four of the organizational variables, namely, sequence, number of pages used, total area encompassed by the figures themselves, and mean horizontal and vertical space between figures were indeed significantly affected by variations in the mode of administration.

In an attempt to focus on perceptual processes in design reproduction while reducing or eliminating manual dexterity, coordination, hand pressure, and other motor functions, Wagner and Schaff (1968) developed a new mode of administration, the *Design Reproduction Test* (DRT). S is requested to reproduce geometric designs presented on cards by moving plastic strips which move along concealed tracks in a specially designed board having an aperture. Error scores were computed based on the deviations from specific points which corresponded to perfect reproductions. This technique seemed to be somewhat successful in differentiating various types of pathologies.

Rosenberg and Rosenberg (1965) addressed the question as to whether the tachistoscopic presentation of the Bender cards (each card shown for five seconds and then removed) prior to the regular administration has any effect on the validity of the regular presentation. It was found that patients drawn from psychiatric and neurological wards could be differentiated from normal Ss, using the *Hutt and Briskin* (1960) *Scoring System,* when the regular, then tachistoscopic, then memory sequence is used ($F = 26.42$, $p < .01$), but not when the tachistoscopic, then regular, and then memory sequence is followed. Therefore, the tachistoscopic presentation appears to lower substantially the discriminatory power of the copy mode of administration, arguing against its use for such purposes.

Also focusing on the relative effects of tachistoscopic versus standard copying procedures in administering the Bender designs, Snortum (1965) investigated the validity of the *Pascal and Suttell* (1951) *Scoring System* for discriminating patients with a functional disturbance from those with organic brain pathology. Groups of twenty-five neurotic, twenty-five alcoholic, twenty-five organic, and twenty-five normal Ss, all males, were administered the Bender figures, first by the tachistoscopic method and then by the conventional copy method. Both methods of administration significantly discriminated among diagnostic groups ($F = 5.54$ and $F = 4.26$, respectively, each significant beyond the .01 level).

On the copy administration, the normal controls were significantly different from each of the three diagnostic groups at the .01 level, but the diagnostic groups did not perform significantly differently from each other.

Using the tachistoscopic method, the controls were found to be significantly different from the alcoholics at the .01 level and from the organics at the .001 level, but they were not significantly different from the neurotics. However, neurotics and organics could be successfully differentiated with the tachistoscopic approach ($p = .02$).

Snortum interpreted these results as supporting his belief that the tachistoscopic phase is a more difficult task than the copy phase, perhaps because it requires increased attentiveness, rapid learning, and short-term retention in addition to the visual-motor functions called for on the copy method. However, the presumed greater complexity of the tachistoscopic approach apparently did not produce greater disruptive effects on neurotics than on normals. The tachistoscopic task improves slightly the ability to discriminate between organics and normals in comparison to the standard method of administration.

Bernstein (1963) found that schizophrenics as compared to nonschizophrenics did more poorly on the Bender, when scored by the Pascal-Suttell system, after being shown each figure for five seconds and then asked to reproduce it. The schizophrenics did more poorly also under standard conditions. The schizophrenic deficit, however, was not significantly greater on the five-second exposure variant as compared to the usual administration.

Taken in combination, the studies by Rosenberg and Rosenberg (1965), Snortum (1965), and Bernstein (1963) suggest that whether the tachistoscopic method of administration does or does not enhance diagnostic accuracy may very well be a function of the specific diagnostic differentiation that needs to be made. Additional research related to this issue is very much needed because of some of the seemingly inconsistent findings reported in the literature.

Verma (1974) attempted to determine whether presenting the drawing paper vertically will affect the frequency of "organic signs" obtained on the Bender-Gestalt Test. The paper on which the designs were to be drawn was positioned vertically for fifty organic patients and horizontally for forty-four patients. There were also 255 nonorganic psychiatric outpatients with 119 being presented the paper vertically and 136 getting the paper horizontally. Changes in orientation of the drawing paper did not affect the incidence of organic indicators for the organic patients, but it did produce significant changes on a number of indicators frequently associated with organicity for nonorganic patients. More specifically, there were significantly greater percentages of rotations, perseverations, separation of lines, and distortions under the condition of vertical paper placement as compared with the horizontal-placement-of-paper condition. The stability of obtained "organic signs" for the organic group, regardless of field orientation, is noteworthy as is the susceptibility of the functionally disturbed patients to these changes in mode of administration.

Another variation in method of administration was designed

by Ko (1972) who required Ss to give detailed oral descriptions of each of the first five Bender figures. The initial request for descriptions was followed by further encouragements that additional descriptions be offered. Ko presents correlations between what he labels the *Bender-Gestalt Visual-Verbal* (BGVV) and various WAIS scores on the one hand, and between the conventional Bender-Gestalt Test—with scoring conforming to a method that he previously devised—and the same WAIS scores, on the other hand. The data reveal higher correlations with intelligence for the new version of the Bender than for the conventional method of administration, but there is no information provided as to whether the difference is statistically significant. Ko asserted that his method is superior for its ability to extract a wealth of information about S's ability to sustain attention and relevant personality dynamics.

The Ko mode of administration, restricting itself to a "description" of the designs, seems to be far more limited in usefulness for personality evaluation than the free-association approach used by Sucek and Klopfer (1952), Tolor (1957), and others.

Bruck (1962) requested Ss to change the appearance of the designs in order to make them "into a picture of something." The Ss were then asked to write what they had made. Bruck reports that these instructions for eliciting elaborations and associations resulted in more meaningful clinical material when applied to hospitalized patients than did Hutt's (1945) instructions to the effect that Ss make the original designs more pleasing aesthetically.

Arguing that organic mental retardates would be cerebrally deficient in coordinating perceptual experiences with motor behavior and therefore less likely to profit from learning, whereas nonorganic retardates would not have such a basic deficiency and therefore would be likely to improve with repetition, Pacella (1965) applied a modified version of the Bender-Gestalt Test providing for three successive administrations. He hypothesized that organically impaired mental retardates could be differentiated from nonorganic mental retardates on the third but not on the initial trial. This refined method of administration did indeed succeed in achieving significant group differences on the third but not on the first two trials of the Bender, supporting the hypothesis.

A comparison by Freed (1964) of hospitalized schizophrenic patient performance on group-administered Benders, when figures are presented via 35 mm slides, with performance based on individually administered Bender-Gestalt figures to another group of schizophrenics, which may or may not have been comparable in intelligence, indicated a significantly greater frequency of rotations for individual administration, X^2 (1) = 8.27, $p < .01$. Freed explained the reduction in rotations under the group-administered condition on the basis of certain orientational cues, such as viewing the designs on an upright screen having "top" and "bottom" references and the projected slides being bounded by a darker area on the screen.

In a follow-up study, Freed and Hastings (1965) varied orientational cues by using the following conditions: Bender-Gestalt cards placed parallel to the top of the paper; the use of horizontally-oriented graph paper held in a fixed position with the cards framed in an apparatus and presented in an upright position; and the use of vertically-oriented graph paper held in fixed position with the Bender cards framed in an apparatus and presented in an upright position. Groups of newly admitted patients and patients ready to be discharged were used for the conditions, and the groups varied in diagnostic representation. Unfortunately, the effects of patient status, patient diagnoses, and method of administration were not systematically analyzed. The author simply concluded that additional orientational stimuli "peculiar to the modes of administration" produced the 2 percent (i.e. fewer than previously reported) rotations under all these conditions combined.

Of all the published innovations over the past sixteen years pertaining to the administration of the Bender-Gestalt Test it is likely that none even approaches in scope and potential value the method introduced by Canter (1966, 1968). The *Canter Background Interference Procedure* (BIP) is intended to be used as an aid in the diagnosis of organic impairment. It requires the S to draw the Bender figures first on a blank sheet of paper and

then on specially designed paper on which various curved intersecting lines are printed. Scoring on the BIP is based on a
comparison of the quality of the drawings made without and
with background interference. Each S, therefore, serves as his
own control. A set of rules is provided for making diagnostic
decisions.

Research (Canter 1968) has demonstrated more than satisfactory inter-scorer reliabilities on the BIP. It has also been
shown (Yulis 1969) that the BIP D-scores, which refer to the
difference between the error scores on both sets of drawings,
are not significantly related to intelligence even though for both
organic and normal groups there was a significant correlation
between error scores based on the standard administration and
intelligence. The finding of independence between BIP D-scores
and IQ assumes considerable importance in view of Tolor and
Schulberg's (1963) observation that most commonly used scoring systems for the Bender-Gestalt Test do correlate with
intelligence.

The BIP is effective in detecting organic dysfunctioning
(Canter 1966; Song and Song 1969). Yulis (1970) hypothesized
that differences in Bender performance under BIP conditions
compared with the conventional administration are due to
varying disruptive effects in perceptual-motor functioning of
increased drive or arousal states and to the presence or absence
of organic brain pathology. As predicted, Yulis found that when
drive was increased experimentally, i.e. from simple repeat
administration of the Bender figures to a condition in which
the Bender was administered followed by Canter's BIP, the test
performance of normals improved. When drive was further increased by following the repeat administration condition with
the BIP procedure administered, either under threat of electric
shock or finally with the actual administration of a single shock,
there was progressive deterioration in Bender test performance
for normal Ss. Thus, for normals, a U-shaped distribution of
scores was obtained.

Brain-damaged patients, on the other hand, as anticipated,
exhibited a progressive deterioration in Bender performance as
drive increased even from simple repeat administration of the

Bender-Gestalt Test to the condition involving the administration of the Bender followed by the Canter BIP.

Canter and Straumanis (1969) found the BIP to be highly successful in differentiating senile patients having chronic brain syndromes from healthy elderly individuals. The BIP seemed to be quite sensitive to the degree of organic pathology associated with senility.

When long-term hospitalized schizophrenics (mean, 12.1 years), short-term hospitalized schizophrenics (mean, 1.5 years), nonschizophrenics, nonorganic psychiatric patients, and organic psychiatric patients were compared on the BIP, Canter (1971) found that both short-term and long-term hospitalized schizophrenics, compared to organic patients, generally failed to reveal a significant loss of functioning on BIP administration. While none of the organic patients revealed significant BIP *improvement*, 29 percent of the long-term schizophrenics and 53 percent of the short-term schizophrenics actually improved on the BIP mode of Bender administration. On the basis of these findings, Canter concluded that schizophrenics tend to respond more favorably to mild arousal than do organics.

Nemec (1978) investigated the effects of verbal and perceptual background interference on patients with lesions in either the right or the left hemisphere. The naming of animals within 30 seconds while *E* named tools was the measure of verbal performance under the verbal interference condition, and Canter's BIP was the measure of perceptual performance under the perceptual interference condition. Of pertinence here is the finding of greatest perceptual interference effect in the right brain-damaged group. In other words, perceptual interference on the Bender did not cause a significant decrement in the performance of controls, but it did have a significant effect on both left and right brain-damaged groups, with significantly greater impairment occurring in the right-hemisphere damaged group than the left-hemisphere damaged group.

While the Canter BIP method appears to be an extremely useful tool, a cautionary note needs to be introduced because there is some evidence (West, Hill, and Robins 1977) that certain demographic variables, such as ethnicity and age, may account for some of the test variance. Furthermore, the validity of this technique with children—especially those under eight years of age—is questionable (Adams and Canter, 1969), and inconsistent results have been reported in attempts to diagnose brain damage in older children (Adams 1970; Adams, Hayden, and Canter 1974; Adams, Kenny, and Canter 1973; Kenny 1971). These issues require further research attention.

Sabatino and Ysseldyke (1972) modified the method of presenting the Bender stimuli by introducing background interference. Two background interference procedures were utilized: (1) the Bender design with an embedded meaningless background (extraneous lines and dots), and (2) a photographic negative of the standard stimulus cards with the most crucial portion of each design obscured.

Although the Ss (readers and nonreaders) in this study did not differ significantly on either the standard or memory administration of the Bender, significant decreases in the performance of nonreaders were found in both background interference conditions. Apparently the complexity of these visual-motor tasks provided the basis for increased discrimination between readers and nonreaders. Unfortunately, there have been no follow-up studies reported.

GROUP ADMINISTRATION

As previously noted (Koppitz 1975b), the group administration of the Bender has been well established. Since the early attempts at group administering the Bender (Keogh and Smith 1961), this technique has been widely employed without any significant loss in reliability, e.g. Becker and Sabatino 1971; Caskey and Larson 1977; Howard 1970; Jacobs 1971; McCarthy 1975; Ruckhaber 1964; and Singh 1965.

Although group administration results in the loss of considerable "clinical" value (the examiner cannot directly observe the child's performance on the task) the substantial savings in administration time increases the utility of the Bender for large-scale screening programs, as well as for research purposes.

Summary

In summary, the research reviewed attests to the incredible ingenuity of psychologists who continue to develop modifications in the administration of the Bender-Gestalt Test to increase its clinical usefulness and to explicate the role of various field cues in accounting for individual differences in performance. Those studies which have introduced administration changes in order to investigate the processes underlying pathological functioning on the Bender-Gestalt Test, such as the work of Pacella (1965), Yulis (1970), Canter (1971), and Nemec (1978) are particularly valuable in that they advance our state of knowledge from the more descriptive level to an elucidation of the visual-motor functions that are involved. On the other hand, the studies that report only minor changes in administration without any evidence of the superiority of the variation over the standard mode of administration evoke a more critical evaluation since they simply lead to a proliferation of methods in the absence of refinement in clinical discrimination or basic understanding of process.

CHAPTER 3

FACTORS INFLUENCING BENDER
PERFORMANCE IN CHILDREN

PERCEPTUAL-MOTOR PROCESSES

ALTHOUGH LAURETTA BENDER (1938) presented a detailed set of Gestalt principles, which could possibly underlie a S's attempt at reproducing the Bender designs, we were unable to find research on these perceptual-motor processes. Nevertheless, Bender (1967, 1970) reiterated, in summary form, her earlier statements concerning the Bender-Gestalt Test. She stated:

> Certain principles determine the maturation of visual motor perception in children:
> 1. Vortical movement, biologically determined in the optic field, gives rise to the most primitive visually perceived forms, such as circles and loops.
> 2. Movement, always present, is directional—clockwise or counter-clockwise—or on a horizontal plane—dextrad or sinistrad.
> 3. By controlling or inhibiting this action-pattern, globes, circles, and arcs are constructed.
> 4. This organizes the visual field into foreground and background.
> 5. Boundaries between objects are delineated.
> 6. Verticalization arises concurrent with body-image maturation as the postural model shifts in the infant from the prone to the upright position.
> 7. Crossed lines, diagonal or slanting relations, and angle formations are a later level of maturation, usually occurring at about six to eight years of age.
> The niceties of all of these relations are often not completed, at least in combination, until the age of 11 years. However, at six to eight years the main principles have matured (Bender 1970, p. 30).

Although Bender (1967, 1970) presented several case studies of normally functioning children, as well as children with be-

21

havioral disorders and learning disabilities, and schizophrenia, there has been a lack of systematic experimentation on her postulates concerning the Bender-Gestalt Test. It is clear that research is still needed to determine the viability of the perceptual principles underlying the Bender-Gestalt Test.

EFFECTS OF DEVELOPMENT

Although the Bender has been and continues to be used in diverse ways, one should not lose sight of the fact that it is "a maturational test of performance in the visual-motor gestalt-function" between the ages of four and 11 (Bender 1938, p. 113). Over the past 16 years there has been considerable research on the effects of development upon Bender functioning.

Koppitz (1964, 1975b) has refined her *Developmental Scoring System* (Koppitz 1960) which consists of 30 items primarily based on four error types: distortion, integration, rotation, and perseveration. Although this system has been widely accepted, there are several points that are worth noting:

1. The scoring system was designed to assess the level of maturity in visual-motor perception of children ages five to 10.
2. Through the younger age levels, the *Developmental Bender* performance undergoes rapid change, especially during the ages of five through seven (Koppitz 1964, 1975b; Smith and Keogh 1963; Snyder and Snyder 1974). Keogh (1969) categorized these changes in the following areas:
   a. improved motor control and accuracy
   b. spatial direction and orientation
   c. organization and integration of details
   d. ability to reproduce more complex relationships
3. The scoring system has little utility for children below five years of age (Plenk and Jones 1967).
4. The Developmental Bender Score has less discriminating power between the ages of eight and eleven.
5. After age ten, only children with marked immaturity or

malfunction in visual-motor perception will show meaningful deviations on the Bender test.

6. Various characteristics of performance have been shown to vary in occurrence with age (Smith and Keogh 1963; Keogh 1968). Primitization and perseveration are very common at age five and remain relatively so even for the older age groups. Integration errors were also shown to be common for five-year-olds, but this type of error was extremely rare for the older age groups. Rotations, which are quite common in young children, were seen in approximately 30 percent of the older children. Truncation, or lack of completion of a design, was seen in approximately 25 percent of the five-year-olds. This error type is virtually nonexistent for all other ages. On the other hand, two other characteristics—erasure and workover—actually increased with age. While 20 percent of the younger children erased, almost 70 percent of the older children did so. Similarly, workover was noted in 50 percent of the younger children and in 80 percent of the older children.

Bender recall performance has also been shown to be related to age (Hutton 1966; Weiss 1970). Weiss (1970) reported norms for Bender recall in five age-groups of Israeli nonclinical Ss. The mean "good" recall scores are the number of figures recalled without (or of no more than) a single slight distortion. The rise in means from grade three to grade nine (third grade = 1.99, fifth grade = 2.59, seventh grade = 3.85, ninth grade = 5.63, and first year university = 5.85) was statistically significant. Only slight improvement was noted after ninth grade.

INTELLIGENCE

Recent research studies (e.g. Becker and Sabatino 1973; Cerbus and Oziel 1971; Henderson, Butler, and Gaffeney 1969; Marmorale and Brown 1975; McNamara, Porterfield, and Miller 1969; Raskin, Bloom, Klee, and Reese 1978) generally support the relationship between Bender performance based on Koppitz's

(1964) Developmental Scoring System and intelligence. However, Koppitz (1975b), in summarizing much of the research on this topic, cautioned that while the Bender may be a good *screening* device of mental ability for children of average or below average intelligence, it is less useful for screening children of above average intelligence.

Doubros and Mascarenhas (1969) reported generally low, but statistically significant, correlations between Bender performance based on the Pascal and Suttell (1951) Scoring System and *WISC Full Scale IQ* ($r = -.43$) and several "organicity-sensitive" subtests (*Similarities, Digit Span, Block Design*). The low magnitude of these relationships, however, makes practical application of these findings difficult.

Simensen (1974), in a multivariate study of Bender-Gestalt functioning, found that while intelligence was the best predictor of Bender performance (based on the Pascal-Suttell [1951] Scoring System) in a mentally retarded sample, rotary pursuit performance also contributed significantly to the regression equation.

EFFECTS OF COGNITIVE STYLE

There has been little research concerning the relationship between Bender performance and conceptual tempo—the characteristic speed and accuracy with which an individual responds to problem-solving situations. Preliminary data reported by Kagan (1965) showed a correlation "in the .70's" between Bender scores and average latency to first response on the Matching Familiar Figures test. Reflective children made fewer errors in Bender reproductions than impulsive children.

More recent research, however, indicated that overall errors on the Bender cannot be explained on the basis of impulsivity-reflectivity. Wallbrown, Wirth, and Engin (1975) found a nonsignificant correlation between the number of Bender errors and total working time on the Bender. Furthermore, they reported only a low correlation between mean latency on the *Matching Familiar Figures Test* and Bender errors, as determined by Koppitz's (1964) system.

In a second study, Wallbrown and Wallbrown (1975) found that conceptual impulsivity constituted a relatively small but statistically significant component of the total variance in Koppitz (1964) errors on the Bender. Taken together, the results of these studies indicate that for normal Ss, conceptual impulsivity, as defined by Kagan (1965), does not constitute a noteworthy aspect of Koppitz (1964) errors on the Bender-Gestalt test.

More recently, Brannigan, Barone, and Margolis (1978) focused on the relationship between cognitive style and Hutt's (1969) indicators of impulsivity. A biserial correlation computed for impulsivity-reflectivity and total Bender-Gestalt errors was significant ($r_{bi} = .60$) for a group of 60 children ($\overline{X}$ age = 10 years, 11 months). Impulsive children exhibited more of Hutt's signs than did reflective children. Response time, but not errors on the MFF Test, was also positively and significantly related to Bender signs ($r = .45$).

Several of the individual signs were also reported (based on chi square analyses) to be significantly related to impulsivity. These signs included: uneven or irregular curves, increased or decreased loops (figure 4 or 6), loops for circles, and circles for dots or dots for circles.

On the whole, while cognitive style did not affect developmental interpretation primarily based on "quantitative" determinants, its effects were clearly in evidence when a more "qualitative" approach to the interpretation of Bender performance was used.

SEX DIFFERENCES

Although Koppitz (1964) reported that girls tend to mature a little earlier than boys in visual-motor perception (girls tend to score better than boys at very young ages), there do not appear to be any statistically significant differences between the *Developmental Error Scores* of boys and girls. In fact, Koppitz (1975), in summarizing the results of studies by Baer and Gale (1967), Condell (1963), Dibner and Korn (1969), Dierks and Cushna (1969), Fiedler and Schmidt (1969), Issac (1971), Keogh and

Vormeland (1970), Koppitz (1973), Sabatino and Ysseldyke (1972), Singh (1965), Smith and Keogh (1963), Taylor and Thweatt (1972), Vormeland (1968), and Wedell and Horne (1969), concluded that, "There is no significant difference between the Bender Test scores of boys and girls regardless of whether they are average public school students or children with emotional and learning problems, provided the groups are matched for age and mental ability" (p. 33).

CULTURAL DIFFERENCES

Results strikingly similar to those reported by Koppitz (1964, 1975b) have been reported for Norwegian children (Keogh and Vormeland 1970), English children (Keogh 1968), Mexican-American children (Gilmore, Chandy, and Anderson 1975), Indian children (Patel and Bharucha 1972), and even Aboriginal children (Money and Nurcombe 1974). In the latter study, the authors attempted to determine the utility of the Bender in assessing the skills of Aboriginal children of Australia's North Coast of eastern Arnhem Land. Although the Ss ($N = 76$) were slightly older than those included in Koppitz's (1964) normative sample, they performed well within one SD of the normative mean Developmental Error Score for 10.6- to 11-year-old children. It should also be noted that this finding is consistent with Koppitz's (1975) norms for 11-year-0-month-old to 11-year-11-month-old children as well.

In conclusion, while it is difficult, if not impossible, to assess the abilities of the members of an ethnic culture apart from the achievements prized by that culture, the Bender stands up well as a cross-cultural assessment tool.

CULTURAL DEPRIVATION

Generally speaking, "culturally deprived" children have reportedly performed more poorly on the Bender than Ss comparable to Koppitz's (1964) normative sample. For example, Marmorale and Brown (1977) administered the Bender to three groups of first graders: nonmiddle-class Puerto Ricans ($N = 74$), nonmiddle-class Negroes ($N = 47$), and middle-class whites

($N = 44$). Both the Puerto Rican and Negro mean Developmental Error Scores were significantly higher than that of the white group.

Taylor and Thweatt (1972) reported that six- and seven-year-old Anglo children made significantly fewer Developmental Errors than Navajo children who lived on the reservation. Although they also reported that 11- and 12-year-old Navajos who lived off the reservation did not differ significantly from Anglo children, this finding is difficult to interpret since the Bender does not discriminate well at the upper age levels. It would have been interesting and more meaningful to compare six- and seven-year-old Navajos on the reservation with those who lived off the reservation.

Snyder, Holowenzak, and Hoffman (1971) reported a mean Developmental Bender Score of 6.3 for a group of culturally disadvantaged, inner-city, third-grade children ($N = 185$), "which is equivalent to expectations for first-grade students." They also noted specific error differences between "average" and disadvantaged groups, but reported no statistical analyses to verify the significance of these findings.

Similarly, Vega and Powell (1970) examined the Bender performance of 33 Negro children ($\overline{X}$ age $= 69.5$ months) in Project COPE, a program of compensatory pre-primary education for culturally disadvantaged children. Although they stated that the means (13.47 and 13.57) of their groups "deviated considerably from that of the comparably aged segment of Koppitz's (1964, p. 33) normative group," they did not report statistical analyses.

Albott and Gunn (1971) compared the Bender Developmental Error Scores of 35 Negro first-graders from a rural, deprived area, with the Koppitz age norms. They found that the Negro sample performed significantly lower than the normative group.

There is one important distinction that should be made concerning these research findings. Although at first glance it appears that Bender performance is related to ethnicity, the Ss in these investigations possessed characteristics which could easily reflect other salient factors, such as socioeconomic class and geographic location. Thus, as Albott and Gunn (1971) suggest, "Until such time that investigations classify the contributions made by all three cultural sources, considerable caution must be exercised in generalizing these results to anything other than hypotheses about etiology of the problems" (p. 250).

Several studies have attempted to examine these cultural, socioeconomic, and geographic factors. For example, Zach and Kaufman (1969) compared the Bender performance of 48 kindergarten children from a Negro "slum" school with the performance of 48 kindergarten children from a white middle-to-high income suburban school. They reported that Negro children made significantly more Developmental Errors than white children on the initial testing. However, a follow-up test within one month showed that, although differences between the groups remained, they were not statistically significant. Consequently, the authors pointed out that the "test-taking" experience serves to benefit disadvantaged children.

This finding is consistent with the Vega and Powell (1970) study which compared the effects of "extensive" practice utilizing specially designed graphic exercises on Bender performance. The experimental group, as opposed to the controls, made significant improvements in Bender performance.

Issac (1973) compared the Developmental Error Scores of 60 white and 60 black disadvantaged first graders and 60 white advantaged first graders. Disadvantaged blacks made significantly more errors than either the advantaged or disadvantaged white groups. However, the latter two groups did not differ significantly on Bender errors.

Unfortunately, there has been no research directly comparing black advantaged and black disadvantaged children. However, recent research by Zuelzer, Stedman, and Adams (1976) incorporated ethnocultural, socioeconomic, sex, and IQ factors in one design. They tested 384 first graders, stratified by socioeconomic level (low and middle), ethnocultural background (Mexican-American, black or white), and sex. Although they, too, reported significant effects of ethnic group and socioeconomic class, the addition of IQ eliminated these effects. The authors concluded that when "IQ (or IQ-mediated variables such as motivation or task orientation) were taken into account, the Koppitz system would be relatively uninfluenced by sex, ethnocultural, and socioeconomic status determinants" (p. 875).

SOCIALIZATION PRACTICES

Lifshitz (1978) compared the Bender performance of kindergarten children from two distinctly different Israeli populations (the Druze and Jews). The most notable finding was that Jewish children drew the Bender forms more accurately than did Druze children. The author also emphasized several significant sex-ethnicity interactional effects on Bender performance and cited differing socialization practices that might account for these results.

TRAINING

Studies (e.g. Keim 1970; Rice 1972; Walker and Streff 1973) examining the effects of visual-motor training on children's Bender performance have yielded equivocal results. Generally speaking though, it appears that children with visual-motor deficits may make some gains with training, but continue to have difficulties in this area.

MISCELLANEOUS FACTORS

There have been several additional studies that have focused on the importance of assessing the influences of perceptual, motor, and cognitive factors on Bender performance.

Pope and Snyder (1970) modified two Bender designs (Cards 3 and 7) to investigate the extent to which the Gestalt principles of proximity and good continuation were functional determinants of the visual perception of first-grade children. They predicted that these Ss "would consistently and correctly reproduce the various designs that followed the Gestalt principle of proximity (Card 3) and that, if graphomotor expectations were reduced in terms of number and difficulty of angulation (Card 7), first graders would demonstrate maturations sufficient for utilization of the principle of good continuation" (p. 264).

As expected, Ss had little difficulty with either the standard or modified version of Design 3. However, a significant difference was noted between the reproduction of the standard and modified versions of Card 7.

Based on the above findings, the authors concluded that the interference of graphomotor skill may obscure "accurate identification of what can and cannot be perceived at this age level."

Zach and Kaufman (1972) administered the Bender and a discrimination test adapted from the Bender to 70 kindergarten children from lower socioeconomic backgrounds. The discrimination test consisted of an original Bender design and four alternatives based on common errors made by children (rotation, integration, perseveration, and distortion.) They reported a low, nonsignificant correlation between the two tasks and concluded that it is possible for a child to discriminate forms well and still obtain a low score (based on Koppitz's system) on the Bender, and the reverse is also true.

Wise (1968) reported a significant correlation of .60 between Koppitz's (1964) Developmental Errors on the Bender and performance on the *Stick Designs Test* in a kindergarten sample. The use of this task in conjunction with the Bender allows the examiner to determine more precisely whether a child's poor performance in copying designs is a function of a specific disability in perceptual spatial relations, a gross motor problem, or both.

Weiss (1969a) noted a low but statistically significant correlation between Bender performance and a "Concept Test" designed to assess the child's ability to differentiate the various elements of the Bender designs (e.g. circle, square, penetrate, touch, row) in kindergarten children but not in first graders.

In a series of studies, Weiss (1969b, 1971a) reported on the directionality of drawing tendencies in normal Israeli children and adolescents. He noted a marked increase in left-right execution with age.

In a somewhat different vein, Murphy (1964) found that children who attended a PM kindergarten session were inferior to AM kindergarten children on the Bender, as scored by the Koppitz (1960) system. Although no rationale for these findings (or the study) was presented by the author, more research on this issue would be helpful

Summary

There has been relatively little research on the perceptual-motor processes underlying the reproduction of the Bender-Gestalt designs in children. Nevertheless, the need for such research is great if a better understanding of Bender performance is to be gained.

Research on the effects of maturation on Koppitz Developmental Error Scores indicated that performance undergoes rapid changes, especially from ages five through seven. This scoring system has considerably less discriminating power between eight and 11 years of age.

The Bender appears to be a good screening device of mental ability for children of average or below average intelligence. However, it is less useful for children of above average intelligence.

Furthermore, cognitive tempo does not appear to influence Developmental Error Scores. However, impulsive children exhibit more of Hutt's signs of poor impulse control than do reflective children.

Generally, culturally deprived children perform more poorly than Ss who are comparable to Koppitz's normative samples. However, when intellectual differences are controlled, the Koppitz system seems to be relatively uninfluenced by sex, ethnocultural, and socioeconomic determinants.

CHAPTER 4

PERSONALITY AND PROJECTIVE USES OF THE BENDER-GESTALT TEST

REVIEWS

In his 1963 review of the Bender-Gestalt Test literature, Billingslea (1963) commented that he could discern no particular direction that research had taken regarding personality and psychodynamic features based on this instrument. He expressed his view that the individual designs probably tended to evoke different reactions based on their symbolic value and, therefore, research dealing with possible psychodynamic meaning should be based on the individual designs. He also cautioned that the sequential influence of each design upon the other designs should be taken into account. Covering the period between 1950 and 1961, Billingslea listed only six different studies in the area of personality.

By contrast, Tolor and Schulberg (1963) cited a large number of studies encompassing the Bender-Gestalt drawings as related to ego-strength, course of hospitalization and future adjustment of patients, severity of psychopathology, specific personality hypotheses, and psychodynamic considerations. Tolor and Schulberg were impressed by the host of methodological defects in many of the studies reported in the literature which tested various aspects of personality functioning or specific personality hypotheses. They concluded that most projective uses of the Bender test still required experimental testing.

In the interval since these two major reviews of the literature were first published, numerous additional reports have found their way into print. These more recent publications have either attempted to illustrate the use of the Bender-Gestalt Test for psychodynamic purposes or have endeavored to establish the validity of specific test patterns.

NEW BOOKS

Drawing extensively upon their clinical experience, DeCato and Wicks (1976) published a number of Bender protocols in a book that attempts to illustrate the process of personality interpretation based on this test. They indicate the type of information that may be gleaned from the Bender productions and relate these data to personality formulations. Employing both child and adult protocols, the authors' interpretive approach assumes clarity. Their intention was not to establish the validity of the specific personality hypotheses, but to provide instead a basic framework for instructing less experienced psychologists to become clinically skillful with this test.

In a different vein, Gilbert's (1978) recent volume attempts to abstract and synthesize data extracted from several major authoritative texts about a variety of test features as they purportedly relate to various aspects of personality functioning. Of the four major psychological tests covered by this reference book, one is the Bender-Gestalt Test. While such a practical interpretive manual may have some value for those who wish to pursue in greater detail the evidence concerning the validity of the interpretations of interest to them, it also creates the possibility of gross misuse by those who may naively and uncritically apply a cookbook approach to interpretations of test data which, it is known, assume clear meaning only when used in combination with other test indicators and within the context of the total situation in which the patient is currently functioning.

Another relatively recent addition to the literature on the Bender is Lerner's (1972) book on the projective use of the Bender-Gestalt Test. It contains much illustrative material but no empirically derived data. Consequently, the contribution this volume makes is limited to providing an intuitive, subjectively based account about the uses of this test.

Hutt's (1977) most recent volume, *The Hutt Adaptation of the Bender-Gestalt Test* (Third Edition), includes a wealth of new clinical and research material. It offers data and insights beyond those which appeared in either the second edition of his book (Hutt 1969) or the first edition, which had been published under the title, *The Clinical Use of the Revised Bender-Gestalt Test* (Hutt and Briskin 1960). Included in this recent work is a discussion of how the Bender technique may be employed to provide access to underlying process phenomena which may then be applied to generate relevant inferences concerning actual psychopathological behavior. These inferences can then be corroborated by checking against other clinical data. It is evident that Hutt is one of the chief proponents of the use of this instrument to develop projective hypotheses about the individual. He attempts to ground projective interpretations in a strong empirical base, blending and integrating very sensitively clinical insights with objective scoring methods.

Hutt also uses a system of configurational analyses, based on patterns of special difficulties in the execution of the Bender designs, to identify different clinical groups.

In referring to the Bender test as an appropriate technique for projective analysis, Hutt goes far beyond the classical Gestalt laws of perception. His interest lies in the understanding of the processes involved in responding and in the final result ". . . in such ways as to maximize the understanding of the behaving individual; his idiosyncratic personality style; his needs, conflicts, and defenses; his level of maturation; and his coping methods and ego strengths" (Hutt 1977, p. 8).

Hutt (1977) distinguishes between an "inferential diagnosis" and a "process diagnosis." The former is based on observations of the sequential steps used in executing the task. The psychologist observes the performance and coping methods of the patient and makes ongoing inferences about the nature of the performance. The latter diagnostic process involves an attempt to clarify the causes of the patient's difficulty by experimentally varying the conditions of testing. Both types of analyses can be appropriately used with the Bender.

In other writings (e.g. Hutt 1968; Hutt 1978) Hutt describes the promising nature of the Bender-Gestalt Test as offering projective clues, and indicates how hypotheses are developed, examined, confirmed or disconfirmed, and finally, how the inferences are integrated to provide explanations to be checked against other available data. Quite realistically, he cautions against regarding interpretations as always conclusive and maintains that other competing hypotheses must be considered. Moreover, he indicates that no stimulus has a universal value to all individuals, but instead responses have an idiosyncratic component even for people sharing the same cultural milieu.

HUTT'S NEW OBJECTIVE SCALES

Among the many contributions made by Hutt to the personality area, as related to the Bender test, there is one that requires special mention, namely, his two objective scales, the *Psychopathology Scale* and the *Adience-Abience Scale*. In several publications (Hutt 1977; Hutt, in press; Hutt and Miller 1976; Hutt and Dates 1977; Hutt, Dates, and Reid 1977) he and his associates outline the development, significance, pyschometric properties, and applications of these two scales.

Regarding the Adience-Abience Scale, the concept of adience-abience pertains to a perceptual expression of a stylistic mode of relating to the inner and outer world. It is regarded as an individual's basic mode of filtering experience and is assumed to be representative of the most primitive aspect of the defensive disposition of the person, namely, as to whether he or she is relatively open (adient) or closed (abient) to visual stimulation and input.

The composition of the Adience-Abience Scale is such that three factors relate to space and size, two factors to organization, three factors to change in the form of the Gestalt, and four factors to distortion. High scores indicate greater adience whereas low scores indicate greater abience. Norms, although based on small samples, are available for normal individuals, for various pathological groups, and for adults as well as children. Scale scores seem to be unaffected by such factors as age in adults, sex, educational level, and estimated intelligence.

Studies have indicated that normals are more adient than organically impaired patients; that deaf and retarded individuals who are more effective intellectually and in adjustment are more adient than deaf and retarded individuals who are less effective intellectually and in adjustment; that therapeutic change is greater for adient than abient patients; that schizophrenics hospitalized for less than six months score higher in adience than schizophrenics hospitalized for more than five years; and that creativity is associated with adience in both schizophrenics and normals. Hutt, Dates, and Reid (1977) found male delinquents to be more abient than a comparable age-group of normal and disturbed youth. Furthermore, adience-abience and recidivism are significantly correlated ($r = .49$, $p = .01$) in juvenile court-referred offenders who did not receive treatment. However, the magnitude of this correlation is not sufficient to permit predictions to be made for individual cases.

The Adience-Abience Scale has been found (Hutt and Dates 1977) to have high test-retest reliability ($r = .91$ for a sample in group treatment and $r = .92$ for a sample in individual treatment); interscorer reliability is also satisfactory (*Kendall's Coefficient of Concordance* for three scorers was .89 and .90 for pre- and post-test records, respectively). Further evidence for the scale's reliability derives from the finding (Hutt and Miller 1975) of a rank-order test-retest correlation of .84 for 20 male and 20 female process schizophrenics for a two-week interval.

The second of Hutt's new Bender-Gestalt scales is the Psychopathology Scale, which provides a global indication of the degree of pathology in the individual. The current version of this scale consists of 17 factors, 16 of which are scored on a scale of 1 to 10 and one of which is scored from 1 to 3.25. Each factor is assigned both a raw and scaled score value. Scoring criteria are presented for each of the factors. Illustrative of the factors included are the following: sequence, position of first drawing, use of space, collision, curvature difficulty, overlapping difficulty, and perseveration. Although Hutt recommended that the Psychopathology Scale not be used by itself for individual diagnoses, many significant group differences emerge when different pathological groups are compared with normal adults and when the various diagnostic groups are compared with one another. Normals scored lower than neurotics and depressive subjects, and these patients scored lower than schizophrenics and organics. Moreover, disturbed children at the 10-, 11-, and 12-year age levels differed significantly in mean scale scores from normal children of comparable ages.

The Psychopathology Scale has a test-retest reliability of .92 over a 40-week interval and a high degree of inter-rater reliability. The Kendall's Coefficient of Concordance for three scorers ranged from .91 to .95 (Hutt and Dates 1977). In another study (Miller and Hutt 1975), 40 process schizophrenics tested over a two-week interval were shown to have satisfactory test-retest reliability (for males and females the rho was .87 and .83, respectively). Interjudge reliability, based on two scorers, produced a rho of .895.

It has been demonstrated that the Psychopathology Scale is sensitive to changes associated with individual and group tutoring and counseling of juvenile offenders (Hutt and Dates 1977). Also the Psychopathology Scale scores are inversely correlated ($r = -.61$, $p < .001$) with the *Tennessee Self-Concept Scale* (Fitts 1965) as reported by Hutt, Dates, and Reid (1977).

Beyond age 10, Psychopathology Scale scores are not significantly affected by age (Hutt 1977); scores are also independent of sex, at least in samples of hospitalized schizophrenics and outpatients (Hutt and Miller 1976).

Turning to the relationship between the Psychopathology Scale and the Adience-Abience Scale, it has been found (Hutt and Miller 1976; Hutt and Dates 1977; Hutt 1977) that there is a substantial correlation between these two measures in hospitalized schizophrenics ($r = -.64$ for males; $r = -.77$ for females), in outpatients seen in psychotherapy ($r = -.39$ for males; $r = -.42$ for females), in delinquents (range of r from $-.40$ to $-.67$), and in a group of 119 unspecified, but seemingly normal, Ss ($r = .69$).[1] Despite the high degree of common variance expressed by these correlations, all of which are statistically significant, Hutt (1977) considers sufficient noncommon elements to remain, warranting the use of both scales to measure the two different constructs.

---

[1] This correlation is reported in Hutt (1977) as .69, but most likely contains an error in sign.

In sum, it would appear that these new scales which measure adience-abience and psychopathology have considerable validity of the construct, concurrent, and predictive types; that they are highly reliable instruments; and that they are valuable adjuncts for personality assessment. We anticipate psychologists will employ these scales more extensively in the future as the scales become further refined and that additional scales dealing with salient personality dimensions will be developed.

INSIGHTS GAINED FROM THE PERFORMANCE
OF NORMALS

Several studies have appeared in the literature that have investigated the performance of nonclinical Ss on the Bender-Gestalt Test. These studies, although designed to provide useful information on normal individuals, permit a better understanding also of the personality functioning of psychologically disturbed persons.

Lieberman (1968) recorded the order of lines and the direction of the lines drawn by sixty-five college students in making the Bender-Gestalt designs. The author presents drawing norms for each design. Examples of interesting findings are the following results: All but six of the Ss drew the circle of Design A in a counterclockwise direction, and sixty of the sixty-five Ss drew the circle first. On Design 4, all Ss made the left-sided figure first before proceeding to the curved portion of the design.

It is also noteworthy that on Design 5, 63 percent of the Ss made the semicircle formation of dots clockwise, and 92 percent drew the straight-line formation of dots outward from, rather than inward toward, the semicircle of dots. On Design 6, 72 percent of the normal respondents drew the horizontal wavy line (left-to-right) first and then made the vertical line (top-to-bottom). Lieberman contrasted this type of performance to the performance in drawing a cross, which usually assumes a vertical followed by a horizontal sequence.

A further illustration of the results obtained by Lieberman is the finding that Ss draw the diamond before making the hexagon on Design 8.

One of the author's overall conclusions was that designs are not drawn consistently in a counterclockwise direction, but that the direction of the drawing is a function of the specific configuration copied. Thus, the modal pattern is for some designs to be typically made with movement orientation in one direction whereas other designs are typically made with movement orientation in the opposite direction. Knowledge of the characteristic responses made by normals, in terms of line directionality and line sequence, should enhance the interpretative skill of the clinician who observes Bender behavior of pathologically organized patients.

Weiss (1970) presents data on the frequency of rotations, perseverations, simplifications, distortions, contaminations, and destruction of designs on both the copy and recall modes of administration by 169 nonclinical male and female Ss, some having 12 years of education and some having only nine years of education. Destruction of the configurations and serious distortions did not occur at all on the copy phase of the administration. Only mild distortions and "moderate" perseverations, defined in terms of specific criteria, occurred in more than 1 percent of the total number of drawn figures that could possibly be affected. The most frequent Bender production deviations on recall were mild distortions and moderate perseverations, but even these deviations occurred in only 3.70 percent and 3.58 percent, respectively, of the possible drawings.

Weiss also examined the distribution of the errors committed on copying Bender figures and observed that mild distortions are relatively more frequent on Designs 2, 5, and 7; that mild rotations are seen most frequently on Design 7; that moderate perseverations are found most often on Design 5; and simplification is limited to Design 3. The distribution of errors for the recall phase, which differs from the pattern of inaccuracies obtained on the copy phase, is also delineated. Weiss concluded that the stimulus value or "card pull" of the different Bender designs for normal individuals may not parallel that reported in the literature for clinical Ss. Thus, the normative data presented in his publication could very well provide the basis upon which a system of differential weightings for each of the error types could be constructed to assist in making a clinical diagnosis.

Turning now to the meaning of the Bender figures and the elements comprising the various designs to normal Ss, Goldfried and Ingling (1964) and Guertin and Davis (1963) report new research in this area. These authors extended Tolor's (1960) use of the *Semantic Differential Technique* to determine the affective impact of each of the Bender designs in four ways: (1) In addition to rating the Bender designs, Ss were asked to rate also a number of critical verbal concepts to make possible a determination of connotative similarities. (2) Some of the semantic differential scales previously used that could relate more to denotative characteristics were omitted. (3) The selection of semantic differential scales was based on the symbolic meanings of the designs that had been postulated by Hutt and Briskin (1960). (4) The data were also analyzed for sex differences.

The mean ratings for each of the Bender designs are reported for the 40 college men and 40 college women comprising the study sample. Eight mean ratings were found to deviate significantly from neutrality for the males, while 26 were significant for females. To summarize Goldfried and Ingling's findings, males found Figure 3 to be slightly active and fast, Figure 6 to be slightly free, active, excitable and fast, and Figure 7 to be slightly masculine and severe. The females rated Figure A as slightly constrained and deliberate; Figure 1 as quite emotional and deliberate and as slightly calm; Figure 2 as slightly active and deliberate; Figure 3 as slightly pleasant, active, and fast; Figure 6 as quite free, active, excitable, fast, and compulsive as well as slightly emotional; Figure 7 as quite strong and rugged, slightly cruel, dangerous, masculine, severe, constrained, and deliberate; and Figure 8 as slightly constrained and deliberate. There were no significant deviations in ratings from the neutral range of Figures 4 or 5 for either sex.

As for the affective similarity between the Bender figures and the verbal concepts, the following results and conclusions were reported by the authors: Design A clustered with "Interpersonal Relations," "Dependency," and "Man" for both sexes; Design 1 was associated with "Dependency" for both sexes; Design 2 was found to be similar to a number of concepts making the symbolic meaning of this figure unclear; Design 3 provided no support for the hypothesized association with the verbal concept, "Anger"; Design 4 did not disclose the clustering with those verbal concepts that would be expected if it related symbolically to male-female interactions; Design 5 only weakly supported the mother surrogate hypothesis but did relate to "Dependency" in males and to "Vagina," "Dependency," and "Interpersonal Relations" in females. Figure 6 showed similarity in meaning to a fairly large number of verbal concepts for females, making interpretation difficult. Design 7 clustered with the verbal concept "Man" for both sexes; women also related "Penis" and "Anger" to this design. Design 8 was associated with "Father" and "Man," along with other concepts in male Ss, and with "Man," "Penis," and "Vagina," along with other concepts, in female Ss, providing some support for the presumed sexual intercourse symbolic value of this figure.

Goldfried and Ingling (1964) concluded that all the results of the study, when taken in combination, offered little empirical support for the symbolic significance frequently assigned to the Bender-Gestalt Test designs. They assert that only the highly emotional symbolic value of Design 6, and the masculine and possibly phallic significance of Design 7, are consistently supported by their data. Therefore, they argue, that interpreting the Bender-Gestalt designs symbolically in clinical practice is generally unwarranted. However, they do acknowledge that ". . . it still remains possible that some consistent symbolic meaning exists for particular individuals" (Goldfried and Ingling 1964, p. 190).

Despite the very high level of experimental design sophistication of the Goldfried and Ingling (1964) study, we feel that their sweeping critical reaction to the possible symbolic significance of the various Bender figures represents too harsh a judgment and is unjustified. There are three major reasons why we believe that the conclusions derived from this research must be viewed with great caution. The first reason is that the data, when re-examined, do indeed contain considerable support for assigning symbolic meaning to some of the designs. The second reason is that the verbal concepts used for comparison of connotative similarities are far from being separate conceptual entities but do, in fact, logically form a cohesive psychodynamic interrelated network. The third reason for exercising more caution in embracing the authors' conclusions is that the method employed may not have constituted an adequate test of the projective hypothesis as applied to the Bender-Gestalt figures.

Turning to the first point, when one examines carefully some of the verbal concepts that do in fact cluster with the Bender figures, one notes considerable support for assigning the kind of symbolic value to them that many clinicians do in their practices. For example, although it is true that there was no association found between Design 3 and the concept "Anger," the wedgelike configuration of Design 3 has led clinicians to assign a penetrative sexual significance, with or without angry overtones, to this figure. The Goldfried and Ingling data disclose considerable support for this interpretation in that Design 3 was associated with the concepts, "Man," "Penis," and "Interpersonal Relations" for male Ss, and with the concepts, "Man," "Vagina," "Woman," "Me," "Sexual Intercourse," "Dependency," "Interpersonal Relations," and "Sexuality" for female Ss.

Another example of what we maintain, contrary to Goldfried and Ingling's position, provides at least some support for the symbolic meaning of the designs may be observed in the data relating to Design 4. Design 4 allegedly taps the nature of the interaction between male and female. The results indicated that Design 4 was similar in meaning to the concept "Dependency" for males and to the concepts, "Interpersonal Relations," "Dependency," "Man," "Penis," "Sexuality," and "Vagina" for females. Therefore, it appears that the results did indeed reveal a consistency with the presumed meaning of this design.

A final example will be drawn from Design 5, which most clinicians regard as containing both vaginal and phallic elements in close spatial proximity. Thus, this design would more likely be a symbol related to sexual impact than to a "mother-surrogate" figure, as Goldfried and Ingling suggested. It is, therefore, noteworthy that Goldfried and Ingling's male Ss rated "Dependency," and that female Ss rated the concept, "Vagina," as being most similar to Design 5. One could argue that these responses are at least suggestively supportive of the hypothesis that Design 5 possesses qualities of heterosexual significance. This conclusion would have special merit if college males' heterosexual drives contained elements of dependent feelings.

Our second contention is that Goldfried and Ingling (1964) should not have treated many of the verbal concepts used in their study as if they represented separate entities. Psychodynamically "Interpersonal Relations," "Sexuality," "Man," "Woman," "Sexual Intercourse," "Vagina" and most of the other verbal concepts constitute an interrelated, psychodynamic network. It is, therefore, difficult to justify their use as conceptual markers for comparison with the Bender designs.

Our third objection rests on the assumption that adequate testing of projective hypotheses may require special activation of the drive or conflict or the selection of Ss of known personality conflicts or drive intensities. In Kwawer's (1977) study of the validity of Rorschach indicators of homosexuality, for example, arousal of unconscious conflicts was accomplished by subliminally exposing to Ss an incest-related stimulus.

Because of the various reasons cited, it is felt that Goldfried and Ingling's (1964) conclusions are somewhat premature, requiring much additional research before any definitive statement may be made concerning the validity of the symbolic interpretations assigned to the Bender designs.

Guertin and Davis (1963) used the semantic differential with 18 undergraduate male students who rated the Bender-Gestalt designs and the elements of which the designs are comprised. There were 30 elements and figures that served as stimuli to be rated on 19 scales. Based on a factor analysis, the results suggested a lack of a single, general meaning that could be assigned to curvilinear elements to differentiate them from rectilinear elements. Instead, curvilinearity and rectilinearity assumed quite different meanings under different conditions. It was also noted that the combination of simple elements into more complex figures did not enhance the meaning of the stimuli appreciably. Neither the integration of similar elements nor dissimilar elements resulted in enhancement of meaning. These findings were interpreted by Guertin and Davis to indicate that the Bender-Gestalt designs could not be used for reliable diagnostic hypotheses. The authors proposed that the test figures be modified by introducing more stimuli and less complexity to provide for improved replication.

MEANING OF DESIGNS FOR CLINICAL SUBJECTS

The semantic differential technique has also been used by Schulberg and Tolor (1962) to investigate the connotative meanings of the Bender designs to psychiatric patients. Ratings of the designs were made on 20 semantic differential scales by a group of hospitalized patients consisting of neurotics, functional psychotics, acute organic psychotics, and character disorders, of whom 85 percent were alcoholics. The results revealed no major differences among diagnostic subgroups in the connotative meanings associated with the designs. In other words, all subgroups tended to characterize the figures in basically similar fashion. However, the nine designs were responded to significantly differently, suggesting that patients assigned different meanings to each of the designs. Knowledge of the stimulus value of the Bender designs to psychiatric patients should facilitate the clinical interpretation of their performance.

PROJECTIVE USE OF THE BENDER-GESTALT TEST

Some reference has already been made to the projective use of the test under the section entitled *New Books,* with Hutt's work assuming a most prominent role. We now cite six specific publications that have directly addressed the issue of the use of the Bender-Gestalt Test projectively.

Brown (1965) described the ways in which the Bender performance could be interpreted in order to predict the degree of acting-out potential. His basic hypothesis is that the sheet of paper on which the designs are copied represents the boundaries of a miniature world within which the respondent is expected to conduct his activities. He indicates that the drawing of each design requires that the person comply nonverbally with an implied external directive. Moreover, the designs vary the demand for control, depending on the degree to which they are bounded, so that differences in regressive trends may be detected in the different figures. Brown cautions that no perfect correspondence between test performance and acting-out behavior should be expected, but an estimate of the likelihood of acting-out is possible.

Among the dimensions that comprise the total patterning of test performance used by Brown to determine acting-out potential are heavy line pressure, substitution of circles for dots, collision, spikes on curves, dot distortion, dashes, compression-expansion in placement, crossing difficulty, integration difficulty, splitting and reduplication, and boundary violation. Underlying the attention paid these test features is a well-conceptualized position concerning the acting-out process with reference to such psychological dispositions as low tolerance for restraint or inhibition, regressive trends, narcissistic traits with associated avoidance of difficult and exacting tasks, and tendency to comply only superficially. The Brown publication is a masterly illustration of the blending of projective skills with insight into basic psychological processes.

De-Levie (1970) reasoned that blunting or cutting off the pointed ends of the hexagons on Design 7 would be suggestive of the S experiencing feelings of a damaged body image, especially an impaired sense of masculinity. To test this hypothesis, the Bender-Gestalt Test was administered to sixty-three Israeli soldiers shortly after they had sustained war-related injuries and to two groups of control Ss, one having long-standing physical and emotional disabilities and one having psychiatric problems. The tachistoscopic method of administration (i.e. presenting each card for five seconds and eliciting drawings from memory) was used. It was found that 30 percent of the injured soldiers produced the blunting or cutting-off of the phallic shape on Design 7, whereas only 18 percent of the first control group and 6 percent of the second control group showed this sign. The group differences were highly significant ($X^2 = 10.76$, $p < .005$), supporting the projective hypothesis that the rendition of Design 7 is related to feelings of potency and, at a deeper level, to phallic competence. Moreover, the degree of recency of the physical injury seemed to be related to the frequency of occurrence of the sign.

It is unfortunate that the three groups of Ss used in this study were not well controlled for intelligence and other characteristics, and that one of the control groups included individuals who also experienced physical problems. Nevertheless, these findings suggest that the Bender may have demonstrable projective utility.

White and McCraw (1975) tested the hypothesis that a downward slant in Designs 1 and 2 reflected a depressive trend. With the MMPI used as the dependent measure, no support for this prediction was obtained.

The MMPI was also employed as a criterion by White (1976) for the hypothesized relationship between variations in Bender constriction and depression. The results indicated that Ss with constricted Bender protocols had significantly higher MMPI Depression scores than those whose Bender protocols were not constricted. However, constriction on the upper half-page compared to constriction on the left side of the page did not yield differences on the Depression scale.

Gavales and Millon (1960) checked the hypotheses that anxiety would be reflected in decrements in the size of the Bender designs, and recall productions would be more sensitive to differences in this variable than the copy productions. Using the *Taylor Manifest Anxiety Scale* to identify High and Low Anxiety Ss, the authors exposed half of each group to an anxiety-producing testing situation (repeated test failures) and half to a non-stress situation. The results indicated the experimentally induced condition of anxiety produced significantly smaller Bender drawings than the non-stress condition, under both copy and recall administrations. The Taylor High Anxiety scorers contributed more to this effect than the Taylor Low Anxiety scorers. Although it was demonstrated that anxiety did indeed relate to figure size, the hypothesis that the recall performance would be more sensitive to this trend than the copy performance was not supported.

In an earlier study of depression in psychiatric patients, Johnson (1973) explored the validity of constriction on the Bender as an indicator of depression. The projective hypothesis tested was that the use of small amounts of space in drawing the nine figures, i.e. constricted use of space, would be associated with clinical depression. Twenty-five patients displaying constriction in their Bender records were compared with 25 patients not showing constriction with regard to their MMPI Depression scores. Constriction was defined as the placing of all Bender designs in less than one-half sheet of paper, with no part of any figure making contact with imaginary center lines separating left and right, or top and bottom halves of the paper. A significant difference was found between the D scores of patients producing Bender constriction and those who did not disclose Bender constriction. Johnson noted, however, that the low incidence of constricted records in the population (only 5.5% of the total) made this sign one of limited practical utility. The research does, however, indicate further support for the projective approach to the analysis of Bender protocols.

RELATION TO PERSONALITY MEASURES

Haynes (1970) investigated the relationship between performance on the Bender-Gestalt and personality variables as measured by the *16 Personality Factor Questionnaire* (Cattell 1962) and the *Guilford-Zimmerman Spatial Orientation and Spatial Visualization Tests* (Guilford and Zimmerman 1947; Guilford and Zimmerman 1953). The Ss consisted of college students, though the sex distribution of the sample was not specified by the author. The Bender protocols were scored according to the Pascal and Suttell (1951) system. Two separate factor analyses were conducted, one on the designs, and one on the deviation categories. The results showed that performance on the Bender-Gestalt was related to personality characteristics. Since a general factor underlying Bender performance was not found, it was concluded that the designs did not measure a unitary dimension of behavior. Furthermore, spatial abilities did not appear to be related to Bender performance, except on Design 7.

Another study relating personality to Bender performance is that of Beyel, Fracchia, Sheppard, and Merlis (1971) who investigated the relationship between errors in reasoning and errors on the Bender-Gestalt Test. The *Raven Progressive Matrices* of eighty-nine hospitalized chronic male schizophrenics were scored for avoidable errors, presumably reflective of pathology-associated changes in consistency and accuracy in intellectual functioning, and for atypical errors, presumably reflective of the psychotic's tendency to select less plausible alternatives. Bender errors were determined by the Hain (1964) scoring method. Total error score on the Bender correlated .41 with atypical errors, but revealed no significant correlation ($r = .01$) with avoidable errors on the Raven. The authors argued that these findings, taken together with the obtained r of −.41 between the two Raven error indices, suggested that atypical errors may be detecting the effects of psychopathology on the perceptual spatial factor.

Roseman and Albergottie (1973) correlated twelve of Hutt's (1969) Bender-Gestalt Test factors with MMPI and 16 PF Questionnaire scales in order to assess relationships with personality variables. Based on the performance of ninety-one vocational rehabilitation clients, it was found that three specific Bender-Gestalt scales, namely, closure difficulty, crossing difficulty, and curvature difficulty, entered into many significant, but low-order correlations, whereas the other nine scales did not yield significant correlations beyond chance expectancy. We regard these results to be difficult to interpret since the personality dimensions measured by the MMPI and the 16 PF Questionnaire are not directly comparable to the personality variables that are allegedly measured by the Hutt scales based on Bender-Gestalt performance.

ADJUSTMENT AND BENDER PERFORMANCE

A number of studies published since 1962 have addressed some facet of the relationship between adjustment level or ego intactness and Bender performance. Questioning whether Bender performance is or is not simply a function of intelligence rather than of adjustment, Taylor (1965) attempted to examine the relationship between Bender-Gestalt performance and adjustment when the effect of intelligence is controlled. In a study of 142 rehabilitation clients (101 males and 41 females) differing widely in adjustment and intelligence, Taylor found correlations of .59, .43, and .62, between Bender-Gestalt scores (using Pascal and Suttell's system) and *WAIS Full Scale IQ, Verbal IQ,* and *Performance IQ,* respectively.

Furthermore, significant correlations ranging from .23 to .51 between Bender-Gestalt scores and all seven adjustment scales, based on the ratings of six supervisors, were obtained. Thus, the Bender-Gestalt was demonstrated to be capable of predicting general adjustment.

Regarding the differential value of intelligence and Bender performance as adjustment predictors, although six of the seven adjustment scales correlated significantly with Performance IQ, only one of the adjustment scales correlated significantly with Verbal IQ, and two adjustment scales correlated significantly with Full Scale IQ. Therefore, it would seem that the Bender is superior in predicting overall adjustment as compared to the intelligence measures. Moreover, when Performance IQ scores were partialed out in computing correlations between Bender performance and the adjustment measures, significance was still maintained on two of the adjustment scales.

The value of the Bender for determining adjustment was underscored by the observation that when the Bender is included with the WAIS in an assessment battery, a statistically significant increment in predicting adjustment would most likely be achieved. These findings led Taylor to speculate that there were three sources of variance in Bender performance: general intelligence, spatial orientation, and personality adjustment.

In a study of the use of ambiguous stimuli to predict competence in dealing with daily life situations, Steinman (1967) found a highly significant correlation ($r = .51, p < .01$) between Bender-Gestalt performance, as scored by the Pascal and Suttell (1951) method, and scores on the *Gestalt Threshold Test,* which measures closure ability. This correlation exceeded that obtained between all WAIS subtest scores, except *Object Assembly* and Performance IQ. It also exceeded the correlation between the Draw-A-Person performance and Gestalt Threshold Test scores. Additionally, the Bender correlated significantly with two of the seven behavioral rating scales. Interestingly, the Draw-A-Person procedure did not correlate significantly with ratings of competence. Virtually none of the WAIS verbal subtests correlated with competence either. In sum, closure ability revealed the highest relationship to performance on the Bender-Gestalt Test and certain WAIS Performance subscales, and the Bender had demonstrable, although weak, association with competence ratings.

Turning now to ego strength as reflected on the Bender-Gestalt Test, Corotto and Curnutt (1962), basing their expectation on selected previous studies (Curnutt and Lewis 1954; Tamkin 1957), predicted a nonsignificant relationship between *Bender* Z scores and those MMPI scales which were identified as measures of ego strength or ego weakness. None of the ten selected MMPI scales was found to correlate significantly with Bender-Gestalt Z scores in a normal population.

Roos (1962) failed to find a significant correlation between Bender-Gestalt Z scores and scores on *Barron's* (1953) *Ego Strength Scale* in hospitalized patients. Both measures of ego strength correlated significantly with age and intelligence. Significant between-group differences were obtained when the performance of schizophrenics, character disorders, and neurotics was compared on the Bender and on the Barron's Ego Strength Scale.

Freed (1966a) compared the Bender performance, raw scores, Z scores, and number of designs recalled by 33 relatively recently hospitalized male psychiatric patients with 30 long-term patients about to be discharged from the hospital. He found no significant differences on these variables. There are some fundamental methodological difficulties with this study, such as the groups not being equated for Z scores on admission and the use of hospital discharge as a criterion of ego strength despite the frequent arbitrariness in determining readiness for discharge.

Despite some questions that could be raised about the adequacy in methodology of the studies done since 1962 in the area of ego strength and Bender performance, the new evidence accumulating seems to suggest that either the Bender taps different aspects of ego strength than do such measures as the MMPI or the Barron scale, or that there is in fact no clear-cut relationship between what is generally conceptualized as reflecting ego strength and Bender performance. This position represents a shift from the conclusion reached in the previous review. At that time it was felt that, "The most general conclusion is that we do not at the present time have sufficient information based on adequate research to know whether or not Bender performance is a good indicator of ego strength" (Tolor and Schulberg 1963, p. 42).

Continuing with our examination of the Bender use for determining adjustment, we shall now focus on acting-out and suicide behaviors. Brannigan and Benowitz (1975) noted several low order, but significant, correlations between three of eight Bender signs that had been selected because they purportedly reflect control problems, on the one hand, and ratings of behavior, on the other, with a sample of 29 male adolescents. The differentiating signs were: progressive increase in figure size, uneven figure size, and exaggerated curvature. On the other hand, the following indicators were nondiscriminating: figures spread widely on page, collisions, dashes for dots or circles, heavy or inconsistent line pressure, and circles for dots.

Addressing the relationship between Bender performance and acting-out in a somewhat different vein, Matranga, Jensen, and Prandoni (1972) published normative data for adult, Negro male offenders fifteen to sixty-five years of age on the Bender-Gestalt, scored on the Koppitz (1964) Developmental Scoring System. The error distribution for the 224 Ss is given for seven IQ ranges.

The three studies investigating suicidal potential provide equivocal results. Sternberg and Levine (1965) found that hospitalized psychiatric patients who drew Design 6 on the Bender penetrating into the open semicircular area of Design 5, which allegedly symbolized both aggression and a desire to return to the womb, displayed significantly greater suicidal ideation than a control group. The presence of suicidal ideation was determined by three psychologists making independent judgments. Eighty-eight percent of the group that produced the predictor criterion also evidenced suicidal thinking.

Leonard (1973) found that various Bender-Gestalt signs of depression and suicide, which had been drawn from the literature, did not differentiate between patients who had made suicidal attempts, were seriously depressed or threatened suicide, and nonsuicidal patients. However, of nine additional indicators, based on measurements of deviations in size and spatial consistency, two yielded significant results. More specifically, suicidal Ss produced more constricted designs and had more difficulty maintaining a horizontal position on Design 2 than nonsuicidal patients.

Finally, Nawas and Worth (1968) found that none of ten specific signs purportedly relating to depression, hostility, dependency, emotional constriction, and rigidity differentiated the Bender protocols of patients who had made an unsuccessful suicidal attempt from those who had not. While one might regard the presumed psychological characteristics, such as depression and hostility, that the authors selected to be possibly associated with suicide to be relevant dimensions, one could question the reliance on some of the signs, such as rotation of Figure 3 as an indicator of hostility.

How sensitive the Bender is to stress and anxiety is a question that bears on the adjustment issue. Here we find (Mordock 1969a) that a stressful condition, defined as testing for preplacement screening of adolescents enrolled in a residential treatment facility, resulted in a greater number of Bender errors than the nonstressful condition, defined as the second test administration which occurred some 10 weeks later, on the average. Bender performance differences were significant for Ss with CNS disturbances but not for Ss with psychiatric problems. Unfortunately, the design of this study did not permit one to conclude with any degree of confidence that obtained test-retest changes in Bender performance were attributable to the effects of stress. As a matter of fact, the rationale for assuming greater stress on first testing is most tenuous indeed.

Lachmann, Bailey, and Berrick (1961) investigated the relationship between self-reports of manifest anxiety and clinicians' judgments of manifest anxiety based on Bender-Gestalt performance. For the five judges who attained the highest degree of reliability, a significant *inverse* relationship was found between psychologists' rankings of anxiety on the Bender and MAS scores. A similar negative correlation was obtained between amount of anxiety inferred from the Draw-A-Person test and the MAS. It should be noted, however, that the judges were instructed to deal only with inferred consciously experienced anxiety, a task which is not particularly congruent with the customary task of clinicians.

PERSONALITY AND PROJECTIVE USES WITH CHILDREN

Prior to 1963 there was little research on the validity of the Bender-Gestalt Test as a tool to evaluate the personality adjustment of children. Recently, however, several studies have appeared in the professional literature.

Bender (1967) studied the Visual-Motor Gestalt function in schizophrenic and normal children. Six- and seven-year-old children were administered the Bender on three different occasions. Interesting differences were noted between the two groups of children. First, the normal children demonstrated "a drive to complete an organized whole experience" each time they took the test. On the first administration of the Bender, an "obvious trial-and-error approach with some primitive organization" was found. Figures were drawn from the center outward in various directions, and horizontally across the top. Erasures, several trials, and disorientation of background with rotated and verticalized figures were also noted. However, on subsequent tests administered one or two months apart, normal children were progressively more mature in their organization and integration of the Bender figures. Stable, usual, or conforming patterns were more frequent. Individual figures also stood out from the background.

In contrast, schizophrenic children did not improve on subsequent administrations. Primitive tendencies were retained and the children were still driven to fill the entire background. Organization was still random, and boundaries between figures often did not exist.

Bender concluded that:

The normal child succeeds through trial-and-error to approach a goal which appears to be mastery of the Gestalt function and integrative competence . . . there is no doubt that it is part, however, of the total maturation pattern, including symbol formation, language and thought, and socialization.

The schizophrenic child is continually lost in his struggle to give into primitive vortex of plasticity, of lack of differentiation (even between foreground and background), of spatial organization of perception, and of controlled object construction (pp. 561-562).

Bender did not use an objective scoring system in this study, but examined each protocol subjectively and intuitively for a variety of principles. For those who argue that her methods are not standardized and therefore not valid, Bender claimed that "no scoring system so far devised is better than a subjective or intuitive evaluation of the test performed by evaluators acquainted with Gestalt principles . . . the more objective approach, despite contrary expectations, does not demonstrably enhance the validity for any purpose (Bender 1967, p. 546)." Furthermore, she claimed that her "intuitive" method is superior because it takes into account "global" and "gestalt" factors which objective scoring methods—having fragmented the visual-motor experience—do not.

Koppitz's (1964) application of the Bender-Gestalt for diagnosing emotional disturbance is considered even by Bender (1967) to be one of the best recognized uses of an objective scoring system for children. Drawing from the work of other investigators (e.g. Byrd 1956; Clawson 1959; Hutt 1960; and Pascall and Suttell 1951), she offered ten Gestalt signs as *Emotional Indicators* and hypothesized that children with adjustment problems would show a much higher incidence of these indicators on the Bender-Gestalt Test than children who were well adjusted. Her investigations of the Bender-Gestalt Test as a clinical tool were based on a study of two groups: 136 "normal" school children who had no history of emotional problems and 136 children who had been referred to a clinic or to a school psychologist because of emotional problems.

She found that of the ten emotional indicators, six differentiated significantly between the disturbed and normal children. The other four factors showed differences between the two groups, but the differences were not significant. The emotional indicators that she identified were confused order, wavy line, dashes for circles, progressive increase in size, large size of drawings, small size, fine line, overwork or reinforced lines, second attempt, and expansion.

Koppitz found that both the individual and the total number of emotional indicators had diagnostic value in the study of children with emotional disturbances. Furthermore, the total number of indicators appeared to be related to the seriousness of the disturbance. She found that more than half of all children with three indicators were emotionally disturbed, four out of five (80%) children with four indicators on their Bender-Gestalt records had emotional problems, and all children with five or more emotional indicators had been referred for psychological evaluation because of serious emotional problems.

Koppitz (1975b) reexamined her ten emotional indicators on the Bender-Gestalt and their implications with respect to more recent research results. She offered additional support that her ten indicators were more frequent in emotionally disturbed children than in normal children. She also added two more emotional indicators to her list of factors which, while occurring very rarely in Bender-Gestalt records, had considerable clinical significance when they did appear. These factors are "box around design" and "spontaneous elaboration or addition to a design." Koppitz (1975b) pointed out, however, that

> Emotional indicators are clinical signs that should be evaluated like any other clinical symptom. They may occur separately or in combination; they are not mutually exclusive. A given emotional problem can be expressed on the Bender Test in different ways. . . . Some EIs involve opposite tendencies that may, on occasion, occur in the same youngster and that may be reflected on a single Bender Test record . . . an interpretation of EIs should be limited to underlying tendencies and attitudes; one should merely develop hypotheses from the EIs that then need to be checked against other psychological data and observations (p. 89).

Thus, even the advocates of objective scoring systems, while finding them useful, caution against using them as sole indicators of personality problems.

Handler and McIntosh (1971) attempted to evaluate the ability of the Draw-A-Person and Bender-Gestalt to correctly identify aggressive, withdrawn, and normal third-grade boys. Their study was an attempt "to establish quantifiable definitions of criteria for withdrawal and aggressive categories rather than employ the vague criterion of 'maladjustment'," as Byrd (1956), Koppitz (1964), and others had done.

First, forty-nine children were classified into either a withdrawal, aggressive, or control (neutral) group on the basis of teacher and peer behavior ratings. Then Draw-A-Person and Bender-Gestalt protocols of all subjects were scored for the presence or absence of aggression or withdrawal signs. The efficiency of the projective instruments in classifying the children was then compared to more direct methods of assessment (i.e. self-ratings and behavioral observations).

Draw-A-Person signs of withdrawal and aggression were adapted from Hammer (1965), Koppitz (1966), and McHugh (1966), while Bender-Gestalt signs were adapted from Brown (1965) and Koppitz (1964). Results indicated that aggressive subjects tended to demonstrate a higher frequency of both Draw-A-Person and Bender-Gestalt aggression signs. Furthermore, the Bender-Gestalt was a better predictor of aggression than the Draw-A-Person. Although withdrawn subjects tended to demonstrate more Bender-Gestalt withdrawal indicators, results did not reach significance. The "direct" method of behavioral observation was the least successful in terms of the total number of subjects correctly classified. On the average, only 40 percent of all subjects were correctly classified by observation (50.7 percent by self-rating), while 67.3 percent were correctly classified using the Draw-A-Person aggression index, 44.4 percent using the Draw-A-Person withdrawal index, 68.7 percent using the Bender-Gestalt aggression index, and 57.7 percent using the Bender-Gestalt withdrawal index.

Findings of the studies mentioned up to this point can be interpreted as strong evidence that the Bender-Gestalt Test can differentiate between children who are well-adjusted and children who are maladjusted. Most of the studies have at least one thing in common—they compare two groups of subjects on a variety of Bender-Gestalt deviations. Some of these research investigators, such as Byrd (1956), have merely pointed out the ability of the Bender-Gestalt Test to discriminate between a disturbed and normal group with regard to these deviations. Other investigators, such as Clawson (1959) and Corotto and Curnutt (1960), offered interpretations for specific deviations and overall differences in protocols in terms of personality dynamics. Many approaches in evaluating the clinical utility of the Bender-Gestalt have been described by the authors cited. Only one of these studies (Handler and McIntosh 1971) has attempted to compare the Bender-Gestalt's actual predictive ability with other modes of assessment. In the main, however, most of the research with both children and adults has involved the use of individual diagnostic signs to distinguish between clinical (disturbed) and nonclinical (normal) populations.

The use of the Bender-Gestalt as an assessment tool to place a child in a diagnostic category (disturbed or nondisturbed) may be helpful in terms of identifying children with emotional problems. A group of children who have been identified as emotionally disturbed, however, may exhibit a wide range of overt behaviors. Several investigators (Brown 1965; Hutt 1969; and Koppitz 1964) have described Bender deviations which have proven to be indicative of psychopathology. Certain Bender-Gestalt signs have been found to be typical of "acting-out" children; other signs have been found to be typical of "withdrawn" children or "severely anxious" children. Yet, rarely have these signs been compared to specific observable behaviors.

There have been two studies that have attempted to correlate Gestalt signs with specific behavior patterns of subjects (Brannigan and Benowitz 1975; Gregory 1977). Gregory (1977) reported low-order but statistically significant correlations between the Koppitz (1964) total emotional indicators and five of the seventeen factors on the *Devereux Child Behavior Rating Scale* (Spivack and Spotts 1966) in a heterogeneous group of elementary school children ($N = 47$) ranging in age from 5 years 6 months to 13 years 4 months ($\overline{X}$ age = 8 years 7 months). They all were referred for psychological services. Those relationships that were significant included: pathological uses of senses ($r =$

.44), poor coordination of body tonus ($r = .33$), unresponsiveness to stimulation ($r = .35$), anxious-fearful ideation ($r = .33$), and inability to delay ($r = .29$).

In the Brannigan and Benowitz (1975) study the Ss were 29 emotionally disturbed male adolescents. Eight Gestalt signs which have been interpreted as indicants of control problems (Hutt 1969) were correlated with antisocial and acting-out behaviors. Behavior ratings were obtained from a house parent who rated each subject on the *Devereux Adolescent Behavior* (DAB) *Rating Scale.*

Significant relationships were found between several Bender-Gestalt signs and antisocial acting-out tendencies in the adolescents. Exaggerated curvature was significantly related to unethical behavior, defiant-resistive behavior, poor emotional control, and inability to delay, while uneven figure size was related to all of the above behavior ratings except poor emotional control. Progressive increase in figure size was related to poor emotional control and inability to delay. Brannigan and Benowitz also noted that the total number of acting-out Gestalt signs was significantly related to poor emotional control and inability to delay.

The authors pointed out that although caution should be used in making a diagnosis based on individual signs, the occurrence of several of these Gestalt signs in a record allows us to place greater confidence in a diagnosis of inadequate control and antisocial tendencies.

The significant correlations obtained between overt behavior and individual Gestalt signs indicated that the Bender-Gestalt may be a useful device for differentiating specific behavioral syndromes as well as for making decisions along the adjustment-maladjustment continuum (Brannigan and Benowitz 1975). Clearly, however, there is a need for more research of this type to establish additional support for a more specific use of the Bender-Gestalt Test.

MISCELLANEOUS STUDIES ON ADJUSTMENT

Farmer (1973) showed that the Bender-Gestalt may be an effective instrument in monitoring changes in functioning during the period of recovery from alcoholism. The Bender-Gestalt was administered to 100 men at an alcoholic treatment center on admission and then again 30 and 80 days later. There was a significant decrease in mean scores, using Pascal and Suttell's (1951) method, between initial testing (when disruption from alcohol toxicity was greatest) and retesting at 30 days, and between 30-day testing and 80-day testing. Moreover, counselor ratings of post-release adjustment were significantly related to whether Bender scores had decreased over time to a normal level as opposed to test scores remaining in the pathological range at the 80-day testing. While this study indicates that the Bender-Gestalt can be effective in detecting changes accompanying an alcoholic problem, it does not clearly distinguish between the changes attributable to organic alcoholic deterioration and those attributable to related or nonrelated emotional pathology.

Can the Bender-Gestalt Test be used to good advantage to predict the response to surgery of patients with intractable duodenal ulcer? Research (Pascal and Thoroughman 1964) would suggest that it can. Patients having hemigastrectomy and vagotomy for intractability in duodenal ulcer were tested with the Bender-Gestalt and a short version of a vocabulary test at the approximate time of surgery (either two to three days before or two to three weeks after surgery). Pascal and Suttell's (1951) Scoring System was used. Follow-up evaluation two years post-operatively resulted in a dichotomous "good" or "poor" judgment, with clear-cut criteria being applied to achieve classifications. Evaluations were made independently of the psychological test results. The 39 patients with good surgical results disclosed a significantly lower mean Bender raw score ($M = 43.0$) than the 30 patients with poor surgical results ($M = 76.1$). There were no significant differences between the groups in age or intelligence. Using the overall group mean Bender score as a cut-off, the Bender incorrectly identified only 17 of the 69 cases. Thus, the Bender appears to be extremely useful in identifying the degree of emotional disturbance associated with poor surgical prognosis for this type of condition.

Also bearing on the validity of the Bender as a measure of adjustment is Weiss' (1977) long-term case study of a single patient who was first examined at age 32 in 1956, retested in 1957, and then retested once more in 1975. During the entire period, the patient maintained psychiatric contact. On the basis of the patient's performance on the Bender and Rorschach, the patient's personality functioning was delineated, and predictions concerning future developments were made and then checked against subsequent psychodiagnostic and clinical data.

Sahay and Singh (1975) focused on the time taken to complete the drawing of the designs as a prognostic indicator of treatment response. All patients were first grouped on the basis of their Bender Pascal-Suttell (1951) Z scores and outcome of treatment into three categories: (1) high Z scores and poor treatment response; (2) low Z scores and good treatment response; and (3) low Z scores and poor response to treatment. The first of these groups took a significantly longer time ($M = 29.70$ minutes) to complete the task than the second group ($M = 7.80$ minutes). The third group took significantly longer ($M = 38.60$) than the second group. Interestingly, when the two poor recovery groups were compared (i.e. the first and third groups) a significant time difference was also obtained. The reason for this result is not at all clear. This study suffers from the fact that different diagnoses were represented in the three categories (e.g. all 10 patients in the third category were obsessive-compulsive neurotics who would naturally be expected to take longer; the first group consisted of 15 schizophrenics and eight patients with affective psychoses; the second group contained 12 anxiety neurotics and 10 patients with conversion reactions). Also, therapeutic outcome was based on only one psychiatrist's assessment. Because of these inadequacies, the authors' conclusions to the effect that the Z score is a significant prognostic indicator for certain diagnostic conditions but not for others, and that the time factor is an important prognostic indicator, seem unwarranted.

Fanibanda's (1973) study tested the basic assumption that the Bender-Gestalt Test is relatively culture free. He compared the performance of 21 East Indian and 21 American college students; both groups were attending the same American university. Results indicated no significant difference for cultural background on Pascall and Suttell's (1951) Scoring System, on

Hutt's (1969) Psychopathology Scale, or on Hutt's (1969) Abience-Adience Scale. There was also no significant interaction between groups and designs. Some minor differences between groups emerged on the elaboration phase. On the whole, this study seems to support the hypothesis that the Bender-Gestalt performance is quite unaffected by cultural factors. However, one should keep in mind that the degree to which the two groups of Ss used in Fanibanda's study were comparable on relevant other variables is unspecified. The study is also flawed by the unknown representativeness of these East Indian students of their own culture. It would seem probable that their enrollment in an American university made them a highly select and atypical sample.

The question of whether emotional disturbance could be simulated successfully on the Bender-Gestalt is a critical question that no study addressed during the time interval covered by this volume. There is one study (Bruhn and Reed 1975), however, which investigated the ability of non-brain-damaged college students to simulate organic dysfunctioning on the Bender. In this study neither the Pascal-Suttell (1951) nor the Canter (1968) Scoring Systems were able to differentiate malingerers from traumatically induced organics. However, two clinicians and a college student were able to identify correctly most protocols of Ss who feigned organicity. Only indirectly, therefore, does this study relate to the more general issue of the susceptibility to simulation of adjustment failure of the Bender-Gestalt.

Summary

In our previous review of the personality and projective use of the Bender-Gestalt Test (Tolor and Schulberg 1963), we made several points. First, we noted that considerable work had been done in investigating the associational properties of the different Bender designs but that few consistent findings emerged. Secondly, we remarked that the results of studies that attempted to link measures of ego strength to the fidelity of Bender reproductions produced equivocal results and did not lend support to the notion that a substantial relationship existed between Bender performance and ego strength. Thirdly, we made a distinction between studies using children as subjects and studies using adult populations with respect to the evidence for the Bender supporting specific personality hypotheses. The child studies seemed to lead to inconsistent results whereas the adult research was somewhat more, but not much more, encouraging. Throughout the review, we mentioned major and recurrent methodological inadequacies in many of the studies.

In depicting the current status of the field we must first indicate that we seem to discern a heightened interest in the projective applications of the Bender-Gestalt Test which speaks perhaps for a renewed appreciation of the psychodynamic assessment process. We take note also of major new contributions that have been made to personality assessment by means of the Bender-Gestalt Test. Publications, such as Hutt's (1977), underscore the surprising robustness of the Bender-Gestalt Test as an instrument for the study of personality functioning. Added to the revived interest in the projective use of the Bender, there has been greater sophistication in the development of objective scales.

There seems to be a trend toward reporting normative data on such performance variables as line sequence, line directionality, and drawing deviations in normal individuals. The accumulation of normative data should be helpful in establishing the boundaries of expected normal and pathological functioning.

The symbolic significance of the designs to both normals and clinical populations remains a vexing problem and has a somewhat elusive quality to it. Whether the designs do or do not possess consistent symbolic significance is still very much an unsettled question and requires further research.

Studies endeavoring to relate performance on the Bender-Gestalt Test to other personality measures have not produced any cohesive pattern, partially because the results have been so inconclusive, and partially because the personality measures that have been selected for investigation have not always been very appropriate. In addition, too few studies of this type have been done. What is needed most is research involving clearly conceptualized hypotheses and more careful attention to the Bender dimensions and personality measures to be selected for testing these hypotheses.

One can report with considerable confidence, however, that

Bender constriction is consistently associated with such negative feelings as depression and anxiety. It also is reasonable to assert that there is considerable empirical evidence to suggest that Bender performance relates significantly to general adjustment as behaviorally determined. When tests of ego strength are employed as criteria, however, a different picture emerges, either that the Bender taps different aspects of ego strength than do these tests or that there is in fact no significant relationship between ego strength and Bender performance. In view of the increasing evidence that the Bender is capable of differentiating between degrees of adjustment as observed by judges, the more likely conclusion is that ego strength is not to be construed as a unitary concept.

The review of the literature on acting-out and suicidal behavior reveals inconsistent results as to whether there are associated Bender characteristics.

With the exception of the studies showing that anxiety is related to Bender constriction, the studies investigating the effects of stress and anxiety on Bender performance have been too few or too poorly designed to permit any definitive conclusions to be reached.

We find that the literature indicates the Bender is a sensitive instrument in monitoring alcoholic recovery and in predicting response to surgery for patients having significant psychological problems. The single study which examined cultural influences on the Bender, although having certain methodological defects, suggests only very minor effects are attributable to cultural origin. The one study addressing the issue of malingering points to the ability of clinicians to be more effective in detecting simulation than are objective scoring systems. However, both of these interesting problems need more systematic research attention.

Studies employing child subjects have produced encouraging results when group differentiation between emotionally disturbed and nondisturbed children are attempted on the basis of individual Bender designs. More recently, efforts at relating Gestalt deviations to more specific types of overt behaviors have been initiated.

CHAPTER 5

THE BENDER-GESTALT TEST
AND ORGANICITY

P REVIOUS REVIEWS OF the literature (Billingslea 1963; Tolor and Schulberg 1963) have concluded that the Bender-Gestalt Test is a diagnostic instrument which can be used successfully to differentiate groups of patients with organic brain disease from other pathological groups and from normal individuals. As we examine the more recent literature regarding the Bender-Gestalt Test as an indicator of organic dysfunctioning, we will pay particular attention to innovative uses that purport to enhance the discriminative power of this instrument for differential diagnoses. We will also endeavor to determine whether there is any evidence that the Bender possesses greater validity for organic assessment than do other diagnostic instruments. Additionally, this chapter will present information on the kinds of organic impairments for which the Bender-Gestalt Test has found application; delineate the findings on rotations as an index of organic pathology; and explore the relationship between intellectual efficiency, organicity, and Bender performance. Other issues addressed are whether a specific kind of Bender performance is associated with left as compared with right hemiplegia; whether there is an examiner effect that influences organic-like performance or diagnosis; whether unique Bender design recall patterns characterize epileptic functioning; whether black patients with organic impairment perform differently than white patients on this test; and whether various scoring systems have differential diagnostic value, especially in comparison to global clinical judgments.

INNOVATIONS TO ENHANCE ORGANIC DIAGNOSIS

In 1963, Canter (1963) first reported on the preliminary development of an experimental technique to help differentiate between deficiencies in performance that may be due to simple motor ineptitude and mental retardation from those that are attributable to psychotic and organic processes. S was asked first to copy each Bender-Gestalt figure on separate blank sheets of paper and then, after an interpolated task, to copy the same figures on sheets of paper which contained a rather dense field of randomly placed intersecting curved lines. The Background Interference Procedure (BIP), as it was called, permitted each S's performance under background interference conditions to be compared with that obtained under standard conditions. At first, Canter recommended that this procedure be used also for other graphomotor tasks, such as the *Benton Visual Retention Test*. He noted that patients with brain syndromes exhibited significantly greater decrements in quality of performance under interference conditions than did nonorganic patients.

Subsequently, Canter (1966) refined the BIP, limiting the graphomotor task to Bender-Gestalt figure drawings and employing specially designed paper having a background with a confusing array of curved intersecting lines. In his test manual, Canter (1976) explained that his method was of serendipitous origin, traced to the time when he resorted by necessity to the use of coffee-stained, faded graph paper in the Bender administration to a neurosurgical patient. At any rate, brain-damaged patients showed significant decrements in Bender performance under the BIP condition compared to the standard condition, whereas little or no change was demonstrated by psychotic, nonorganic and by nonpsychotic, nonorganic patients under the BIP condition. In this comparison, all scores were based on a modified version of the Pascal-Suttell Scoring System (Pascal and Suttell 1951).

Since it was found that the organic patients differed significantly from nonorganic patients also on standard administration, the question arose as to whether the BIP was more sensitive than the conventional method in the diagnosing of organicity.

An analysis of the data indicated that by employing the BIP criterion of decrement in performance, there was far less group overlapping than employing scores based solely on standard administration. Therefore, one may confidently assert that the inclusion of the BIP does indeed enhance the accuracy of organic diagnosis.

Canter's tentative criteria for identifying brain pathology were the following: BIP total score at least four points greater than the total score based on the standard administration *and* three or more of the eight designs (excluding Design A) drawn more poorly (by at least two points) on BIP than on standard administration. Criteria were also formulated for the "Borderline or Equivocal" and "Nonorganic" designations. Employing these criteria, a high success rate was obtained in differentiating organics from nonorganics in a cross-validation study. The maximum error of 9 percent was recorded.

Later (Canter 1968), the BIP was further refined in regard to administration (e.g. a board was designed to prevent inadvertent paper or card rotations) and in regard to scoring (e.g. Design A could now be scored and other scoring difficulties were overcome). Reliability in scoring for an experienced clinical psychologist and a nonclinician psychometrist was demonstrated. Moreover, the sensitivity of the BIP as a diagnostic screen was again established for populations having different organic base rates, regardless of scorer.

In a further validational study, Canter (1971) compared organic patients with two groups of schizophrenics, one hospitalized for more than four years ($M = 12.1$ yrs.) and one hospitalized for less than three years ($M = 1.5$ yrs.). He also used a nonschizophrenic group of nonorganic patients—unfortunately considerably younger in age—as an additional control group. The results revealed a strong impairing BIP effect, defined as a D-score of four or more points, for 94 percent of the organics, 24 percent of the long-term schizophrenics, 13 percent of the short-term schizophrenics, and 13 percent of the nonschizophrenic, but nonorganic patients. By contrast, the interference procedure *improved* the performance of 53 percent, 38 percent, and 29 percent of short-term schizophrenics, nonschizophrenics, and long-term schizophrenics, respectively. None of the organics showed improved performance. Thus, it appears that the BIP condition leads to arousal and improved integration in a substantial number of nonorganic patients, but to disruption of integration in most or all organically impaired patients.

Pardue (1975) compared 20 organic, 20 schizophrenic, and 20 nonorganic normal controls, matched for age and intelligence on Canter's BIP, and found that the BIP, as scored by the Pascal-Suttell (1951) system, produced significant differences between groups, whereas the standard administration, similarly scored, did not. The *Hain* (1964) *Scoring System* applied to the BIP also yielded significance but not when applied to the standard administrations of the Bender.

Research (Canter and Straumanis 1969) has shown that senile patients with chronic brain syndromes associated with arteriosclerosis (mean age, 75 years) to be adversely affected by the BIP in comparison to healthy elderly (mean age, 72 years) individuals still functioning in the community. Although the standard Bender also differentiated between these two groups, as did the WAIS Vocabulary and Block Design scaled scores, the BIP appeared to be more efficient diagnostically than the other measures.

That for nonparanoid schizophrenics performance on the BIP was significantly poorer than performance under standard conditions, and that paranoids showed no difference on these two tasks was reported by Horine and Fulkerson (1973). They also reported that the performance of the paranoids on the BIP was superior to that of nonparanoid schizophrenics. These findings were interpreted as supporting the notion that nonparanoid schizophrenics have an attentional disorder and that process nonparanoid schizophrenics resemble brain-damaged patients on the BIP. While the attempt to distinguish types of schizophrenias from a highly heterogeneous overall classification represents an improvement over Canter's methodology, this study provided far too few subjects in each of the subgroups, making some replicative attempt a highly desirable procedure.

Hypothesizing that retardates with organic brain disease would disclose a greater adverse BIP effect than would retardates without organic brain disease (i.e. those with cultural or familial retardation), Song and Song (1969) compared these two groups having different etiologies. A third group, consisting of emotionally disturbed, nonorganic mental retardates, was also used. On the BIP the organically based retardates differed significantly from the cultural familial retardates and from the emotionally disturbed retardates. The two nonorganic groups did not, however, differ significantly from each other, confirming the hypothesis. It is regrettable that the three study groups had not been equated for intelligence, although a redeeming factor is that intelligence was found not to be significantly correlated with D-scores for all Ss combined. The study also disclosed that all retarded groups have performance decrements under BIP and that the three groups exhibit much overlap of D-scores.

Norton (1978) compared the relative validity of the BIP and the *Trail Making Test* for organic diagnosis. The 598 Ss comprising the overall sample were categorized as "normal," "abnormal," or "borderline" on the basis of the Trail Making Test and BIP scores. The Ss were also placed into these classifications on the basis of a more complete neuropsychological evaluation, including neurological criteria. Although a highly significant association between BIP performance and classification based on neuropsychological evaluation was reported, Norton indicated that 47 percent of the abnormal Ss fell within the BIP normal group. These disappointing results should be weighed, however, against the very low (4%) false positive rate. The Trail Making Test, according to Norton, also misclassified 21 percent of abnormal patients as normal.

Norton failed to address the issue of the adequacy of "the whole psychological examination" or "the neurological criteria" as adequate criteria of organicity. Instead, he is extremely critical of the BIP and the Trail Making Test both individually and in combination as valid screening devices.

As did Yulis (1969), Norton found that the BIP D-scores are independent of IQ. Adams (1971) attempted to determine what aspects of the BIP accounted for its ability to tap organic malfunctioning. He devised a form in which the background lines were peripheral and compared the performance of brain-damaged and nonbrain-damaged psychiatric patients on this new form with the usual form. Although the organic patients did more poorly on the BIP than the control group, performance on the two forms did not differ significantly.

The Canter Background Interference Procedure, in our opinion, represents a highly creative and sophisticated modification of Bender-Gestalt Test use for the diagnosis of organic pathology. There has been considerable published research with this technique which in itself attests to its viability. The research has indicated that the effort in the development of this technique has paid off well. A careful examination of the studies suggests that often the BIP enhanced the diagnostic acuity of the Bender, and that this improved efficacy is generalizable to a number of patient comparison groups, including schizophrenics, retardates, and the elderly. We wonder whether practicing clinicians have taken sufficient advantage of this diagnostic aid, which has proven to be so useful for group screening.

THE BENDER'S VALIDITY FOR ORGANICITY

In an excellent review of the problem associated with the assessment of organic brain damage by psychological tests, Haynes and Sells (1963) present the diverse conceptions of the behavioral effects of brain damage as found in the literature. The published research appears to accept the term, "brain-damage," as a diagnostic unitary entity even though the evidence overwhelmingly indicates that the nature of brain pathology is highly complex and multi-dimensional. Haynes and Sells conclude that only a few investigators have used multiple variable batteries, and most research focuses on diagnostic signs, single variable tests, scatter patterns, and qualitative techniques.

This mode of approach is also evidenced in the literature dealing with the Bender-Gestalt Test, according to Haynes and Sells. Those reviewers regard the Bender-Gestalt Test to be one of several tests of brain damage that focuses on only one aspect of behavior for diagnosis. They argue that although such tests are capable of group differentiation, they frequently identify too many false positives and false negatives. Their second objection is directed at the assumptions underlying the diagnostic process itself, assumptions which pertain to organismic variables while allegedly disregarding the stimulus properties and the nature of the task. That this later objection is not largely justified with respect to the Bender can be gleaned from an examination of the work of several investigators who have meticulously studied the Bender figure characteristics and have also studied the aspects of the task required for completion of the Bender figure drawings.

Test Comparisons

In a major review of some studies in which more than one test was used in establishing an organic diagnosis, Spreen and Benton (1965) were able to identify 21 studies for this type of comparative analysis. In setting the stage for the evaluation of the psychological instruments, Spreen and Benton indicated that physical measures of organicity yield the following respective hit rates: electroencephalogram, around 70 percent on average; radiological techniques, including pneumoencephalography, arteriography, and ventriculography, about 72 to 96 percent; and the brain scan, about 92 percent of all lesions. By contrast, the psychological measures, based on 196 individual predictions in various reports, provided a mean prediction rate of 74 percent, with a range from 33 percent to 99 percent. For single test measures, the mean prediction rate was 71 percent; for combined or weighted multiple test measures, which were fewer in number, the mean prediction rate was 82 percent. These accurate identification rates appear to compare favorably with those obtained when physical diagnostic techniques are employed.

Spreen and Benton also endeavored to address the question as to whether some psychological tests predicted brain damage better than others. Of the studies considered, only two implicated the Bender-Gestalt Test. In Korman and Blumberg's (1963) study, the optimal Bender-Gestalt cut-off score correctly identified 74 percent of brain-damaged patients when compared with a mixed psychiatric patient group. This represents about the same hit rate as the mean of 76 percent reported in the literature for 14 individual tests, such as the *Spiral Aftereffect Test*, the *Trail Making Test*, and the *Memory for Designs Test*. In the Kerekjarto (1962) study cited by Spreen and Benton (1965), the recommended Bender-Gestalt cut-off score produced a hit rate of 63 percent which is nearly identical to the mean hit rate of 62 percent based on seven psychological measures, including the *VRT Form C, Block Designs,* and the *Shipley-Hartford Conceptual Quotient.* Therefore, it would appear that the Bender-Gestalt Test achieves about as much success in its diagnostic accuracy for organic pathology as do other psychological instruments when used individually or in combination, and that the Bender-Gestalt maintains a respectable position in comparison to various physical measures of organicity.

Spreen and Benton (1965) concluded that psychological tests in general are more sensitive to left-hemisphere than right-hemisphere lesions and to brain damage in the dominant hemisphere (and to diffuse or bilateral lesions) than to the non-dominant hemisphere (or focal lesions). All of the findings, however, were to be qualified by the fact that data available varied greatly for the studies examined, that the control groups used often included diverse psychiatric patients, that the brain-damaged patients varied in severity of impairment and site of pathology, and in other respects. The importance of these variables was stressed by Smith (1962) who has indicated that the psychological test performance of organics is a function of type of lesion, age of the individual when the lesion first developed, and time interval between onset of the damage and the testing. Despite these qualifications, Spreen and Benton (1965) assert that composite psychological measures and weighted scores enjoy an advantage for organic diagnosis over single measures although the gain is not proportionate to the extra time required to administer the batteries of tests. Moreover, for general screening purposes, they argue, there is little justification for administering an entire battery of tests sensitive to organic pathology. This recommendation has obvious implications for the use of the Bender-Gestalt Test as a screening device, especially in view of its validity for organic diagnosis.

Continuing with individual studies of the relative validity of the Bender-Gestalt Test for organic diagnosis, Anglin, Pullen, and Games (1965) reported validity coefficients (point-biserial correlations) of .55 and .67, not significantly different from each other, for the Bender-Gestalt Test and the Memory-for-Designs Test (MFD), respectively. Raters had scored the MFD and made global judgments of the Bender-Gestalt protocols of 60 patients admitted to a state hospital. The ratings were compared with the hospital staff diagnoses divided into organic vs. non-organic categories. Scorer agreement was significantly higher on the Memory-for-Designs Test than the Bender-Gestalt Test.

Ascough and Dana (1962) investigated the concurrent validities of objective scoring and clinical judgments of the Bender-Gestalt Test and the *Lowenfeld Mosaic Test* (Lowenfeld 1954) by using as criteria independent medical diagnoses of organicity. Three clinicians made diagnostic judgments based on the Mosaic records. These records were also scored on certain signs and objective criteria. Similarly, three clinicians made diagnostic judgments based on the Bender protocols. The protocols were also scored by the Pascal and Suttell system (Pascal and Suttell 1951). The Ss were patients in a rest home, of which 19 and 10 were diagnosed organic in the validation ($N = 28$) and cross-validation ($N = 15$) samples, respectively. The Bender-Gestalt scoring significantly differentiated organic from nonorganic groups in both validation and cross-validation samples. Successful clinical validation was also obtained on this test, but there was successful cross-validation only for the most experienced clinician. Some of the Mosaic criteria also survived cross-validation, but cross-validation for clinical judgments of the Mosaics was not achieved. The results are difficult to evaluate because of the small number of clinical judges, their varying degrees of experience, and the peculiarities of the base rates of normal and organic subjects in the samples used.

Brilliant and Gynther (1963) investigated the predictive validity for organicity of the Bender-Gestalt Test, the Benton Visual Retention Test (Benton 1945, 1955), and the Graham-Kendall Memory-for-Designs Test (Graham and Kendall 1946, 1960). Based on 120 patients tested at the time of admission to the hospital—where the base rate of organicity was 30 percent —and later diagnosed by the psychiatric staff, it was found that when the effects of age, IQ, and education are statistically controlled, all three psychological tests predicted the clinical diagnosis of organicity at the .001 level of significance. It is noteworthy that the Bender-Gestalt Test was found to be the best single measure, with an 82 percent of correct identification of all patients. The Benders had been scored with the Hutt and Briskin (1960) system.

Korman and Blumberg (1963) studied the relative discriminating power of several tests which purport to be sensitive to organic brain disease. Forty cerebrally damaged patients were matched in pairs for age, education, and sex with a control group of nonbrain-damaged patients. The tests administered were the following: the Bender-Gestalt Test, scored by Pascal and Suttell's (1951) system, the Trail Making Test (Reitan 1956), the Graham-Kendall Memory-for-Designs Test (MFD) (Graham and Kendall 1960), the Spiral Aftereffect Test (SAET) (Psychological Research and Development Corporation 1958), the L scale of the MMPI, and the Wechsler-Bellevue I Vocabulary Test. All tests were able to differentiate significantly between the two groups of patients, but there were marked differences in the tests' efficiency. Using artificial base rates of 50 percent brain damage and 50 percent nonbrain damage, optimal cutting scores were generated for the several measures. A Bender cutting score between 44 and 45 correctly identified 77.50 percent of the patients with cerebral brain damage and 70.00 percent of those without cerebral brain damage, yielding an overall accuracy level of 73.75 percent. This accuracy rate was somewhat better than the discrimination reported for Trails A minus Trails B (70% total correct), Vocabulary (67.50% total correct), and the L scale (63.75% total correct). However, it was somewhat less efficient than the MFD, SAET, Trails B, Trails A and B combined, and Trails A, which yielded total accuracy in identification rates from 76.25 percent to 90 percent. It was also reported that the Bender correlated significantly with the MFD, with the SAET, with the Trails, and with Vocabulary, but the highest common variance of only 36 percent was obtained with the uncorrected MFD.

Among other studies comparing Bender performance with diverse tests of organic dysfunctioning are those of McGuire (1960), Wagner and Evans (1966), Quattlebaum (1968), and

Reinehr and Golightly (1968). McGuire (1960) compared male patients having known organic pathology with a control group consisting of mostly healthy males. The Bender protocols were evaluated by five experts, with agreement on the part of three, four, and five judges, respectively, used as criteria of varying stringencies. The flicker and Bender, with agreement on the part of three judges as the criterion, correctly identified virtually the same number of cases (30 and 29, respectively), but the specific subjects identified by these two methods were not necessarily the same.

Wagner and Evans (1966) found no significant differences between the Bender-Gestalt Test and two graphomotor tasks selected from *Reitan's Aphasia Screening Test* in differentiating organic from nonorganic psychiatric patients. The protocols were classified by three experienced judges in each case.

Quattelbaum (1968) reported a correlation of .85 between scores on the Graham-Kendall Memory-for-Designs Test and the Bender-Gestalt Test, scored by the Hain system. The sample was a heterogeneous group of psychiatric patients.

The Bender-Gestalt Test and the *Organic Integrity Test* (Tien 1960) were found by Reinehr and Golightly (1968) to correlate .34. All Ss were hospitalized alcoholics.

The ability of several tests (i.e. the Bender-Gestalt, using the Pascal and Suttell [1951] Scoring System, the Graham-Kendall Memory-for-Designs, and some of the Benton Visual Retention Test measures) to differentiate brain-damaged patients from schizophrenics was studied by Watson (1968). Of the three visual-motor tests, the Bender-Gestalt and the Memory-for-Designs could not achieve significant differentiation. Since there was a .58 correlation between the Bender and Shipley raw scores, and .60 between the MFD and the Shipley, the author felt that whatever discriminating power these tests possessed could be a function of intellectual differences.

Levine and Feirstein (1972) tested organics, schizophrenics, and medical groups with measures that included the Bender-Gestalt Test, five tests selected from the Halstead-Reitan test battery, and the Trail Making Test. Organics were differentiated significantly from both schizophrenics and from medical patients on the Bender. The Halstead test battery also achieved diagnostic accuracy, albeit to a lesser extent (since it could not differentiate organics from schizophrenics), as did Part B and Part A and B combined of the Trail Making Test.

Lacks, Colbert, Harrow, and Levine (1970) had also found that the short and easily administered Bender-Gestalt Test, scored by the Hutt and Briskin (1960) method, was as effective for screening organicity as the Halstead-Reitan battery. Moreover, the Halstead tests seem to be inferior to the Bender in classifying nonorganic patients, since the former could achieve only a 62 percent accuracy rate compared to the 91 percent accuracy rate for the latter.

The conclusion to be reached, on the basis of the studies reviewed that deal with the efficacy of the Bender relative to other measures, is that in general the Bender-Gestalt Test is not only capable of making group differentiations in a highly successful manner, but that it is capable of doing so as efficaciously as do most other psychological and physical measures with which it has been compared. Moreover, there is little evidence that more extensive screening batteries are substantially superior to the Bender-Gestalt Test for organic diagnosis. However, as Garron and Cheifetz (1965) have indicated, comparisons of measures of organicity may produce equivocal results because of the fact that different brain structures govern different psychological functions so that lesions in one structure may not necessarily be detected by a measure that is sensitive to other functions.

Indirect Evidence

Still addressing the issue of the Bender's validity for detecting organic pathology, we might refer to several reports that offer less direct evidence. Eichler and Norman (1965) studied the effects of ammonia intoxication in normal volunteers on the serially administered Bender. Their findings were interpreted as indicating that hyperammonemia blocks the accurate perception of the configurations, the integration of the perceptions, and the "recording" of the integrated percepts, but does not interfere with those percepts that had already been integrated. This study found no evidence of a practice effect on the Bender.

Cooper, Dwarshuis, and Blechman (1967) applied a technique which they had developed (Cooper and Barnes 1966) for measuring the proportional accuracy with which any two-dimensional stimuli are reproduced to the Bender-Gestalt renditions. Forty Ss who had either cerebral vascular accidents or degenerative brain disorders (with sex of Ss not specified) were rated for severity of neurological deficit, as indicated by Ss' psychological reports. The Bender performance of the Ss was scored by their technique. The correlation between the severity rating score and the Bender was .39. Age and intelligence were not significantly related to severity of organic impairment. While this study supports the Bender's validity for determining severity of organic dysfunctioning, and indicates some utility of the new scoring method, it provides no leads concerning the relative usefulness of this method of scoring accuracy of the drawings compared to others.

As Munz and Tolor (1955) had done previously with a number of such patients, Bruell and Albee (1962) administered the Bender-Gestalt Test to one patient following cerebral hemispherectomy. Also using a case study approach, Russell (1976) compared the results derived from the Halstead-Reitan neuropsychological battery and the Bender-Gestalt Test in a single, severely brain-damaged, 53-year-old male patient. The performance on the Bender-Gestalt was well within the normal range while the results of the Halstead-Reitan battery clearly indicated brain damage. The inability of the Bender to detect the brain injury, which was known to have occurred in the left temporal area, led the author to suspect that the Bender is limited in its usefulness to diffuse slowly progressive and right-hemisphere damage. He recommended the Halstead-Reitan battery ". . . when the highest possible accuracy in determining the existence of brain damage is required or when an extensive evaluation of that damage is required" (Russell 1976, p. 361).

Arbit and Zager (1978) compared the factor analysis (linear) and hierarchical cluster analysis (nonlinear) of a neuropsychological battery of tests which included the Bender. The aim was to understand better the components of the diagnosis of organic brain disease. The Bender was administered as a five-second memory task as well as a direct copy task and was scored by Koppitz's (1964) method. It was concluded that the Bender relates to memory ability, whereas the Graham-Kendall Memory-for-Designs Test loads higher on the perceptual-motor ability factor.

The indirect evidence of the Bender's validity for organic diagnosis is equivocal. The studies cited in this section seem to provide interesting leads but require further supportive research before more definitive conclusions can be reached.

Group Comparisons

Studies of concurrent validity, in which organics are compared with various clinical groups or with normals, solely on the Bender are less numerous. Hain (1964) found fifteen of thirty-one signs to discriminate between brain-damaged and nonbrain-damaged groups. When the protocols of cross-validation samples of brain-damaged and psychiatric samples are scored by using the discrimination weights of the signs derived from the original sample, significant differentiation again was obtained. It should be noted that in Hain's (1964) study, the normal control group used before cross-validation did not differ significantly from the psychiatric patients in Bender performance and was, therefore, treated as a single nonbrain-damaged group. Furthermore, in the selection of organic patients for cross-validation, organic patients with seizures were omitted because their Bender performance was deemed to be atypical in relation to the other organics.

Hain's system shows that a high score has a high probability of identifying brain damage, but a low score does not necessarily reflect absence of brain damage. Therefore, discrimination leads to few false positives, but many false negatives.

Using Hain's (1964) method, Verma, Wig, and Shah (1972) found normals could be significantly differentiated from psychotics and from organics, and neurotics could be differentiated from psychotics and from organics. However, groups of organics and psychotics did not perform differently.

Kramer and Fenwick (1966) were able to differentiate 18 organic from 24 functionally disturbed patients on the Bender-Gestalt Test on both the Hain (1964) and Pascal and Suttell (1951) Scoring Systems. The latter system also distinguished significantly both patient groups from normals (staff members), although the Hain system did not reveal a significant difference between the functional and normal groups. The Hain system, with suggested cut-off score, correctly placed 76 percent of the patients while a clinical expert, without benefit of observation of drawing behavior, did somewhat better (81% accuracy).

Neurotics, alcoholics, organics, and controls were administered the Bender-Gestalt Test under conventional and tachistoscopic conditions by Snortum (1965). Performance was evaluated using the Pascal and Suttell (1951) Scoring System. The copy procedure differentiated the diagnostic groups from the controls significantly, but did not differentiate the various diagnostic groups from one another. By contrast, however, the tachistoscopic procedure discriminated significantly organics from neurotics, and controls from alcoholics and organics. Organics were characterized by the poorest performance of all groups.

Stoer, Corotto, and Curnutt (1965) had Ss copy the Bender designs on a card like the one on which the stimulus is printed. The S was also presented with eight choices of the same design, six of these choices consisting of deviant reproductions of varying degrees (previously ranked for deviancy by three judges), one consisting of a nearly identical reproduction of the stimulus, and one consisting of the S's own reproduction. The task was for S to select the design most like the stimulus and the design least like the stimulus. Also Ss were asked to order the remaining six choices for degree of similarity with the stimulus.

The matching task, thought to be reflective of perceptual ability, did not differentiate organics, schizophrenics, and normal controls; however, the reproduction task, thought to be reflective of motor ability, did significantly differentiate controls from organics, controls from acute schizophrenics, and controls from chronic schizophrenics. The two types of schizophrenics did not, however, draw their designs differently than the organic group. Instead of deviant visual perception, the disturbance revealed by the Bender was concluded more likely to be motoric or integrative.

Ko (1971) reported the frequency of eye movement on the Bender-Gestalt Test (considered a measure of attention breadth) to be significantly greater for organic, as compared with schizophrenic patients, but not to be different from neurotics.

Rosecrans and Schaffer (1969) found two groups of brain-damaged patients, differing in age, to perform significantly less well on the Bender than a group of psychiatric patients. Time scores did not have a consistent discriminative function between the groups.

In a study of group differentiation between organics and normals at varying intellectual levels, Johnson, Hellkamp, and Lottman (1971) found that the Bender, as scored by the Hutt and Briskin (1960) method, is most efficacious in the IQ range from 70 through 89. The high correlations between Hutt-Briskin error scores and WAIS IQ (range —.53 to —.59) raises some questions about the scoring system.

Hirschenfang, Silber, and Benton (1967) used Pascal and Suttell's (1951) Scoring System to compare institutionalized patients with alcoholic neuropathies and patients with metabolic or infectious neuropathies. Mean scores were not significantly different. On Design 6, however, those with alcoholic neuropathy drew the figure significantly worse. This study presented little rationale for this type of group comparison and also suffers from a lack of control for possibly relevant variables, except for age.

In another rather poorly designed study (Silber, Hirschenfang, and Benton 1968) among several psychological tests administered by one clinical psychologist to 36 patients with a history of either diabetes or alcoholism, some of whom developed peripheral nerve damage and some of whom did not, was the Bender-Gestalt Test. Pascal and Suttell (1951) scores are presented for the designs separately and jointly. Since there was no analysis of the scores, one does not know whether the Bender performance for patients with neuropathy differs from those without neuropathy, or whether diabetics differ from alcoholics. The contribution, if any, which the Bender made to the authors' conclusion that underlying personality patterns played a significant role in patients who developed peripheral neuropathy remains unknown.

There are two studies, both by Armstrong (1963, 1965), dealing with group differences in Bender recall. Armstrong (1963) did not attempt to ascertain whether group differences existed, but her main purpose was to determine whether the complexity of Designs 3 and 4 or their serial position accounted for the infrequency of their recall. An incidental finding, relevant here, however, was that organic patients always recalled significantly fewer designs than did either the functionally psychotic or the nonpsychotic patients. Regarding her main concern, she concluded that the complexity of the designs, or possibly their psychological impact, contributed more to their infrequent recall than their position in the series.

In her other study, Armstrong (1965) compared the copying and recall performance of the Bender-Gestalt of several diagnostic groups, including organics. Organics differed significantly from the functional disorders in producing consistently poorer copying and recall scores. Thus, the quality of the organic group's poor copying performance relative to the functionally disturbed group's is evident also on recall. However, organic patients produced no significant correlation between copying and recall performance. Organics recalled significantly fewer designs, 3.85, on average, compared with 6.00, 5.57, 6.09, and 6.06, for schizophrenics, depressives, neurotics, and character disorders, respectively.

In a very recent publication, Holland and Wadsworth (1979) described a study in which the Bender-Gestalt Test was administered under standard, recall, BIP, and BIP-recall conditions to twenty organically involved and twenty schizophrenic male hospitalized patients. After the effects of intelligence were controlled, only the recall conditions, both regular recall and BIP-recall, based on number of scorable designs, differentiated the two groups significantly. When these recall scores were expressed as difference scores corrected for base level, there was no significant increase in group differentiation, and a substantial multiple correlation with intelligence was found. The results of this study raise doubt as to the value of calculating difference scores and correcting for base level. They also highlight the sensitivity of the recall measure for group diagnosis.

Garron and Cheifetz (1965) criticized much Bender-Gestalt work involving recall because of what they regard as a simplistic view of memory. They remind us that poor productions of designs on recall may result from either impaired memory or impaired perceptual and/or execution functions, or possibly from a combination of both. The locus of lesion and degree of pathology could also affect the nature of the memory defect to be expected.

A final study (Weinstein and Johnson 1964) of the Bender's concurrent validity, which failed to find differences between schizophrenics and lobotomized epileptics, was critically evaluated by Bender (1965). Weinstein and Johnson (1964) employed a tiny sample of 12 epileptic patients and tested them prior to and following unilateral temporal lobectomy. They also compared their performance with 12 schizophrenics. Eight clinical psychologists were asked to differentiate protocols of pre- vs. post-operative patients, six were asked to differentiate pre-operative vs. schizophrenic protocols, and six were asked to differentiate post-operative vs. schizophrenic protocols. None of the psychologists was successful beyond chance expectations in making these judgments, although the overall psychologists' 65.4 percent correct identification rate exceeded chance. The Pascal-Suttell (1951) method did not show improvement over clinical judgments. Laymen asked to differentiate post-operative from schizophrenic drawings had a success rate of 62.5 percent. On the basis of these and related findings, Weinstein and Johnson (1964) recommended that the test no longer be used for organic diagnosis.

Bender (1965) retorted that the use of epileptics as representative of a broader range of organic individuals was a most inappropriate choice since epilepsy has no specific organic cortical pathology that would be reflected on the Bender-Gestalt Test. Also, lobectomies, she argued, result in only temporary disruptive influences on perceptual-motor functions. She also expressed reservations about the selection of the schizophrenic sample and the ways in which the test task was framed. Certainly,

Weinstein and Johnson's (1964) sweeping recommendation seems totally unwarranted considering the various problems that apply to the study as performed.

The studies brought together under the section, *Group Comparisons*, are not very numerous. The preponderance of the evidence available supports the concurrent validity of the Bender-Gestalt Test for discriminating organics from functionally disturbed patients and from normals, although there are some exceptions to this general trend. The Bender's discriminative ability appears to be independent of the specific method of analysis employed (i.e. the nature of the scoring system, or whether clinical judgments, recall quality, or number of designs recalled are used as the basis for diagnoses).

TYPES OF ORGANIC CONDITIONS

The following section illustrates the kinds of organic pathologies which have been studied in recent years using the Bender-Gestalt Test. There is one report (Schwartz and Dennerll 1969) relating Bender recall to epileptic seizure types. Grand mal and psychomotor seizures combined, relative to other epileptic seizure types, revealed the poorest recall. The results were not due to differences in the number of seizures experienced, nor to lateralizable EEG abnormality.

There is one study (Lyle and Gottesman 1977) in which the Bender-Gestalt Test was used, along with other measures, to identify premorbid indicators of Huntington's disease. Marked differences were found in a comparison of premorbid Bender recall scores obtained 15 to 20 years previously from a group that later developed Huntington's disease and a group that did not develop any symptoms of this disease. A hierarchy in degree of impairment, from those who did not display symptoms 15 to 20 years later, through those who were free of Huntington's disease at the time of initial testing but who had subsequently developed symptoms, through those who already had symptoms at time of initial testing, was found. More specifically, the still normal group recalled a significantly ($p < .01$) greater number of Bender designs than the premorbid group ($M = 5.7$, $SD =$

1.3 vs. $M = 4.3$, $SD = 2.4$). The still normal group also recalled a significantly greater number of designs than either the early onset subgroup where Ss developed symptoms within two years of testing ($M = 3.7$ designs) or the late onset subgroup where Ss developed symptoms six to 18 years after testing ($M = 4.8$ designs). However, those with early appearing symptoms were not significantly different from those with later appearing symptoms in designs recalled.

In this study, the Bender recall yielded a 78 percent rate of true negatives and a 58 percent rate of true positives for predicting the future Huntington's disease status of Ss, all of whom had a 50 percent chance of inheriting the disease.

Shapiro, Shapiro and Clarkin (1974) reported test findings derived from 24 male and six female patients with Giles de la Tourette's syndrome. The test battery consisted of the WAIS or WISC, Bender-Gestalt, Rorschach, and for some patients the Draw-A-Person Test, *Thematic Apperception Test,* and MMPI. A wide age-range from eight to 64 years (mean, 14 years) was represented in this sample. Similarly, there was great variability in duration of illness with a range of 3.5 to 54.0 years. Regarding the Bender results, based on independent ratings made by psychologists employing, as appropriate, either the Hutt and Briskin (1960) or Koppitz (1964) systems, a definite and statistically significant trend toward organic performance was noted in these patients. Three psychological tests, namely, the WAIS or WISC, Bender-Gestalt, and Rorschach, in combination, produced an impression of at least mild organic impairment in 77 percent of the sample. These findings were interpreted to support the hypothesis that organic factors are implicated in Giles de la Tourette's syndrome. However, in the absence of a control group, conclusions remain very tentative at best.

The aging process has also been investigated by using the Bender-Gestalt Test along with other psychological measures (Ames 1974). Older individuals, ranging in age from 57 to 92 years, were classified on the basis of their Rorschachs into normal, intact presenile, medium, and deteriorated senile groups, and their performance on the other psychological tests was recorded. Normals and intact preseniles combined produced significantly fewer Bender errors than medium and deteriorated Ss combined. Thus, the Bender was capable of distinguishing between different levels of deterioration or intactness in old age, as operationally defined on the basis of Rorschach performance. It should be noted that Ames (1974) used only five of the Bender figures.

In an extremely important study of elderly male patients with a mean age of 68, all of whom exhibited severe deterioration in cognitive functioning, Jacobs, Winter, Alvis, and Small (1969) found that increased arterial oxygen tension resulted in highly significant gains in cognitive functioning over pretreatment levels. Among the tests of psychological functioning was the Bender-Gestalt Test to which was applied a weighted scoring system to measure memory traces on the recall phase. The study was marked by meticulous attention to experimental controls for tester bias, the effect of increased attention devoted to S, and effects that might be attributed to the environment or to high barometric pressure itself. Even when these controls were instituted, the improvement as a consequence of elevation of alveolar oxygen tension was maintained on all tests.

In discussing psychological techniques that can be used advantageously with the aging, Oberleder (1967) advocates the use of the Bender-Gestalt Test as the test of choice when a whole battery of tests is not feasible.

In sum, then, this test has found useful application for such diverse organic problems as epilepsy, Huntington's chorea, Giles de la Tourette's disease, and the aging process. In each of these pathological conditions the Bender has made some contribution in elucidating relevant clinical issues.

ROTATIONS

The large number of reports on rotations of Bender figures appearing in print underscores the continuing interest which this concept has held for many clinicians and researchers using the Bender-Gestalt Test.

In a series of studies, Freed (1965, 1966b, 1969) offered data on the incidence of rotations among mentally defective psychiatric patients as well as other types of psychiatric patients. Defining a rotation as an angular displacement of at least 45°, Freed (1965) observed that 39.4 percent of psychiatric patients falling within the mentally defective range on the Wechsler scale produced one or more rotations. With use of the Pascal-Suttell (1951) Scoring System, including a modification to account for Design A, 68.2 percent of these patients made at least one rotation.

In an attempt to enhance the understanding of the perceptual contribution of the individual designs, Freed (1966b) studied the frequency of the rotation susceptibility of each of the designs. For a mixed diagnostic inpatient psychiatric population of 1091 male patients, rotations occurred most commonly on Designs 3 (28%) and A (17%) and least often on Designs 6 (2%), 2 (5%), and 1 (6%), when a 45° displacement is the criterion of rotation. Using the Pascal-Suttell (1951) criteria for rotation of part of the figure on Design 4, 5, 6, and 7, and a greater than 45° rotation of the diamond on Design A and of part of the figure on Design 3, it was found that the incidence of this type of rotation was 61 percent on Design 7, and on Design 4 it was 20 percent. Freed concluded that Designs 3 and A are most susceptible to gross rotations, whereas Design 7 yielded the greatest frequency of rotation of part of a figure. Those figures that were least frequently rotated also have a clear horizontal orientation in relation to a similarly oriented stimulus card.

Following Tolor and Schulberg's (1963) suggestion that rotation data be reported by diagnostic grouping with the effects of intelligence partialed out, Freed (1969) tabulated the incidence of rotations for general diagnostic groups according to the two types of rotation criteria previously outlined. Those patients who produced rotations scored significantly lower in intelligence than those who did not produce rotations. Partialing out the effects of IQ canceled any between-group differences in number of gross rotations of designs, but did yield some significant differences on the more subtle Pascal and Suttell (1951) criteria of rotations of portions of designs.

When a 45° or greater angular displacement was the measure

of rotation, Silverstein and Mohan (1962) found that 46 percent of a group of 200 hospitalized mentally retarded individuals of both sexes (median age, 16) had at least one rotation on initial testing, and 52 percent had at least one rotation on retesting about three years later. This difference was not significant. There was a low order, but significant (phi coefficient = .26, $p < .001$), relationship between rotations on the two testing sessions. On initial testing, there was no relationship between rotations and age, sex, IQ or organic vs. nonorganic diagnosis, but on retesting a significant inverse relationship between rotations and intelligence was found. A significantly greater number of female retardates rotated (65.7%) than did males (44.6%) on retesting only, but this may have been an artifact due to intellectual differences between the sexes at retesting.

A replication study with another group of 200 mentally retarded individuals who had only been tested on one occasion showed 39 percent to rotate at least once. This incidence of rotations did not differ significantly from the original sample. For this group, the background variables were unrelated to rotation tendency.

Jernigan's (1967a) publication, supplemented by personal communication, indicated that of 1,475 state hospital patients tested, 1,081 gave scoreable Bender records. Twenty-three percent of the scoreable records revealed at least one rotation, with 31 percent making counterclockwise rotations, 41 percent clockwise rotations, 5.5 percent mixed rotations, and 22.5 percent indeterminate rotations.

Further data on rotation style (Jernigan 1967b) were based on the performance of three groups of patients: (a) patients tested by the psychology service and described as "general medical," (b) a replication sample of "general medical," and (c) a psychiatric population at the same hospital. For all groups it was found that rotators were significantly older, less intelligent, and less educated than nonrotators. Diagnosis was related to rotations only in the first sample with patients having central nervous system disorders being significantly more often represented in the group that rotated designs.

The rotation style in the medical groups was quite similar

with counterclockwise rotations occurring most often (46%), clockwise rotations occurring in about 31 percent of the patients, and mixed rotations occurring in about 10 percent of the patients. The psychiatric patients differed from the medical patients in producing a significantly higher incidence of indeterminate rotations (38% vs. 13%), and fewer, but not significantly fewer, clockwise rotations (10% vs. 31%). There was some tendency for general medical patients who were assigned a psychiatric diagnosis to make more clockwise rotations than those assigned a physical or CNS diagnosis, but this finding failed to be replicated. Jernigan also felt that counterclockwise rotations might be associated with regression and chronicity, although the confounding effect of several variables that were not well controlled, but which apparently covary with rotations, render such conclusions quite tentative.

Indicating that rotations were a poorly understood phenomenon and that theories pertaining to this type of test behavior were not widely accepted, Royer and Holland (1975) reasoned that an adequate theory of test rotation should account for its occurrence in normals and pathological groups, should specify the conditions that facilitate its occurrence, and should explain the observation that organics produce a greater number of spontaneous rotations but have greater difficulty making rotations when specifically requested to do so.

While a presentation of Royer and Holland's (1975) theoretical formulations and methodology for testing the theory go far beyond the scope of this review, they should be commended for their contribution to an understanding of the psychological processes required to process information. Group differences obtained appeared to reflect the differences in the integrity of the psychological processes involved. The authors did not examine these processes with the Bender-Gestalt Test, but employed stimuli that varied systematically the figural and spatial orientational information. Yet, the results have implications for Bender performance as well.

Understanding of the phenomenon of rotations was also promoted by the development of the *Minnesota Percepto-Diagnostic Test*, which consists of six gestalt designs the S is requested to copy. As a matter of fact, Fuller and Laird (1963a) developed this new measure specifically around the concept of rotation. This test, which is not identical to the Bender-Gestalt Test, is based on the research of Fuller and Chagnon (1962) and Fuller (1963) and focuses on rotations to facilitate group diagnosis.

On the Minnesota Percepto-Diagnostic Test (MPD), two Bender designs—Design A and 3—appear on six cards. The orientation of the ground is varied for the different cards, sometimes appearing rectangular, diamond-shaped, or horizontal, or vertical, so that each of the two designs appears in association with three different grounds. The task consists of copying the design without turning the card or the paper. The test is alleged to provide a rapid and objective method to determine whether adults have brain damage, a personality disorder, or are normal; and whether children are schizophrenic, more moderately disturbed emotionally, or are normal. Additionally, the MPD is purported to be capable of determining the etiology of a child's reading disturbance in terms of the organic pathology or retardation. The MPD has been standardized on over 1,200 children and adults.

In commenting about the problem of rotations, Fuller and Laird (1963b) distinguish between paper rotation, card rotation, and perceptual rotation, which have not always been distinguished in previous research on the Bender. They also remark about the failure to use a consistent and reliable scoring procedure and about the lack of conceptualization in accounting for group differences in producing rotations. The MPD is designed to overcome these limitations.

An interesting and relevant comment made by these authors is that a 1° to 20° rotation can be expected from normal individuals. Neurotic and psychotic individuals perceive stimuli that are incongruent or ambiguous with greater rotation, and organics perceive them with even greater degrees of rotation (about 60°) because of their inability to utilize cues in the immediate environment.

Uyeno (1963), using the MPD, found that carefully matched organics and pyschotics differed significantly ($p < .001$) in degree of rotation with organics rotating 77 degrees and psychotics rotating 34.40 degrees.

Overall, the studies on rotations provided considerable data on the frequency of rotations in pathological groups as well as data on the susceptibility of specific Bender designs to rotation. The evidence showing that there are consistent rotation styles associated with diagnostic status is more equivocal. There is some indication that incidence of rotation is related to diagnosis, with organics tending to rotate significantly more often than others, but the evidence is only suggestive, partially because control for intelligence and other variables has not always been instituted. Royer and Holland's (1975) and Fuller and Laird's (1963a) work is particularly encouraging, since these investigators are endeavoring to elucidate the underlying processes related to rotations. Serious methodological questions, such as, who administered the Bender-Gestalt Test, under what conditions have records been elicited (e.g. by allowing the stimuli and/or paper to be rotated), what constitutes a rotation, is the focus on gross rotations of whole designs or, more subtly, on parts of designs, have been raised by Fuller and Laird (1963b) and others. Attention to these issues should produce greater theoretical and methodological refinements in future research in this area.

EFFECTS OF ELECTRIC SHOCK

There are three studies dealing with the effects of ECT on Bender performance. Erwin and Hampe (1966) did serial administrations of the Bender-Gestalt following shock therapy administered to 20 psychiatric patients. The mean number of ECT treatments was seven, but the range was three to 16. Although it is reported that there was deterioration in Bender performance in 18 of the 20 patients, as determined by the Pascal-Suttell (1951) system, the authors found the variability in subject response to be so great as to make the Bender an unreliable measure for this purpose.

Garron and Cheifetz (1968) found that ECT did not cause any lasting impairments on the Bender-Gestalt as scored by the Hain (1964) method. Pre- and post-ECT protocols of 19 psychiatric patients were compared with controls who did not experience ECT. For the ECT group, retesting occurred two days, on the average, after treatment.

Goldman, Gomer, and Templer (1972) focused on the long-term effects of ECT on patients who had more than 50 such treatments. Dealing with carefully matched groups of ECT and non-ECT male chronic schizophrenic patients, the authors found a significantly greater number of Bender errors, as scored by the Pascal-Suttell (1951) system, for the ECT group tested some 10 to 15 years since the last course of ECT. While these results seem impressive and suggested to the authors that ECT causes irreversible brain damage, there may have been selective factors accounting for the specific patients treated with shock therapy. In the absence of baseline Bender scores for both groups, the authors' conclusions seem unwarranted.

Therefore the studies of the effects of ECT leave the issue unsettled of what effects, if any, shock therapy has on Bender performance.

OPEN-HEART SURGERY

The reasoning for suspecting that open-heart surgery might lead to brain dysfunctioning is that the heart-lung machine creates microemboli in the blood that could cause neurological damage. Landis, Baxter, Patterson, and Tauber (1974) assessed the effects on Bender-Gestalt performance, as scored by the Pascal and Suttell (1951) system, of a new filter designed to remove emboli. Noting changes in Bender drawings obtained one or two days preoperatively and five to eight days postoperatively in a double blind controlled study of a group of patients receiving filtered blood and a group of patients receiving extracorporeal blood without the benefits of the filter, it was found that the filter patients exhibited significantly less Bender deterioration than the nonfilter patients. Moreover, Bender scores paralleled ultrasonic counts of microemboli. This study clearly revealed the sensitivity of the Bender to certain types of neurological changes.

RIGHT COMPARED TO LEFT HEMIPLEGIA

Is there a distinctive Bender pattern for right as compared to left hemiplegia? This question has received some research attention. Diller and Weinberg (1965) assumed that alterations of vertical and horizontal planes experienced by hemiplegics in three-dimensional space would be reflected in Bender performance. The right hemiplegics were 18 males and four females; the left hemiplegics were 11 males and five females. Their mean age was 54 years. The controls were matched for age and duration of disability. All control patients were leg amputees and were right-handed. They were requested to make the Bender figures with both right and left hands to equate for the inability of the right hemiplegics to draw with the right hand. Left hemiplegics consistently displaced their drawings in a counterclockwise direction in both vertical and horizontal planes and revealed disturbances in integrating vertical and horizontal planes. The left hemiplegics also had significantly more rotations, omissions, and additions. The Bender appeared to be sensitive to processes very much like those required for judging vertical and horizontal planes in a dark room. The S seems to "yield" to the disturbing forces (i.e. the unilateral hemiplegia), not compensate for them.

Hirschenfang, Berman, and Benton (1967) reported that left hemiplegics performed significantly worse on the Bender-Gestalt Test, as scored by the Pascal-Suttell (1951) method, than did right hemiplegics. The right hemiplegics had cerebral lesions in the left, dominant hemisphere. All patients who were previously right-handed had sustained a cerebrovascular accident caused by embolism, thrombosis, or hemorrhage. It is regrettable that the significance levels for each of eight designs, for configuration score, and for the overall score are not given. Also, since the mean age for left hemiplegics was 59 years and for right hemiplegics was 55 years, one wonders whether there was a significant age difference between the two groups, to say nothing of other relevant variables.

There is another report (Hirschenfang, Schulman, and Benton 1968) which refers to the administration of the Bender-Gestalt

Test, WAIS, and Wechsler Memory Scale to groups of right and left hemiplegics. However, there is no further mention of these patients' performance on the Bender or Wechsler Memory Scale. Although intellectual distributions are given by sex and by right vs. left hemiplegia classification, one wonders whether the Bender was at all helpful in elucidating differences between right and left hemiplegia.

It is obvious from the studies cited that there probably is relatively greater impairment in left hemiplegics than in right hemiplegics. This type of conclusion is consistent with Nemec's (1978) finding that perceptual interference had greater effect on perceptual functioning for patients with lesions in the right cerebral hemisphere than on patients with lesions in the left cerebral hemisphere. However, the problem of achieving adequate intellectual control in studies of this type, where verbal skills are generally more impaired in right hemiplegics and performance skills are relatively more impaired in left hemiplegics, needs to be resolved.

ETHNICITY AND ORGANICITY

There is one study (Butler, Coursey, and Gatz 1976) that indicated there is no ethnic bias in Bender scoring by the Pascal-Suttell (1951) or Hain (1964) systems of hospitalized patients diagnosed as either brain damaged or psychiatrically disturbed. The one exception was the Pascal-Suttell (1951) system with a subgroup of nonepileptic patients in which case blacks scored significantly better than whites. However, neither scoring system was able to achieve much success in diagnostic group differentiation.

It may, therefore, be concluded that the Bender does not discriminate adversely against blacks in organic diagnosis.

EXAMINER EFFECT

An earlier study (Pacella 1962) supported the contention that the Bender-Gestalt is not susceptible to inter-examiner differences. Nine normally adjusted women were administered the Bender-Gestalt Test by four examiners, with the order of administration being randomized. Three of these examiners used standard instructions for administration; one made hostile, critical, and disapproving remarks. On the Pascal-Suttell (1951) Objective Scoring System there were no significant differences in Bender performance for the four different administrations. In addition, judges were not successful in identifying the protocols produced by each S under the critical condition.

With this study as background, we now turn to another study (Wohlford and Flick 1969) which focused on the question of whether there is an examiner influence specifically on organic diagnosis. Accordingly, four male and four female clinical psychologists (Ph.D. trained and of similar experience) did a blind analysis of Benders and Memory-for-Designs elicited from 15 male and 15 female neuropsychiatric inpatients, all of whom were suspected of organic pathology. The judgments made by male and female raters correlated highly with the objective Bender scoring by the Pascal-Suttell (1951) method of the same protocols. However, female psychologists rated the protocols significantly more organic than did the male psychologists. Also, male patients received significantly more severe organic ratings than did female patients.

There were no rater sex differences in confidence level of ratings made nor in the indicators employed for diagnosing organicity.

This study suggests only minor rater differences attributable to sex in the evaluation of Bender protocols for organic pathology. The fact that the medical criterion itself was an indirect measure of organicity consisting of ratings by the two authors of various neurological, EEG, and anamnestic data available is somewhat disconcerting.

SCORING SYSTEMS COMPARED WITH EACH OTHER AND WITH CLINICAL JUDGMENTS

Mosher and Smith (1965) examined the usefulness of the *Peek and Quast* (1951), Hain (1964), and Hutt and Briskin (1960) scoring systems in differentiating neurological patients with brain lesions from schizophrenic patients and from patients with suspicion of, but subsequently unconfirmed, brain damage.

Only five of the Hutt and Briskin signs were scored. Twelve of the 30 signs drawn from all three systems of scoring significantly differentiated the brain damaged from the control group. Moreover, the organic group revealed a significantly greater number of organic indicators than the control group on the Hain and on the Peek-Quast systems. These two systems correlated .79 for the organic patients and .55 for the control Ss. Even when brain-damaged and control patients were matched for intellectual functioning, both the Hain and Peek-Quast scoring systems were still able to achieve significant group differentiation. However, over 70 percent of the organic cases were misclassified using the best cut-off scores for the two systems, although relatively few false positives were obtained. The authors cautioned against employing the Bender-Gestalt Test for truly questionable organic patients and for individual diagnosis. They also felt that when base rates of organicity were low, the Bender would probably increase the diagnostic error above an acceptable level.

Cooper and Barnes (1966) developed an objective measurement technique designed for use with all types of drawing reproductions of two-dimensional stimuli, including the Bender-Gestalt figures. The method does not depend much on subjective judgments. It focuses on the degree to which the proportional relations of the linear dimensions of the copied version correspond to the proportional relations of the original figure. Using Designs A, 3, 4, 5, 7, and 8, the authors first identified and measured with a ruler certain "reference dimensions" in the stimulus figures. They then identified and measured "component dimensions" which refer to linear dimensions, and these appear to define the shape of each figure. Finally, they calculated the ratio of each component dimension to the reference dimension.

Determining the proportional accuracy of the drawings entails measuring reference and component dimensions of the reproduction, calculating the ratio of the component dimensions to their reference dimensions, subtracting the absolute difference between the criterion ratios (based on the stimulus) and the ratios found on the reproductions, and summing the differences across the component dimensions of the drawings.

The system was capable of differentiating organic patients from nonorganic psychiatric patients and from normals. However, normals and psychiatric patients were not distinguishable.

Despite this encouraging finding, and the observation that the system results in high reliability (.93), we question the use of such an extremely time-consuming and elaborate scoring system, which would be of little interest to clinicians, especially when we are not afforded any information on the degree to which this system compares with others that are based on more subjective impressions or even with gross clinical judgments.

The previous review of Bender studies (Tolor and Schulberg 1963) led to the conclusion that clinicians who used a global impressional approach succeeded as well as more detailed objective scoring systems in establishing the test's validity. With this conclusion in mind, Lyle and Quast (1976) attempted to determine whether experienced clinicians making global judgments of Bender-Gestalt records could differentiate normals from patients with brain lesions associated with Huntington's chorea and from individuals who later developed Huntington's chorea. The clinicians' judgments were compared with Bender recall, based on one point for each correct design and a half point for part of the design recalled.

The Bender recall significantly differentiated normals from premorbids and normals from patients with Huntington's chorea. The recall means for normals, premorbids, and those affected with Huntington's chorea was 5.89, 4.34, and 4.60, respectively. As for the three clinicians who had extensive experience with the Bender, the clinical consensus resulted in 65 percent correctly predicted normals, and 68 percent correctly predicted organics when normals are compared with premorbid Huntington's chorea patients. The clinicians' consensus when normals are compared with currently affected patients was 72 percent of the normals correctly identified, and 62 percent of the organics correctly identified. The clinicians' overall hit rates were almost identical to the hit rates for Bender recall. Despite the only slightly higher predictive accuracy with Bender recall over clinical judgments, the authors stressed the superiority of actuarial over clinical prediction, an emphasis that we feel is not justified. However, their contention that these group differences are not large enough for individual diagnosis is fully endorsed.

In sum, the studies reviewed in this section suggest that various objective scoring systems are capable of achieving group differentiation when an organic population is compared with nonorganic groups. However, the clinical approach also enjoys considerable success in achieving group differentiation. However, as indicated previously, both methods have serious limitations when employed for individual diagnosis.

INTELLIGENCE AND RETARDATION

Low levels of intelligence, it has been postulated (e.g. Carter 1966; Kennedy 1968), may very well be inextricably related to organic dysfunctioning, even when cultural and familial factors are implicated. The apparent clear-cut distinction in the etiology of retardation between central nervous system pathology and environmental influences becomes very much blurred when one considers that a host of pre- and peri-natal factors, such as sensory deprivation and nutritional deficits, could result in irreversible nervous system changes. It is with this rationale in mind that we now examine the relationship between Bender performance and intellectual differences.

There are several studies that have focused on the Bender-Gestalt Test performance of mentally retarded adolescents or adults.

Sternlicht, Pustel, and Siegel (1968) used two groups matched for CA and IQ, one of organic retardates and one of cultural-familial retardates having no known or suspected organic defect. The mean IQ was 53.8, and the mean CA was 16.4 years in each group. The Bender-Gestalt Test, when scored by means of the Pascal-Suttell (1951) system, but not the Koppitz (1964) system, was able to significantly ($p < .05$) differentiate the two groups. Interestingly, the Memory-for-Designs Test did not achieve discrimination in this study.

Andert, Dinning, and Hustak (1976) extended Koppitz's (1964) Developmental Scoring System for the Bender-Gestalt Test from the original normative data based on a standardization sample of children between the ages of 5 and 10 years, 11 months to a group of 510 adult resident retardates. Separate data are given for "borderline," "mild," and "moderate" ranges of retardation, as determined by the WAIS, and for "moderate" and "severe" ranges, as determined by the Stanford-Binet (Form L-M). Bender error scores correlated −.72 with Full Scale WAIS IQ (−.59 with Verbal IQ and −.73 with Performance IQ) and −.68 with the Binet IQ. The mean Bender errors for "borderline," "mild," and "moderate" retardation was 4.86, 8.17, and 16.44, respectively. The authors advocated the use of the Koppitz system with adult retardates.

Krop and Smith (1969) found that participation in a six-week special educational program, and especially a period of instruction on the drawing of geometric designs, can improve significantly the performance on the Bender-Gestalt Test, as measured by a newly developed *Hamburg-Bender Scoring System,* of adult female residential mental retardates. None of these Ss had any known organic brain damage.

Andert, Hustak, and Dinning (1978) reported that in mentally retarded male and female adults the time to complete the Bender task significantly correlated inversely with WAIS intelligence (time and WAIS IQ $r = .22$, $p < .01$) but not with Binet-measured intelligence. The duration of the Bender reproductions also related significantly ($r = .27$, $p < .01$) with Koppitz (1964) scores. Moreover, the relative time to complete the Bender protocol significantly varied for levels of retardation: (borderline) $M = 6'58''$; (mild) $M = 9'00''$; (moderate) $M = 9'42''$).

Allen (1968b) evaluated the performance of a group of educable mental retardates with a mean age of 13.3 years on the Bender-Gestalt Test, as scored by the *Keogh-Smith* (1961) *System,* and on the *Developmental Test of Visual Perception* (DTVP). The Bender figures were administered by having each S draw on a field identical in size and shape and axial orientation to the stimulus field (See Allen and Frank 1963). In addition to comparing the performance of Ss on the two measures, the author described differences in functioning on the two measures by high and low perceivers. Since the identification of an individual as a high or low perceiver was based on the total DTVP raw score, there is gross contamination of predictor with criterion variables. Also, since there was no control group of nonretard-ates, the mere presentation of mean scores and *SD*s for the two measures can hardly be said to support the hypothesized poorer Bender and DTVP performance of mentally retarded individuals compared to nonretardates. In this study, the Bender correlated significantly with Total DTVP and the subtests, but not with MA or CA.

Phelps (1968) administered the Bender to 76 young (mean age, 19 years) adult females who were mildly or moderately retarded. Forty-three of these *S*s were judged as rehabilitated, and 33 were not rehabilitated on a 12-month follow-up. The mean WAIS IQ for the rehabilitated *S*s was 63 and for the nonrehabilitated *S*s 61. The protocols were scored for Hain's (1964) 15 differentiating signs for identifying organicity. There was no significant between-group difference either in incidence of critical scores or in mean scores on the Bender.

Wagner, Klein, and Walter (1978) used three measures—the Rorschach, the Bender-Gestalt Test, and the Hand Test—in an attempt to discriminate low intelligence *S*s with exogenous trauma, from low intelligence *S*s with no history of brain trauma. Trauma appears to be used idiosyncratically in this investigation, not to signify a blow to the cerebrum but as any disease affecting the CNS. No significant difference was found on the Bender between groups as scored by the Pascal and Suttell (1951) method, but Bender scores did significantly differentiate low from high intelligence groups. As a matter of fact, the rho between Bender scores and intelligence was a substantial —.45. These results suggested to the authors that projective tests were more sensitive to intellectual impairment than to brain damage *per se*.

In a population of institutionalized mentally deficient males, Temmer (1965) found that nonorganic *S*s scored higher in all intelligence scores and produced fewer Bender errors than organic *S*s. An inverse relationship was obtained between number of Bender errors and intelligence with nonorganic re-tardates. Considering the Bender distortions scored, the number of sides and the accuracy of angles were most highly correlated with intelligence. For the organic subgroup, no significant cor-relation existed between intelligence and Bender scores.

Pacella (1965), employing a modified version of the Bender-Gestalt Test, found that on the third trial, though not on the initial trial, organic mentally retarded patients were significantly less accurate than cultural-familial mentally retarded individuals. The Bender-Gestalt was scored using the Pascal-Suttell (1951) system. The Ss' age range, from twelve to thirty-five years, was broad indeed, and the sample sizes were small.

In a group of mixed nonretarded patients admitted to a psychiatric service of a city hospital, Aylaian and Meltzer (1962) found substantial significant correlations between WAIS scaled scores and WAIS quotients on the one hand, and Pascal-Suttell (1951) Bender Scores, on the other hand, ranging from .33 to .57. Even when the effects of age on WAIS full scale scores were partialled out, the correlation between the Bender and the WAIS was not changed much ($r = .556$). There were significant differences on the Bender attributable to diagnosis. It was concluded that overall intelligence should be considered in evaluating the Bender-Gestalt performance for emotional or organic pathology. The correlation between the performance scale and the Bender was the highest of all correlations. It should be noted that the sample had an average age of 28 years, and that the predominant diagnosis among the 127 Ss was character and personality disorder.

The *Quick Test* (Ammons and Ammons 1962), which measures intelligence, correlated $-.55$ ($p < .01$) with the Bender-Gestalt Test, scored by the Hain (1964) method, and the Memory-for-Designs Test (Graham and Kendall 1960) correlated .69 ($p < .01$) with the Bender, according to Quattelbaum and White (1969). The sample consisted of 180 neuropsychiatric patients with a mean age of 32 years. Age did not add significantly to the prediction of Bender scores. Intelligence accounted for approximately one-third of Bender-Gestalt variance.

Armentrout (1976) found that the ability to recall Bender designs is significantly correlated with intelligence (Verbal IQ $r = .34$; Performance IQ $r = .52$; Full Scale IQ $r = .44$), but the degree of association is not great enough to replace the WAIS Vocabulary alone as a predictor of above average or below average intelligence. In this study, 42 males and 69 females in a vocational rehabilitation service, with a mean age of 23 years, were used. Bender recall was assigned either a full or a half credit, based on degree of completeness.

Rogers and Swenson (1975) attempted to determine whether the Bender-Gestalt measured intellectual efficiency or memory. Near perfect recall scores correlated .74 ($p < .0001$) with the *Wechsler Memory Scale* (Wechsler 1945), and partial recall scores correlated .70 ($p < .0001$) with the *Wechsler Memory Total*. Factor I on the Wechsler Memory Scale, which pertains to memory storage (Davis and Swenson 1970), correlated .76 with near perfect Bender recall scores whereas Factor II, which pertains to freedom from distractibility, correlated less robustly (.40) with near perfect Bender recall scores. Since the two correlations were significantly different, it was concluded that immediate recall is a valid measure of memory, but not necessarily of mental efficiency as it related to freedom from distractibility.

In sum, the studies reviewed in this section lead to the following conclusions: (1) There is considerable supportive evidence that organically brain-damaged retarded adults reveal significantly greater Bender-Gestalt Test disruption than do non-organically brain-damaged retarded adults. (2) The Bender-Gestalt Test, when used to identify changes related to special training in the mentally retarded, may be a sensitive indicator of improvement. (3) There is convincing evidence that performance of adult mentally retarded individuals on the Bender-Gestalt Test is related to their relative levels of overall intelligence. (4) Time consumed on the Bender task correlates with intellectual efficiency in adult retardates. (5) On the other hand, the Bender-Gestalt when used with adult retardates has not been demonstrated to identify degree of rehabilitative success or to distinguish "trauma" from "nontrauma" status.

Regarding nonretarded adults, there is confirmation for a significant relationship between Bender efficiency in memory and intelligence, and there is some indication that Bender performance in general is associated with intelligence.

A further point should be made, namely, that studies in this area are characterized by the reliance on different scoring systems, some of which show positive results, and some negative results. Not only does one get an impression of a lack of uniformity in the use of these various systems, but one also observes that there is disagreement on the efficacy of some of the scoring systems.

STUDIES OF ORGANICITY IN CHILDREN

As Koppitz (1975b) noted, over the past 15 years there has been a growing awareness and concern about the relationship of neurological impairment to learning and behavior problems in children. In this section we will explore the innovative uses of the Bender-Gestalt Test in the assessment of brain damage, minimal brain dysfunction, hyperactivity, and other neurological disorders in children.

In a 1962 study, Koppitz reported that the Developmental Error Score, as well as many of the individual scoring items, successfully differentiated between children with and without brain damage. Although these findings are questionable primarily due to problems in sampling, some supportive results have been reported over the past 15 years. For example, Wikler, Dixon, and Parker (1970) noted a significant difference between hyperactive children and *matched* controls on Koppitz's (1964) Developmental Error Score. No significant difference was noted for a similar comparison involving nonhyperactive children with scholastic and/or behavior problems. Similarly, Developmental Error Scores have been found to differentiate between children diagnosed as minimally brain damaged and normal controls (Klatskin, McNamara, Shaffer, and Pincus 1972), and between organic and emotionally disturbed children (Hartlage 1970) and adolescents (Oliver and Kronenberger 1971). Furthermore, McConnell (1967) reported that these Error Scores were significantly related to *degree* of organicity in children. And, in a related study, Wiener (1966) noted statistically significant correlations between Bender scores, based on seven variables comparable to the general error categories (i.e. distortion, rotation, perseveration, integration) on the Developmental Scoring System, and neurological deficits associated with minimal brain damage in children 8 to 10 years of age.

Nevertheless, there have also been studies that have reported questionable findings or failed to find any significant differences between neurologically impaired children and adolescents and other controls (e.g. Dykman, Peters, and Ackerman 1973; Friedman, Strochak, Gitlin, and Gottsagen 1967; Palkes and Stewart 1972). In addition, Holroyd (1966), using *high cut-off scores* to minimize false positive predictions, found that both the Peek and Quast (1951) Scoring System and Koppitz's (1964) Developmental Scoring System correctly predicted 10 out of 25 children (considered abnormal or suspiciously abnormal on the basis of a neurological examination and/or the EEG) as brain damaged with one false positive each.

Research (e.g. Friedman et al. 1967; McConnell 1967; and Oliver and Kronenberger 1971) on Koppitz's (1964) *Brain Damage Indicants and Emotional Indicants* has been unsuccessful (or has added little information beyond the Developmental Score) in differential diagnosis of neurologically impaired Ss. Lambert (1970), in a large-scale study, examined the validity of 82 Bender "signs" for predicting the correct diagnosis of children diagnosed as either emotionally handicapped or neurologically handicapped. She also noted the relationship between Bender "signs" and several more specific clinical problems such as eccentric-bizarre behavior, withdrawn or shy behavior, acting-out aggressive behavior, and neurological handicaps. In this research there were no significant differences in Bender signs between the emotionally and neurologically handicapped groups. Furthermore, the Bender "signs" examined were generally unrelated to specific clinical problems as well. The author concluded that these findings seriously challenged the utility of specific Bender signs for differential diagnosis.

Taken as a whole, therefore, research utilizing Koppitz's (1964) criteria, or similar criteria, has yielded inconclusive results. It is doubtful however, as Koppitz (1975b) suggested, that any one test (or one score) would be able to consistently identify children with neurological impairments.

BACKGROUND INTERFERENCE

Studies of the Background Interference Procedure with children have not demonstrated consistently the efficacy of this diagnostic technique. In one of the earliest studies, Adams and Canter (1969) examined the BIP performance of normal children ranging in age from six to 14 years. They found that error scores decreased steadily with age whereas D scores decreased sharply at eight years of age and tended to vary more narrowly after age 10. A low, but statistically significant correlation ($r = -.25$) was found between BIP D scores and age. No significant relationships were found for BIP D scores and either intelligence or sex. The authors cautioned, however, that allowances need to be made in interpreting the BIP performance of children under 13 years of age, and especially those under eight years of age, because of the occurrence of a "normal decrement." Further, in an examination of ethnic influences on the BIP, Adams and Lieb (1973) found significant differences between Caucasian and Negro Headstart children on the error score and number positive score, but not the D score.

Subsequent studies have focused on the diagnostic utility of this instrument. However, the results have also been equivocal. For example, Hayden, Talmadge, Hall, and Schiff (1970) compared the performance of brain-damaged ($\overline{X}$ age = 130.1 months, $\overline{X}$ IQ = 91.0) and emotionally disturbed children ($\overline{X}$ age = 130.1 months, $\overline{X}$ IQ = 90.8) on the Canter BIP and Koppitz's (1964) Developmental Error Score. Although Koppitz's errors did not differentiate the members of the two groups, BIP error scores and D scores did (brain-damaged Ss performed more poorly than emotionally disturbed Ss). Similarly, Kenny (1971) compared the BIP performance of brain-damaged, emotionally disturbed, and normally functioning children at five age levels ranging from eight to 12 years. The D scores of the children with neurological dysfunction were significantly higher than those of the emotionally disturbed and normal children. The latter two groups did not differ significantly. The age factor also was not significant. However, Adams (1970) examined the BIP performance of brain-damaged and non-brain-damaged, mentally retarded children ($\overline{X}$ CA = 124.5 months, $\overline{X}$ MA = 89.5 months, and $\overline{X}$ IQ = 72.7) and found that while the error score differentiated between the two groups, the D score did not.

A reanalysis of Kenny's (1971) data by Adams, Kenny, and Canter (1973), using a revised scoring system to determine the accuracy of identification of children with neurological dysfunction, replicated the earlier results. The accuracy of classification was 84 percent for the BIP conditions combined as compared to 71 percent for the Bender-Gestalt Test alone. Similarly, in a study designed to explore the Canter BIP performance of hyperkinetic children, Adams, Hayden, and Canter (1974) found a greater decrement on the D score in the hyperkinetic groups ($\overline{X}$ age = 120.4 months) as opposed to the control group ($\overline{X}$ age = 118.1 months). However, in an analysis of the discriminative power of this measure for the two groups, the authors found that the "hit" rate for D scores was low, even though it was statistically significant. For this reason, they cautioned against the use of the technique in making decisions concerning the differential diagnosis of children.

More recently, Adams, Peterson, Kenny, and Canter (1975) attempted to enhance the utility of the Canter BIP with children by using an item analysis aimed at selecting and weighting the scoring items from a revised scoring system for optimal differentiation between children with neurological dysfunction and other groups (i.e. emotionally disturbed and normal children). In comparing these three groups in the age range of eight to twelve years, the authors noted a striking difference between ten- and eleven-year-olds and indicated the need for separate scoring items and criteria of classification for younger and older children. The overall "hit" rate was 92 percent for eight- to ten-year-olds, but only 76 percent for eleven- and twelve-year-olds. However, when the older group was reassessed using adult scoring procedures (with newly established criteria for combining the basic scores), a "hit" rate of 94 percent was obtained. Although these results seem promising, the authors emphasized that careful cross validation is required before they can be applied to the clinical situation.

SCANNING STRATEGIES

Locher and Worms (1977) systematically examined the visual scanning strategies of neurologically impaired, perceptually impaired, and normal children while viewing the Bender-Gestalt designs. The primary purpose of the study was to describe and compare the visual encoding and copying performances of the three groups. The authors noted qualitative and quantitative differences in the scanning strategies of each of the three groups.

The scanning strategies of the normal children (median age, 8.4 years) were characterized by the efficient use of fixations which tended to center upon the salient structural features of the stimuli. These children selected parts high in information content, and they encoded in such a way as to lead to the greatest internal organization of the stimulus.

By contrast, perceptually impaired children (median age, 8.1 years) tended to use more fixations, encoded fewer salient features per design, and exhibited scanning strategies which were less well-organized in terms of the structural organization of the stimulus. Furthermore, they tended to fixate on non-informative areas of the stimulus and refixated areas previously examined.

Neurologically impaired children (median age, 10 years) exhibited certain deficits in scanning strategies. The authors described the strategies "as a rapid, random encoding of structural features, with fixations frequently placed off of the stimulus or on noninformative areas of the stimulus and characterized by the periodic halting of the encoding process" (p. 153).

An examination of Bender reproductions indicated that the neurologically impaired group performed significantly more poorly (based on a rating for each design for goodness of reproduction, i.e. the accuracy of a drawing in depicting all structural components) than either the normal or perceptually impaired groups. Although the latter two groups did not differ significantly from each other in copying the designs, the perceptually impaired Ss spent more time scanning the designs and used more fixations per second examining each design than normal Ss.

The authors concluded that the evaluation of scanning

strategies may provide considerable information to aid in the process of differential diagnosis.

ROTATIONS

Smith and Martin (1967) examined the comparative ability of neurologically impaired and non-neurologically impaired children (who exhibited a variety of social, emotional, and/or academic problems) to use learning cues to correct rotations of Bender designs.

Based on the rationale that some rotations may be the result of "carelessness, temporary distraction, or inexperience with drawing," the authors devised a five-stage system (becoming progressively more directive) to determine the precise nature of the errors. They found that the neurologically impaired children produced a significantly greater number of rotations than controls and required significantly more cues for correction. Sixteen of 21 neurologically impaired Ss who made rotations required two or more cues for correction, whereas all nine of the control Ss who made rotations corrected them on the first cue. Therefore, rotations, as well as the ability to correct rotations, should be considered for greater accuracy in differential diagnosis.

Similarly, Weiss (1971b) examined the incidence of rotations of Bender figures in normal third-, fifth-, and seventh-grade Israeli children. He concluded that rotation in many cases is a developmental phenomenon rather than the result of brain injury.

MENTAL RETARDATION

Research on the Bender performance of retarded children and adolescents, although somewhat unsystematic in nature, suggests that this test may offer useful information in the diagnosis of mental retardation.

Although no statistical analyses were presented, Condell (1963) reported some large differences in Developmental Errors in five groups of children classified according to mental functioning: trainable retarded ($\overline{X} = 11.00$), educable retarded ($\overline{X} =$

6.14), borderline ($\overline{X}$ = 4.50), dull normal ($\overline{X}$ = 4.25), and average ($\overline{X}$ = 3.60).

Maloney and Ward (1970) found that mentally retarded adolescents with organic etiology made significantly more Developmental Errors (Koppitz 1964) than those diagnosed as functionally retarded. The groups did not differ in age or IQ.

Richardson and Rubino (1971) investigated the effectiveness of the Bender (Koppitz's [1964] Scoring System) in differentiating between normal, perceptually handicapped, and mentally retarded children. They found that while the Bender was generally successful in group differentiation, individual prediction was only moderately successful.

Allen (1969), and Allen and Adamo (1969) noted that the Bender performance (based on the Keogh-Smith [1961] Scoring System) of educable mentally retarded Ss was significantly poorer than that of normal Ss.

Allen, Adamo, Alker, and Levine (1971) found that retarded children performed more poorly than normal children on Bender recognition and reproduction tasks (based on the Keogh-Smith [1961] scoring criteria). They also noted, however, that the deficit in the more complex reproduction tasks was markedly greater than in the recognition task.

Throne, Kaspar, and Schulman (1964) found a significant relationship between Bender performance time- and brain-damage ratings in a group of male retardates ranging in age from eleven years to fourteen years, eleven months.

SEIZURE DISORDERS

Hauer and Armentrout (1978) compared the Bender performance of two matched groups of children: one group composed of children with medically documented seizure conditions; and another group of controls, matched in age (within 12 months) and Wechsler overall intelligence, who had no history of organic impairment. All Ss exhibited emotional and behavioral problems. The pairs ranged in age from 9 years, 1 month to 16 years, 7 months ($\overline{X}$ = 13-4, SD = 26 months). The mean IQ was 87.7 (SD = 12.9). While the members of each pair were closely matched, the pairs varied considerably in age and intellectual level. The Developmental Error Scores for the seizure disorder $(\overline{X} = 2.7,\ SD = 3.4)$ and nonseizure disorder $(\overline{X} = 2.8,\ SD = 2.2)$ groups did not differ significantly.

Similar results were obtained in a study by Schwartz and Dennerll (1970). These investigators examined the Bender *recall* performance of 26 nonconvulsives, 32 questionable convulsives, and 82 convulsives ranging in age from 9 to 15 years. The children were referrals from physicians because of actual epileptic seizures, seizurelike episodes, or learning and/or emotional disorders in whom brief interruptions in consciousness akin to epilepsy were noted. Final placement in one of the three groups was based primarily on seizure history and EEG. The groups did not differ significantly in age, education, or sex. Although the groups differed significantly on the WISC, they did not differ on Bender recall, using the *Reznikoff and Olin* (1957) *Scoring System.*

One difficulty in interpreting the results of these studies concerns the nature of the populations. Both studies included Ss with multiple problems, and the Bender does not seem to be useful in these instances.

CEREBRAL PALSY

Working under the assumption that cerebral palsied children have certain disturbances in visuo-spatial integration, in addition to their physical and mental handicaps, Patel and Bharucha (1972) examined the Bender performance of 34 cerebral palsied children and 80 "normal" controls of comparable age and socioeconomic backgrounds.

The cerebral palsied group had relatively little impairment of the arms. However, IQs ranged from 60 to 112 $(\overline{X} = 83)$. Chronological ages ranged from six to 12 years $(\overline{X} = 9\text{-}2)$, and mental ages ranged from five to nine years $(\overline{X} = 7\text{-}7)$. In order to minimize the IQ differences between the normal group and the cerebral palsied group, mental age, rather than chronological age, was used in grouping and comparing the two groups.

The authors noted that while Developmental Errors decreased steadily with increasing age in both groups, the number of errors was higher in the cerebral palsied group and their number decreased at a slower rate. Of the six age levels compared (five to 10 years), three yielded statistically significant differences (five, nine, and 10). Cerebral palsied children also made significantly more errors involving rotation and substitution of circles for dots. The two groups did not differ significantly in other specific error types, such as distortion of angles, perseveration, integration, and loss of shape.

ENCEPHALITIS

Sabatino and Cramblett (1968) designed a study to examine the personality and behavioral sequelae of 14 children between seven months and two years after their hospitalization with California encephalitic virus infection. The children ranged in age from five to fourteen years at the time of follow-up assessment.

In comparison to Koppitz's (1964) normative sample, nine Ss had significant visual-motor coordination deficits (below 1 SD). Severe auditory deficits were also noted. In addition, the authors noted that the children had no difficulty in the higher language functions or in the conceptual skills associated with verbal intellectual functioning. However, these children were described by parents as nervous, hyperactive, restless, disruptive, distractible, easily frustrated, tense, preoccupied with self, and irritable.

SICKLE CELL ANEMIA

Flick and Duncan (1973) designed a pilot study to examine the Bender performance (among other variables) of children with sickle cell anemia—a blood disorder in which erythrocytes may be deficient in carrying oxygen to the brain. Twenty-two female and 20 male black children with sickle cell anemia, and 10 female and eight male black children, served as controls. All Ss were selected from the Collaborative Child Development Program at Charity Hospital.

Children with sickle cell trait (seven years of age) were

found to make significantly more errors on the Bender than the control group, which suggested that these children had a perceptual-motor deficit. There was also a tendency for the children to be described as awkward and poorly coordinated. Nevertheless, the authors urged caution in the interpretation of their results until more extensive research is conducted.

LOW BIRTH WEIGHT

Wiener and his associates (Wiener, Rider, Oppel, Fischer, and Harper 1965; Wiener, Rider, Oppel, and Harper 1968) conducted a series of studies on the neurological and psychological functioning of children with low birth weight (under 2,501 gm.). When tested at six to seven years of age, low birth weight children performed significantly more poorly than controls on the Bender as well as on several other variables, such as intelligence, speech maturity, gross motor coordination, and reasoning skills. Children at eight to 10 years of age revealed comparable results.

A similar study (Abrams 1969) with upper-weight-level, premature children (birth weight between three and one-half and five pounds) reported no significant Bender differences in comparison to control Ss.

PHYSICAL HANDICAPS

Newcomer and Hammill (1973) examined the Bender performance of 90 motor-impaired children. Using the Koppitz (1964) Scoring System, the authors reported progressively poorer performance on the Bender as severity of the motor handicap increased. They also noted, however, that these children functioned appropriately for their chronological age on the *Motor Free Test of Visual Perception* (Colarusso and Hammill 1972). These findings point out the importance of assessing the adequacy of motor skill and visual perception separately, as well as the integration of these functions.

MUSCULAR DYSTROPHY

Marsh (1972) examined the Bender performance of 21 boys (six years, 10 months to 13 years, two months) with a medical diagnosis of Duchene muscular dystrophy, which is characterized by muscular wasting and physical disability. The author reported that Developmental Error Scores of 14 of the 21 subjects showed mild to severe visual-motor impairment (in comparison to Koppitz's norms). However, she also noted that Bender scores were significantly related to WISC IQ scores (the mean Full Scale IQ score was 87.9).

DEAFNESS

There have been several studies of the Bender performance of deaf children. Gilbert and Levee (1967) reported significant differences on the Bender-Gestalt Test between a sample of deaf children and a control group. Deaf children performed significantly more poorly on the Bender, based on the Pascal and Suttell (1951) Scoring System.

Similarly, Clarke and Leslie (1971) reported Bender scores for deaf children that were considerably higher than those of normal children, based on Koppitz's (1964) norms. However, the results of this study are contaminated by the fact that many of the deaf children had below average IQ scores and/or learning disabilities.

In a more elaborate study, Keogh, Vernon, and Smith (1970) were concerned with the validity of visuo-motor tests for differential clinical assessment of deaf children. More specificially, they tried to address three specific questions: (1) whether etiological factors that produced both deafness and brain damage resulted also in impaired visuo-motor performance; (2) whether the impaired visuo-motor performance is an effect of auditory deprivation or neurological structure and organization; and (3) whether there is an interaction effect of both factors.

The authors found that while deaf children generally performed two to three years below normally hearing children on the Bender, their scores were not related significantly to either the degree of hearing loss or the etiology of deafness.

DRUG EFFECTS

In a comparison of the effects of stimulant drugs on visual-motor performance, Arnold, Huestis, Wemmer, and Smeltzer (1978) noted significant improvement in the Bender scores (based on Koppitz's errors) of 31 hyperkinetic minimally brain dysfunctioned children ($\overline{X}$ age = eight years) administered dextroamphetamine, but not levoamphetamine, even though the two are thought to have comparable effects on behavior.

Summary

In recapitulating the general conclusions derived from the review of the literature which encompasses the topic of this chapter, namely, the Bender-Gestalt Test and Organicity, we would like to make the following points:

1. The Canter Background Interference Procedure represents a highly desirable modification and refinement in technique for organic diagnosis and offers as well the promise of making considerable theoretical contribution to the understanding of the processes underlying pathological functioning.

2. Despite numerous conceptual and practical problems in conducting adequate research on the relative validity of the Bender-Gestalt Test in comparison to other measures of brain damage, the predominant evidence points to the ability of the Bender-Gestalt Test to achieve group differentiation as successfully as do most other psychological and physical measures with which it has been compared. Even more extensive screening batteries, in general, are not demonstrably more efficient in making valid organic diagnoses.

3. When indirect evidence for the Bender's validity for detecting organic change is examined, there is too much conflicting data for definitive conclusions.

4. However, studies of the Bender's concurrent validity,

while not numerous, provide substantial support for the test's validity for discriminating brain-damaged patients from patients with psychogenic disturbances, and brain-damaged patients from normal individuals. This type of differentiation can be demonstrated with a variety of scoring systems (including those that focus on recall) and with more impressionistic clinical judgments.

5. The Bender has found application with various special kinds of organic pathologies, including epilepsy, Huntington's disease, Giles de la Tourette's syndrome, encephalitis, cerebral palsy, sickle cell anemia, and the aging process.

6. Investigations of rotations of Bender figures abound in the literature, with data accumulating on the frequency of rotations, susceptibility of specific designs to rotations, and characteristic rotation styles. Additionally, the effects of diagnostic status and intelligence, and the conditions that facilitate or inhibit rotations, have been studied.

7. The precise influence of shock therapy on Bender performance remains unclear.

8. The sensitivity of the Bender to brain dysfunctioning associated with open-heart surgery seems to have been well established.

9. Studies appear to point to greater Bender impairment in left than right hemiplegics.

10. No evidence for a racial bias in organic diagnosis exists on the Bender.

11. There are no major sex biases either.

12. A variety of scoring systems, as well as clinical judgments, have been successfully employed for group differentiation of organics and other pathological groups.

13. The Bender performance of retardates who are organic is significantly poorer than that of nonorganics, and the level of retardation is significantly related to adequacy of the Bender reproductions. The amount of time devoted to making the Bender drawings relates to intellectual efficiency. The sensitivity of the Bender to the rehabilitation of adult retardates is dubious, although some success in detecting changes as a consequence of special educational efforts has been reported. In nonretarded adults,

memory, intelligence, and Bender performance seem to be intercorrelated.

14. The wide range of children's organic problems in which the Bender-Gestalt Test has found useful application attests to its contribution with this type of population as well.

CHAPTER 6

THE BENDER-GESTALT TEST
AND PSYCHOSIS

T HROUGHOUT THIS VOLUME, reference has been made to psychotic patients when they were used as Ss comprising a comparison group as, for example, in relation to patients having organic brain disease. Psychotics have also been mentioned in studies of the Bender-Gestalt Test's validity. In this chapter, however, we plan to cite only those studies published since 1962 that focus on some specific aspect of psychotic functioning. The number of studies that fall within this category is quite limited, perhaps because of the more extensive conceptual foundation required for such research.

Nahas (1976) based his investigation of 30 newly admitted acute paranoid schizophrenics (15 men and 15 women) on the widely accepted view that schizophrenics have a fundamental perceptual or sensorimotor defect. Nahas sought to explore the relationship between the symptomatology of these schizophrenics and their Bender productions. Each patient's symptoms observed during a mental status examination were recorded and quantified on the *Rockland and Pollin Scale* (1965). The Bender-Gestalt Test was scored using the Pascal-Suttell (1951) system. A highly significant difference between scores for this schizophrenic group and the norms for a normal group was reported. In addition, there was a high correlation ($r = .88$, $p < .001$) between the degree of deviations on the Bender and intensity of observed symptomatology. Significant correlations were also obtained between the amount of Bender deviation and 11 of 16 mental status variables, with the highest occurring for facial expression ($r = .72$), mood ($r = .67$), involvement with examiner ($r = .65$), and judgment and abstract ability ($r = .64$).

A factor analysis of scores on the mental status examination and the Bender-Gestalt Test revealed that the one factor that had significant loading on the Bender-Gestalt Test was associated with disturbance in affect, mood, speech, sensorium, and hallucinations. Therefore, the study provided further indication that Bender performance relates to many of the psychotic symptoms often found in association with paranoid schizophrenia.

Employing scores on the 16 dimensions of the Rockland and Pollin (1965) Scale as predictor variables and the degree of deviation on the Bender as the criterion variable, it was found by use of multiple regression equation that hallucinations constituted the single best predictor, accounting for 25 percent of the criterion variance. This finding would suggest that hallucinations produce gross interference with the selective perception required to draw the Bender designs with fidelity.

Changes in body image following sensory deprivation in schizophrenics were investigated by Reitman and Cleveland (1964) who cited previous work which had documented the deleterious effects of sensory deprivation in normals. Among the adverse effects reported for normal individuals was general disorganization, including delusions, hallucinations, and disorientation. By contrast, however, previous work had suggested that in pathologically organized individuals the effects of sensory deprivation may be different, actually providing these patients the opportunity to achieve some measure of reorganization. In the Reitman and Cleveland (1964) study, the focus was specifically on body image changes as a consequence of sensory deprivation.

Of special interest to us is that the Bender-Gestalt Test was one of several instruments used to serve as a control for possible changes in visual-motor coordination or for a possible general perceptual shift after the sensory deprivation experience had occurred.

The Ss were 40 hospitalized schizophrenics and 20 hospitalized anxiety reaction and character disorder patients who were used as controls.

While this study's results demonstrating the differential effects of sensory deprivation on the perceived body image of schizophrenics (who exhibited a reintegrative trend) and of non-psychotics (who exhibited further disintegration) are most intriguing, they will not be detailed here. What is relevant, however, is the finding that the mean size of the drawn Bender-Gestalt figures was not significantly different for schizophrenic as compared with nonpsychotic groups, nor was there elicited any significant pre-deprivation vs. post-deprivation difference. It would seem, therefore, that sensory deprivation does not cause any size difference in the Bender renditions of schizophrenics. It remains to be determined, however, whether sensory deprivation results in other kinds of Bender deviations in psychotic individuals. One might hypothesize improved general Bender performance if indeed there is a general reintegrative effect on perceptual processes for schizophrenics exposed to sensory deprivation conditions.

Depressives are known to be generally more constricted behaviorally and less productive ideationally than nondepressive patients. To ascertain whether psychotically depressed female patients use less total area in their Bender renditions as compared with schizophrenics, and compared with patients diagnosed as character disorders, was the purpose of Salzman and Harway's (1965) research. The size of each design drawn was determined by superimposing a transparent grid that had been ruled in tenths of an inch over the designs. Psychotically depressed female inpatients were not found in this study to make their Bender figures significantly smaller in size than the other two patient groups. Therefore, the hypothesized reduction in productivity in the psychotically depressed could not be confirmed.

It is of some interest that using a different graphomotor technique (i.e. the human figure drawing test) once more resulted in an absence of any significant relationship between depression and size of drawing in psychotically depressed women.

Donnelly and Murphy (1974) compared the Bender-Gestalt protocols of 37 bipolar depressives, having a history of depression and mania, with 30 primary affective disorder patients presenting only a history of depression (unipolar depressives).

The differential diagnosis was based on interviews with patient and family, previous hospital records, and psychological testing. The sex of the Ss was not specified in the report.

The Bender records of patients were independently scored for successive positions (sequence) of the designs on the paper. The scoring categories, following Hutt (1969), were: normal or methodical, in which one shift in sequence of placement occurs; overly methodical, in which no shift occurs; irregular, in which more than one shift occurs; and confused or symbolic, in which no plan is discernible.

The bipolar depressed patients were inclined to produce irregular sequence, and the unipolar depressed patients were inclined to produce overly methodical sequence. The difference was statistically significant. Additionally, patients with irregular sequence scored significantly higher on the *Ma* scale of the MMPI than patients with methodical sequence. On the MMPI *Psychasthenia (Pt) Scale*, patients with irregular sequence scored lower than did patients with overly methodical Bender sequence. These findings suggest that lack of impulse control—as evidenced by irregular placement of Bender designs, high hypomania, and low psychasthenia—characterizes the bipolar depressed person; and that greater impulse control—as evidenced by a more compulsively organized placement of Bender designs, less hypomania, and greater obsessive, compulsive, and phobic tendency (high *Pt*)—characterizes the unipolar depressed person.

Although an incidental finding in Carlson's (1966) study was that chronic undifferentiated schizophrenics obtained significantly higher Pascal-Suttell (1951) scores on the Bender than acute undifferentiated schizophrenics, the main focus of the study was a comparison of the performance of black and white schizophrenics on this test. Black and white schizophrenics, recently hospitalized, were matched for rated degree of impairment on the *Proverbs Test* and on the *Ammons Full-Range Picture Vocabulary Test*. The age range was limited to 15 to 55 years because of Tolor and Schulberg's (1963) finding that within that age range, age does not constitute a significant variable. There were 21 female and 10 male Ss in each group.

Overall, black schizophrenics produced significantly ($p <$

.025) poorer Bender records than did whites. More specifically, Designs 4, 6, 7, and 8 were rendered less accurate by blacks as compared to whites. The mean number of errors committed by the black schizophrenics was 15; for white schizophrenics it was 10. Also, the frequency of errors and the time taken to complete the task was significantly greater for blacks as well. However, there were no systematic differences in specific types of errors nor the number of errors for any particular figure.

The author indicated that educational differences could not have accounted for these results, since the blacks actually had significantly more formal education than the whites, and since there was a significant negative correlation ($r = -.36$) between education and total raw score; blacks should actually have done better on the Bender. Age differences also could not account for the differences between blacks and whites, since age did not correlate significantly with Bender score.

Although it is possible that the schizophrenic process has a more devastating effect on blacks than on whites, in the absence of pre-morbid baseline data, this remains only one of several possibilities.

Korin (1974) compared the Bender-Gestalt Test performance in psychiatric patients, some psychotic and some nonpsychotic, who were using heroin and those who were using other drugs. The study was prompted by some previous observations that heroin-dependent patients often showed marked perceptual distortion on the Bender even though many were nonpsychotic and had recently been detoxified.

The very small size of the samples is indicated by the fact that there were only five in the psychotic, heroin-user group, 11 in the psychotic nonopiate group, 22 in the nonpsychotic heroin group, and six in the nonpsychotic, nonopiate group. The patients' ages ranged from 19 to 33 years.

The Bender-Gestalt protocols were scored for 17 factors on the Psychopathology Scale (Hutt and Gibby, 1970) without knowledge of patient's status. The effects of psychosis and drugs were analyzed by use of a 2 × 2 factorial analysis of variance design.

A significant drug effect was found with heroin patients

performing significantly worse than nonheroin users. No significant effects were found for psychosis or interaction between psychosis and drug use.

The correlation between mental ability, as determined by the Kent Series of Emergency Scale (Kent, 1942), and Bender-Gestalt Psychopathology Scale scores was —.57 in the heroin group, and —.65 in the nonopiate group. Adjustment of Bender scores for the effect of variation attributable to mental ability, by means of analysis of covariance, produced an enhancement of the drug effect on the Bender performance.

Korin also analyzed the performance of the heroin and nonopiate groups separately for the 17 scored Bender variables and found that on the following three factors significant differences emerged: use of space (between designs)—greater constriction for the heroin group; perseverations—more in the heroin group; and rotation—more frequent in the heroin group.

Means for the total Bender-Gestalt Test scores were not different for detoxified and nondetoxified subgroups.

This study suggests that heroin produces marked perceptual-motor disturbance, even in nonpsychotic individuals, whereas marijuana usage does not have this type of effect. The psychosis-nonpsychosis status seemed not to be reflected in Bender performance. Of course, in view of the small size of the samples, and the possibility that heroin use might lead to organic changes of the brain, these results need further clarification through better controlled research.

Finally, in one of the few studies involving severely emotionally disturbed children, Safrin (1964) examined the possibility of "perceptual-deficit" in psychotic children. However, no significant difference was noted in the Bender performance (based on the Pascal-Suttell [1951] scoring system) of psychotic ($\overline{X}$ age = 117.4 months) and nonpsychotic children ($\overline{X}$ age = 119.9 months).

Summary

To recapitulate, there appears to be a relationship between degree of psychotic pathology and Bender-Gestalt Test disturbance. Hallucinatory symptomatology, in particular, is reflected in deteriorated Bender performance. Sensory deprivation does not seem to be accompanied by changes in the size of the Bender renditions produced by schizophrenic patients, but it is still not known whether other, more important, Bender alterations are not accompaniments of the sensory deprivation experience. Reduced size in Bender drawings is not a consequence of psychotic depression in women. Bipolar depressed patients perform differently on the Bender-Gestalt Test than unipolar depressed patients by being less systematic in their placement of the designs on the paper. It appears that black schizophrenics produce more deviant Bender protocols than white schizophrenics, although some uncertainty about the generalizability of this result remains. The effect of heroin usage appears to be quite markedly adverse on fidelity of Bender reproduction, and it is far greater than the effect of psychosis *per se*. These assertions all represent tentative conclusions requiring replications before being fully accepted.

CHAPTER 7

THE BENDER-GESTALT TEST AND SCHOOL PERFORMANCE

Sᴵɴᴄᴇ ᴠɪsᴜᴀʟ-ᴍᴏᴛᴏʀ coordination is thought to play an important role in children's learning, especially in the early grades, a considerable amount of research has focused on the relationship between Bender performance and school achievement. However, due to wide variations from study to study in design and analysis, sampling, criterion measures, target populations, and Bender administration and scoring procedures, it is difficult to draw definitive conclusions.

In an attempt to integrate the research findings, the studies in this chapter will be classified according to two criteria: (1) Bender administration and scoring procedures, and (2) target population studied. Within these individual sections, issues concerning sample characteristics, criterion measures, and design and analysis will be further considered.

KOPPITZ DEVELOPMENTAL SCORING SYSTEM

Elizabeth Koppitz (1958, 1960, 1964, 1975b) has devoted considerable time to the development and refinement of the *Developmental Bender Scoring System*. The system consists of 30 items primarily based on four error types: distortion, integratiton, rotation, and perseveration.

Since the scoring system was validated against achievement in the first two grades, Koppitz anticipated that Bender scores would be useful predictors not only of achievement in the first two grades but also in other grades. Indeed, the early research of Koppitz and her associates (Koppitz, Sullivan, Blyth, and Shelton, 1959; Koppitz, Mardis, and Stephens, 1961) was interpreted in support of the relationship between Bender performance and achievement in the first grade. In the latter study, Koppitz, Mardis, and Stephens (1961) reported significant correlations between the Bender and *Metropolitan Achievement Test* scores in six of seven first grades tested (range $= -.29$ to $-.71$, median $= -.58$), the Bender and *Lee-Clark Reading Readiness Test* scores in three of five first grade classes (range $= -.21$ to $-.64$, median $= -.33$), and the Bender and the *Metropolitan Reading Test* scores in two classes tested (r's $= -.41$ and $-.73$).

Since this time, numerous studies have been conducted to examine this relationship in children at various grade levels in both regular and special education classes.

REGULAR CLASS STUDENTS

The results of recent research generally support the notion that Bender performance is related to the school achievement of regular class children, especially in the early grades. For example, Snyder and Freud (1967) reported a significant correlation ($-.47$) between the *Developmental Bender Score* and the Lee-Clark Reading Readiness Test in 667 Caucasian first graders of average and above average intelligence.

Similarly, Norfleet (1973) investigated the feasibility of the *Developmental Bender Score* as a predictor of reading achievement in the first grade. Special attention was devoted to (1) the accuracy of Bender cut-off scores in predicting successful and unsuccessful reading achievement, and (2) the relationship of the *Developmental Bender Score* to teachers' judgments of reading achievement. The Ss were 158 boys and 153 girls in the first grade of a predominantly white, middle-class school in a semirural area. The *Gates-MacGinitie Reading Test* and teachers' ratings were used as reading criterion measures. Poor, average, and good Bender groups were selected based on cut-off scores. Chi-square analyses for reading achievement (above versus below the mean) in Vocabulary, Comprehension and Total Score were all significant. As expected, Bender performance was positively related to reading achievement. Similar results were obtained for a comparison of good and poor Bender groups on teacher ratings of reading achievement, although the results were much stronger for girls than for boys.

The author stated that, on the whole, good Bender performance was a useful predictor of success in reading, but poor Bender performance was not valuable in identifying poor readers. She concluded, therefore, that "the Bender should be supplemented with other measures for individual prediction, particularly in those screening programs that are primarily interested in identifying potentially poor readers."

Henderson, Butler, and Gaffeney (1969) focused on the effectiveness of the *Developmental Bender Score* in predicting arithmetic and reading achievement for white and nonwhite seven-year-old children. The sample included 120 white Ss and 83 nonwhite Ss (95% Negro and Negro-white mixture and 5% Oriental American or American Indian). The arithmetic and reading (word recognition) sections of the *Wide Range Achievement Test* were used as criterion measures.

Low to moderate, yet statistically significant, correlations between Bender performance and the achievement measures were reported for both the white (r reading $= -.26$; r arithmetic $= -.41$) and nonwhite (r reading $= -.32$; r arithmetic $= -.36$) samples. However, when intelligence (WISC) was partialled out, the Bender was found to add very little to the prediction of reading and arithmetic achievement. The authors concluded, therefore, that while the Bender may be a useful predictor of achievement, *it is not as effective as the WISC.*

Carter, Spero, and Walsh (1978) designed a study to determine the usefulness of the *Developmental Bender Score* as a discriminator of below average achievement in reading and arithmetic in seventy-eight children (37 males, 41 females) representing four socioeconomic levels based on the *Warner-Meeker-Eells Scale,* and three age-groups: 6-4 to 7-3, 7-4 to 8-3, and 8-4 to 9-3. Their mean IQ (WISC-R) was 102.6 ($SD = 17.61$). The criterion measures were the Reading Comprehension, Vocabulary, Math Concepts, and Math Problem-Solving sections of the *Iowa Test of Basic Skills.*

Children in the three age categories were subdivided into

two groups for each of the achievement measures, based on grade equivalent achievement scores nine months or more below the average grade equivalent expectancy (below average group) or any other grade equivalent score (average group). An analysis of covariance showed that Bender scores were successful in discriminating average and below average achievers in vocabulary, math concepts, and math problem-solving, *but not reading comprehension.*

Obrzut, Taylor, and Thweatt (1972) examined the *Developmental Bender Score* as a predictor of reading achievement of 289 children, randomly selected from grades one, three, and six. The following subtests of the Stanford Achievement Tests were used at the various grade levels:

1st Word Reading
    Paragraph Meaning
    Vocabulary
    Word Study Skill
3rd Word Meaning
    Paragraph Meaning
    Word Study Skill
6th Word Meaning
    Paragraph Meaning

Pearson product-moment correlations between the *Developmental Bender Score* and reading achievement subtest scores were generally low (range: $-.22$ to $-.37$) but statistically significant (with the exception of first grade paragraph meaning—$r = .15$—which was not significant).

The author also examined the relationship between individual Koppitz signs and reading achievement using chi square analyses (based on extreme cut-off scores on the arithmetic subtests and presence or absence of the particular Bender sign). Seven of the 30 Koppitz signs were significant at the first grade level, two at the third grade level, and one at the sixth grade level. However, with such a large number of analyses, several significant results may be due to change. Therefore, the results are of little value in individual prediction.

In a more extensive study, Dibner and Korn (1969) evaluated

the *Developmental Bender Score* as a predictor of school performance in children ($N = 492$) from kindergarten through fourth grade. The Ss were from a suburban area, with a high socioeconomic level. In addition to the *Developmental Bender Score*, the *Koppitz Total Emotional Indicators Score* (one was dropped—expansion; three were added—constriction, overlapping, and boxing in) was examined. The criterion measures were based on teachers' ratings (using a five-point scale) of the Ss in the following areas:

1. General adequacy of school performance
2. Arithmetic
3. Reading
4. General Intelligence
5. Emotional Control
6. Prediction of success in the next grade if promoted

Correlations between *Developmental Bender Scores* and both original and new teacher ratings were generally low to moderate but statistically significant. Emotional Scores were not significantly related to original teacher ratings. However, these scores were significantly related to new teacher ratings in the first and second grades. Overall, the authors suggested that the *Developmental Bender Score* was a useful predictor of school performance, *but its value diminished rapidly after the first grade.*

Keogh (1965a) found low (range from −.21 to −.32) but statistically significant correlations between kindergarten Bender performance and five measures of third grade reading (a) a seven-point teacher rating scale and (b) the Word Recognition, Following Direction, Word Form subtests and the Total Score of the *California Reading Test*. Similar results were obtained for third grade Bender Scores (range from −.14 to −.27). However, with intelligence (CTMM) held constant, the majority of these relationships became statistically nonsignificant.

In an attempt to gain greater predictive accuracy the author set cut-off scores on the kindergarten Bender at approximately plus and minus one-half standard deviation. Subjects were trichotomized on the basis of Bender scores and dichotomized on the basis of reading performance (the author did not state cut-off score used). Chi square analyses revealed significant relationships. Significance was mainly attributable to the following finding: poor Bender performance was not indicative of reading difficulty, but good Bender performance was indicative of success in reading.

Along these lines, Wallbrown, Wallbrown, and Engin (1977) designed a study to determine the relative effectiveness of the Bender and the *Minnesota Percepto-Diagnostic Test* in identifying achievement-related errors in visual-motor perception of older children. One hundred and fifty-three children (78 boys and 75 girls) from a third grade in a suburban upper-middle class (based on education and occupation of fathers) area, served as Ss. The mean IQ (Cognitive Abilities Test) of the sample was 116.9.

The criterion measures were the Reading Vocabulary, Reading Comprehension, Math Computation, Math Concepts and Problems subtests of the California Achievement Test. Very low (range −.18 to −.27), but statistically significant correlations, were found for the Developmental Bender Score and all areas of achievement. However, the MPD was found to be a much more sensitive measure of achievement than the Bender with older children.

LONGITUDINAL STUDIES

There have been two longitudinal studies of Bender performance and achievement. In the first study, Keogh and Smith (1967) examined the utility of the Bender in predicting school achievement in the middle and upper elementary school years. They compared kindergarten Bender performance with achievement in the third and sixth grades. They also examined the predictive value of third and sixth grade Bender performances. The achievement measures were the reading and spelling sections of the California Achievement Test at third grade, and the reading, spelling and arithmetic sections of the Iowa Test of Basic Skills at sixth grade.

Low to moderate, but generally (11 of 15) statistically significant, correlations were obtained for the Developmental Bender Scores and the achievement measures. The authors concluded that the kindergarten Bender was a remarkably good predictor of both good and poor achievement at sixth grade. Although using the cut-off scores ($\pm$ 1 SD) was helpful in predicting good and poor achievers, a large number of children were not correctly identified. Therefore, the authors concluded that the Bender should be used in conjunction with other assessment devices.

The second longitudinal study was conducted by Koppitz (1973) who followed children from kindergarten through eighth grade. The Bender was administered to 101 kindergarten children from a middle-class, suburban elementary school. The following criterion measures were also administered:

(1) In the fourth grade, the California Test of Mental Maturity and the Metropolitan Achievement Test
(2) In the seventh grade, the Differential Aptitude Test
(3) In the eighth grade, report card grades in English, Social Studies, Mathematics, Science and the average of the four subjects.

Chi squares were computed to compare the Bender scores at or above the mean and below the mean with both high and low IQ scores and Metropolitan Achievement Test scores, respectively. Bender performance was related significantly to fourth grade IQ scores and reading and arithmetic achievement.

Similar analyses were performed at the seventh grade. However, only two of the eight areas sampled by the Differential Aptitude Tests (Abstract Reasoning and Space Relations) were found to be related significantly to kindergarten Bender performance.

Eighth grade analyses revealed significant relationships between kindergarten Bender scores and Science grades and grade averages, but not English, Mathematics, or Social Science grades.

Of the 43 Ss available for eighth grade comparisons, 20 children with average (less than 1 SD below the mean) to above average (more than 1 SD below the mean) Bender scores were performing at least at an average level, and 17 of the 20 were performing at an above average to outstanding level.

However, a low average to poor kindergarten Bender score (1 SD above the mean) was not a good predictor of a given child's eighth-grade performance. These children's grades ranged from excellent to failing.

There also have been studies (Giebink and Birch, 1970; Coy, 1974) which did not find significant relationships between Bender performance and school achievement. Giebink and Birch (1970) related Developmental Bender Scores in kindergarten and first grade to reading performance assessed at the beginning of second grade. One hundred and forty-two boys and girls ($\overline{X}$ age = 7.67 years, $\overline{X}$ IQ = 109.31) from a small, semi-rural school system served as Ss. Reading achievement was measured by the California Achievement Test during the first semester of second grade. The correlations between both kindergarten and first grade Bender performance and reading achievement were not significant.

Coy (1974) investigated the predictive validity of the Developmental Bender Score as it relates to achievement in reading and arithmetic in third graders. Fifty-one (21 males and 30 females) children, from a predominantly white school, served as Ss. The criterion measures were the Wide Range Achievement Test (Reading and Arithmetic sections) and the Cooperative Primary Reading Test. The Ss represented high and low achievers (the top and bottom 27% on the achievement tests).

Correlations were computed on the Bender scores and achievement test scores, but no significant relationships were found. The author reported, however, that integration errors occurred significantly more frequently in the low reading achievement as opposed to the high reading achievement group. No differences were noted for distortion, perseveration, or rotation errors.

Overall, the research surveyed reported statistically significant relationships between Developmental Bender Scores and school achievement. However, the magnitude of the relationships is usually not large enough to permit individual prediction. Even Koppitz (1975b) has reevaluated her earlier statements concerning the relationship of Bender performance and academic achievement, stating ". . . I seem to have overestimated in the earlier studies the significance of visual-motor perception for school achievement . . . one cannot neglect other equally important factors, especially language development, oral-visual integration, sequencing, recall of symbols and information, and concept formation. Children's ages, attitudes, gender, and family and social backgrounds also influence their achievement in varying degrees. A youngster's progress in school depends on a combination and interaction of all of these factors" (pp. 60-61). Furthermore, the Bender seems to be a more effective predictive instrument for younger children than older children, and therefore may warrant consideration for inclusion in a readiness battery.

MULTIVARIATE STUDIES

Several research studies have focused on the combined effectiveness of the Bender and other educational assessment instruments in predicting school achievement.

A study by Wallbrown, Engin, Wallbrown, and Blaha (1975) was designed to investigate the relationship between selected facets of perceptual-cognitive development at the kindergarten level and subsequent reading achievement during first grade. One hundred Ss from three social strata (43 outer city, 18 transitional, 39 inner city) were randomly selected from the total kindergarten enrollment in the school sample. The mean IQ was 104.1 ($SD = 16.7$) and the mean age at the time of the kindergarten testing was 74.2 months ($SD = 4.2$).

The battery was comprised of the Bender-Gestalt test and nine other predictor tests: *Slosson Intelligence Test, Wepman Auditory Discrimination Test, Illinois Test of Psycholinguistic Abilities* (Auditory Sequential Memory and Visual Sequential Memory subtests), *Tapped Patterns, Horst Reversals Test, Language Comprehension,* and the *Word Recognition Tests I and II.* The Developmental Bender Score was based on six cards (A, 1, 2, 4, 6, and 8).

The Gates-MacGinitie Reading Test was used to obtain criterion measures for first grade reading vocabulary and reading comprehension. Analysis of the regression of the Vocabulary subtest on the predictor variables indicated that the Slosson Intelligence Test was the most effective single predictor of first grade reading vocabulary. The Bender-Gestalt test and three additional *perceptual* variables (Tapped Patterns, Word Recognition I, and Language Comprehension) resulted in significant increments in R^2. Subjects with higher error scores on these tests tended to have lower scores on the Vocabulary subtest. The authors concluded that, "Those Ss most likely to achieve highest in vocabulary at the end of first grade were not only higher in general intelligence but also relatively free of deficiencies in visual-motor integration, auditory-motor integration, direct word learning, and oral comprehension." They also noted that in children free of deficiencies in one or more of the perceptual areas, general intelligence is the best predictor of reading vocabulary.

Analysis of the regression of the Comprehension Subtest on the predictor variables indicated that the Bender was the most effective single predictor of first grade reading comprehension. Four other variables (Slosson Intelligence Test, ITPA Sequential Memory, Sex, and Horst Reversals) also contributed to the significance of the regression equation. The authors concluded that "The child who achieves well in reading comprehension at the first grade level tends to show the following characteristics at the end of kindergarten: free from deficits in visual-motor integration, higher in general intelligence, higher in visual sequential memory, free from deficits in visual discrimination, and more likely to be female."

These findings suggest that both general intelligence and visual-motor integration are important components of overall first grade reading achievement, and that comprehension involves a broader range of visual skills than vocabulary. Also, it appears that comprehension is a more complex phenomenon than vocabulary in that it involves a wider range of perceptual-cognitive skills.

Telegdy (1975) examined the effectiveness of selected readiness tests to predict first grade success. The tests were the following:

1. Bender-Gestalt Test
2. Screening Test of Academic Readiness

3. First Grade Screening Test
4. *Metropolitan Readiness Test*

All tests were administered to 56 children (28 boys and 28 girls) at the end of their kindergarten year ($\overline{X}$ age = 5.6 years). Upper, middle and lower socioeconomic levels were represented in the sample from both inner city and suburban areas.

The Ss were administered the criterion measures (Reading, Spelling and Arithmetic subtests of the Wide Range Achievement Test and the Passage and Comprehension section of the *Gray Oral Reading Test*) one year later.

Although the MRT and the STAR were better predictors of first grade achievement, the Developmental Bender Score was also a highly significant ($p < .001$) predictor of academic achievement. Furthermore, the stepwise multiple regression procedure showed that the combination of the Bender, human figure drawing, Metropolitan Readiness Test (Alphabet), and STAR (Letter) scores was the best predictor of all five criteria of what the author considered "overall readiness." He concluded that the basic skills required for good first grade achievement were: (1) good visual-perceptual ability, (2) letter or alphabet knowledge, and (3) the ability to attend to detail or a relatively high motivation level.

Werner, Simonian, and Smith (1967) administered the Bender and the Primary Mental Abilities test to 369 boys and 381 girls ages 10 and 11, and residing in Hawaii. Low but statistically significant relationships were reported for *Developmental Error Scores* and both reading grade (.31) and reading test score (.31). However, apart from the total PMA IQ, the best predictor of early grade achievement was the Verbal Comprehension factor. The addition of the Bender and all other PMA factors did not significantly improve prediction.

Overall, the results of multivariate studies favor the use of the Bender in a readiness battery. When used appropriately in combination with other educational assessment tools, the Bender adds significantly to the prediction of achievement in *young* children. However, again, its usefulness is greatly diminished with older children.

ACHIEVEMENT OF EXCEPTIONAL CHILDREN

Disadvantaged Children

As with the results of regular class students, research with disadvantaged children has reported positive relationships between Bender performance and school achievement. Mlodnosky (1972) compared the utility of the Bender as a predictor of first-grade reading achievement among children from an economically deprived neighborhood. Ninety-three first graders (90% black, 6% Mexican-American, 2% Oriental-American and 2% Caucasian), from a school that qualified for federal aid to impoverished areas, were selected as Ss. She found moderately high, statistically significant correlations between the Developmental Bender Score and the nine measures of reading achievement listed below:

(1) Gates-MacGinitie Reading Test (Vocabulary and Comprehension)
(2) California Reading Test (Vocabulary and Comprehension)
(3) *Stanford Achievement Test* (Word Study Skills, Word Reading, Vocabulary and Paragraph Meaning), and
(4) a measure of classroom reading level based on the reading series being used.

Baker and Thurber (1976) investigated the relationship between the *Developmental Bender Score* and reading (Wide Range Achievement Test) performance of 147 disadvantaged children ranging in age from six years to 14.11 years (median = 9.5 years). The Information Subtest of the WISC was also administered to all Ss.

The authors reported a highly significant correlation between the Bender and word recognition scores for the entire sample. However, separate correlations performed on groups divided by age (above and below the median), showed that the magnitude of the relationship declined sharply for the older Ss. In addition, partial correlations with age and/or intelligence held constant showed that the relationship between Bender scores and achievement remained significant for the younger group but not the older group. Their findings support previous research which reported a loss of predictive utility for the Bender with older children.

Gifted Children

Chang and Chang (1967) investigated the relationship between Developmental Bender Scores and reading achievement of 100 gifted second and third graders. The Ss were dichotomized into low and high Bender groups (at each grade) based on percentile cut-off scores. Gates Reading Test Scores were obtained for each S, and correlations with low and high Bender groups were computed for each grade. They reported moderate, statistically significant relationships between Bender performance and reading achievement at the second grade but not the third grade.

Mentally Retarded Children

Research with mentally retarded children has not shown a significant relationship between Bender performance and school achievement.

Cellura and Butterfield (1966) designed a study to examine the validity of the Bender as a predictor of reading achievement among mildly mentally retarded institutionalized adolescents who were matched on CA, MA, and IQ, but who differed in reading achievement (Metropolitan Achievement Test). Bender protocols were scored by both the Pascal and Suttell (1951) and the Koppitz scoring systems. The groups were not found to differ significantly on either measure.

Kelly and Amble (1970) tried to determine whether there would be an increase in prediction of academic achievement among educable mentally retarded students by using both Wechsler Intelligence Test scores and Bender scores. The authors used a multiple regression analysis, controlling for chronological age differences. The Wechsler Verbal and Performance IQs and the Developmental Bender Scores were used in the prediction of WRAT achievement in reading, spelling, and arithmetic.

Moderate, statistically significant correlations were reported between the Bender and all the achievement areas. However, given CA, VIQ and PIQ, Bender scores did not add significantly to the prediction of reading or spelling. The only area where Bender scores added significantly to the predictive equation was arithmetic.

Morgenstern and McIvor (1973) designed a study to further explore the relationship between Bender performance and WRAT achievement in reading and arithmetic among retarded children. Seventy-six children, ranging in age from 9 years, 10 months to 15 years, 11 months, and WISC IQ from 45 to 84, served as Ss. The correlation between the Developmental Bender Score and reading achievement was not significant. However, a moderate, statistically significant correlation was found between Bender performance and arithmetic achievement. Although partialling out both CA and IQ substantially reduced the magnitude of this correlation, it was still statistically significant.

Deaf Children

Clarke and Leslie (1971) administered a battery of tests, including the Bender, to 59 deaf children ranging in age from eight to twelve years. Based on their Performance IQ and reading level (Gates-MacGinitie Reading Test), 27 Ss were divided into the following three groups:

(1) reading was retarded by more than two years, and WISC performance IQs were less than 90
(2) reading was retarded by more than two years and WISC performance IQs were greater than 90
(3) reading was retarded by less than two years and performance IQs were greater than 90

The groups were matched on CA ($\overline{X} = 9.9$ years), hearing level, age of onset of deafness, and length of attendance at school.

Although Groups 1 and 2 were found to be significantly different on the profile including the five WISC performance IQ subtests, the Bender, and the Memory for Designs, there was no significant difference between the average profile of Groups 1 and 2 and the profile of group 3. The authors did not report a comparison of the three groups on the Bender.

The study was generally poorly conceived and executed. In fact, the authors did not report information on how the Bender was scored or the mean IQs of the groups. Nor did they adequately describe their sample, especially in terms of overall academic skills. Although they did report on reading, all we know is that two groups were deficient in reading by more than two years and one by less than two years.

With the range of deficiencies possibly great it is not unexpected that Bender performance would be generally poor. In fact, the authors reported that 21 of the 27 Ss had Bender scores 1 *SD* below the mean for normal children.

THE KEOGH-SMITH SCORING SYSTEM

Keogh and Smith (1961) developed a five-point rating scale designed to yield a single total score based on "discriminated degrees of quality of production." The scale ranges from a score of one (design figures not recognizable) to a score of five (all parts of the design are present and recognizable).

Several studies (Smith and Keogh 1962; Keogh 1965a; 1965b; Keogh and Smith 1968) have been conducted on the relationship of this scoring system to school achievement.

REGULAR CLASS STUDENTS

In a follow-up to their 1961 study, Smith and Keogh (1962) compared children's kindergarten Bender performance with (a) kindergarten teachers' reading readiness ratings of each child on a seven-point scale ranging from total lack of reading abilities to ready to begin reading; (b) the *Lee-Clark Reading Readiness Test*; (c) first grade teachers' ratings of each child's reading achievement on a seven-point scale; and (d) the *Lee-Clark Reading Achievement Test*. Correlation coefficients for the Keogh-Smith total Bender score and all of the reading measures were statistically significant (range from .39 to .54).

Further follow-up at third grade (Keogh, 1965a) revealed low (range from .18 to .28) but statistically significant correlations between the kindergarten Bender performance and five measures of reading: (a) a seven-point teacher rating scale, and (b) the Word Recognition, Following Direction, Word Form Subtests and the Total Score of the California Reading Test. Similar results were obtained for third grade Bender scores (range from .21 to .29). However, with intelligence (California Test of Mental Maturity) held constant, the majority of these relationships became statistically nonsignificant.

In an attempt to gain greater predictive accuracy, the authors set cut-off scores on the kindergarten Bender at approximately plus and minus one-half standard deviation. Subjects were trichotomized on the basis of Bender scores and dichotomized on the basis of reading performance (the author did not state the cut-off score used). Chi square analyses revealed significant relationships. Good Bender performance was associated with good to adequate reading ability, but poor Bender performance was not useful in predicting reading ability.

Keogh and Smith (1968) correlated the Bender performance of kindergarten children with classroom teachers' ratings of their reading readiness on a one-to-five scale. The sample consisted of 74 boys and 66 girls ($\overline{X}$ age 63.35 months). The Bender was administered during September, November, February, and May of kindergarten. The protocols were scored by the Keogh and Smith (1961) five-point rating scale.

Correlations between the teacher ratings and all four Bender scores were moderately high and statistically significant.

GIFTED STUDENTS

Keogh (1965b) considered the use of the Bender-Gestalt Test as a screening test for the early identification of potentially successful school achievers by examining the third grade achievement of children who had been above average in Bender performance in kindergarten. One hundred twenty-seven third graders from a predominantly Caucasian, middle socioeconomic area who had been administered the Bender in kindergarten served as Ss. Using the Keogh-Smith (1961) scoring system, 40 Ss were classified as good Bender performers and the third grade achievement data were then analyzed.

Scores from the California Test of Mental Maturity and the California Achievement Test were used as criterion measures. The results indicated above average achievement in all areas of school performance for the group.

More specifically, 32 of the 40 children classified as good or superior on the Bender at kindergarten were achieving above actual grade placement at the third grade, while eight were below actual grade placement on two or more of the evaluation criteria.

Of the 56 children achieving above grade placement, 57 percent were correctly predicted by good Bender performance in kindergarten. The author concluded that "Children who do well on the Bender at the kindergarten level are apt to achieve well in other areas of the school program." However, she goes on to state that "If the Bender had been the only screening measure used at kindergarten, a sizable number of potential good achievers would not have been identified, and a small number would have been incorrectly identified. This reflects in part, no doubt, the error potential in using any single measure for prediction of a complex behavior and/or school learning."

THE deHIRSCH SCORING SYSTEM

deHirsch, Jansky, and Langford (1966) reported low to moderate statistically significant correlations between Bender performance and reading ($r = .44$), writing ($r = .33$), and spelling ($r = .45$) in a group of 53 children (30 boys and 23 girls) from a racially mixed, lower middle-class area. The Ss were administered the Bender in kindergarten and the criterion measures in second grade.

The writing test consisted of four sentences dictated to the Ss who were free to choose between printing and cursive writing. The reading test was a combined score derived from the Gates Advanced Primary and the Gray Oral Reading tests. The spelling test was taken from the Metropolitan Achievement Test, Primary II Battery.

The authors used a modified Bender involving six of the nine designs (A, 1, 2, 4, 6, and 8). In collaboration with Dr.

Lauretta Bender (1938, 1967) the authors devised the following scoring system. "The score is the number of copies, from 0-6, on which the child fails to reproduce the essential features of the Gestalt. One point is added if he is unable to arrange the designs on the paper—if, for instance, designs are superimposed on one another. Another point is added if he rotates three or more of the figures" (deHirsch, Jansky, and Langford, 1966, p. 107).

Similarly, Jansky and deHirsch (1972) reported moderate, statistically significant correlations between the Bender and reading ($r = .41$) and spelling ($r = .44$) in a group of 347 racially mixed, kindergarten children from a large metropolitan area.

A more refined scoring system, which included more specific criteria for scoring the six figures, was presented. The reading and spelling criterion measures were the same as those employed in the previous study. Again, the Bender was administered in kindergarten and the criterion measures were given in second grade.

BENDER "SOFT" SIGNS AND SCHOOL ACHIEVEMENT

Thweatt, Obrzut, and Taylor (1972) developed a scoring system for the Bender, which was based on "a systematic exploration of mild or soft parameters of visual-motor-perceptual performance." Based on the assumption that inadequate perception in space handicaps a child in many ways—especially in academic tasks—the authors developed an objective scoring system to measure an individual's directional orientation to the Bender-Gestalt Test.

The Ss were 99 first graders, 98 third graders and 92 sixth graders. The total sample was composed of 69 percent white and 31 percent non-white children. All subjects were administered the Bender and the Stanford Achievement Test. The Bender was scored according to a 33-item soft-sign system. Subjects were classified as good or poor readers based on their reading performance on the SAT. A high reading level was defined as a percentile score of 77 or better and a low reading level was defined as falling at or below the twenty-third percentile.

Chi square analyses revealed that nine of the 33 Bender signs were significant at the first grade level, five of 33 at the third grade level, and only three of 33 at the sixth grade level. Although the authors did not report the relationship of "total" signs to reading level, they did mention that many signs showed "a trend in their predictive power."

Overall, it appears that the system may have some utility for predicting "early" reading achievement, but its power decreases with age.

BENDER RECOGNITION AND SCHOOL ACHIEVEMENT

Labrentz, Linkenhoker, and Aaron (1976) examined the relationship between the Bender copying task (Koppitz Developmental Score) and a Bender-Gestalt multiple choice recognition test to reading achievement. Initially 132 pre- and primary school children were administered the recognition task followed by the copying task. Two years later, these scores were correlated with the results of Metropolitan Reading Achievement scores. The exact number of Ss in each group was not reported. The results for both procedures were moderately high and statistically significant for second grade children but were not significant for first grade children. The authors attempted to account for the lack of significance at the first grade level on the basis of a difference in reading instruction in the two groups. The first graders were involved in a program featuring a phonetic approach (Initial Teaching Alphabet), whereas the other group was instructed through the "traditional" method.

MISCELLANEOUS STUDIES ON SCHOOL ACHIEVEMENT

There are two additional studies on the relationship between Bender performance and achievement. However, these studies are difficult to assess because they do not note which scoring system was used for the Bender.

Lessler and Bridges (1973) designed a study to examine the academic performance of children in a low socioeconomic, rural school district. Eighty-seven boys and 109 girls were administered the following battery of tests at the beginning of first grade:

Metropolitan Readiness Test
Lee-Clark Reading Readiness Test
California Test of Mental Maturity
Peabody Picture Vocabulary Test
Bender Gestalt Test
Bean Bucket Game (a measure of social maturity)

Two criterion measures (California Achievement Test and a teacher rating of overall performance) were administered in the spring of both the first and second grades. Although low to moderate, statistically significant correlations were found between the Bender and the first grade reading measure (no results were reported for second grade achievement and Bender performance) the best single predictor of reading performance was the Metropolitan Readiness Test. The Bender did not add significantly to the predictive effectiveness of the group tests.

Similarly, Lessler, Schoeninger, and Bridges (1970) designed a study to compare and combine three different instruments (the Bender, Lee-Clark Reading Readiness Test, and Peabody Picture Vocabulary Test) in the prediction of first-grade performance. The Ss were 154 white children representing a range of socioeconomic levels. The two criterion measures were teachers' ratings and the California Reading Test.

Although the Lee-Clark was the best single predictor of both reading achievement and teachers' ratings, low to moderately high correlations were reported for the Bender and these criterion measures. However, with the Lee-Clark partialled out, the Bender contributed very little to prediction.

Summary

Significant relationships between Bender performance and school achievement have been reported. However, when the effects of intelligence are taken into consideration these relationships are reduced. Generally speaking, therefore, the magnitude of these relationships—with the possible exception of studies of early elementary school aged children—is not large enough to be of significant predictive value.

Multivariate studies indicate that when used in conjunction with other instruments, the utility of the Bender as a predictor of *early* school achievement is increased considerably.

CHAPTER 8

THE BENDER-GESTALT TEST AND LEARNING DISABILITIES

A<small>LTHOUGH</small> T<small>OLOR AND</small> S<small>CHULBERG</small> (1963) reported only scant research on the relationship between Bender performance and learning disorders, there has been a considerable amount of research on this topic over the past 16 years. This is due primarily to the popularity of the *Koppitz* (1964) *Developmental Scoring System*.

As mentioned previously, the *Developmental Scoring System* was validated on the Metropolitan Achievement Test (Koppitz 1964). Only those items that differentiated consistently between above and below average students were included. Therefore, one might expect the Bender to be a useful LD assessment tool.

Although several studies have been conducted on the relationship between Bender performance and "learning disabilities," most of the research has been concerned with the relationship between Bender performance and reading impairment. The Bender's usefulness for children having learning disabilities and those who have reading difficulties will be treated separately in this chapter.

LEARNING DISABILITIES

While numerous case histories, which examine the Bender performance of learning disabled children, have been published (Bender, 1970; Koppitz, 1971; 1975b), there have been very few research studies on this population. This is in part due to the fact that the term "Learning Disability" encompasses a wide variety of disorders varying in severity. For example, a learning disability, as defined by the Children with Specific Learning

Disabilities Act of 1969, is "a disorder in one or more of the basic psychological processes involved in understanding or using spoken or written language. These may be manifested in disorders of listening, thinking, talking, reading, writing, spelling, perceptual handicaps, brain injury, minimal brain dysfunction, dyslexia, developmental asphasia, etc. They do not include learning problems which are due primarily to visual, hearing, or motor handicaps, to mental retardation, emotional disturbance, or to environmental disadvantage."

One of the earliest studies of learning disabled children was conducted by Koppitz (1971) who examined the Bender performance of 177 pupils enrolled in special public school classes for the educationally handicapped. The 152 boys and 25 girls in the study ranged in age from five to 12 years ($\overline{X}$ = eight years, 11 months). The Benders were scored for Developmental Errors and placed into one of four categories:

(1) Good—scores more than one *SD* above the mean.
(2) High Average—scores between the mean and one *SD*.
(3) Low Average—scores between the mean and minus one *SD*.
(4) Poor—scores more than one *SD* below the mean.

Approximately 90 percent of the children in this study showed visual-motor immaturity in comparison to same-aged normal children. One hundred two Ss obtained poor scores, and 53 obtained low average scores. When mental age was incorporated into the comparison, 77 percent of the children still showed visual-motor immaturity.

A five-year follow-up on the Bender performance of LD pupils who returned to regular classes, LD pupils who remained in special education classes, and LD pupils who were referred for residential treatment showed that only the residential treatment group showed a significantly higher frequency of "poor" Bender performance.

Koppitz (1975b) later showed that the visual-motor integration skills of learning disabled students mature at a rate slower than normal, although this rate depends on the child's age and mental ability. Based on an examination of over 1,200 Bender protocols of special-class pupils, she reported that while the average child at age five and one-half achieved a Bender score of 10, LD children with IQ scores of 100 or higher did not reach this level of maturity of visual-motor integration until six years of age, and those with IQ scores of 85 to 99 did not obtain this score until seven years of age. Learning disabled children of borderline mental ability achieved a Bender score of 10 at eight years of age and moderately retarded LD children achieved this score at nine and one-half to 10 years of age.

Consistent with these findings, Kerr (1972) reported a significant difference between the Developmental Bender Scores of 122 poorly ($\overline{X} = 10.13$), and 134 average ($\overline{X} = 5.99$), achieving children. The samples were selected on the basis of teachers' evaluations, and consisted of those Ss who would not advance to the next grade or level in school and a group of children randomly selected from the remainder of the classes. The sample was composed of 64 kindergarten, 100 grade one, and 92 grade two children.

Similarly, Ackerman, Peters, and Dykman (1971) reported that a significantly greater proportion of children diagnosed as "learning disabled," as opposed to a normal control group, had Developmental Error Scores above the mean for children of equivalent ages in Koppitz's (1964) normative sample. The LD sample consisted of 82 boys identified by a Child Guidance team composed of a child psychiatrist, psychologist, social worker, and an educational specialist. Each of the Ss met *at least one* (and in most cases more than one) of the following criteria:

(1) failure of a grade, requiring retention
(2) impending failure coupled with scores at least one year below grade level on the Gray Oral Reading Test or on either the reading, spelling, or arithmetic subtests of a standard educational battery
(3) impending failure attributable to severe dysgraphia.

All of the Ss were Caucasian and ranged in age from eight years to 11 years, 11 months. Most of them were from middle-class homes. Furthermore, each child came from a culturally advantaged background, was judged to be emotionally stable, had no limiting physical handicaps, and was of average intelligence (either a Verbal or Performance WISC IQ of 90 or above).

The authors reported several other noteworthy findings:

(1) The LD group made significantly more rotation and distortion errors than the control group.

(2) The LD group was significantly faster than the control group in completing the designs.

(3) A greater proportion of LD Ss, as opposed to normal controls, showed confusion in ordering the designs.

(4) Neither the total emotional indices nor any single sign differentiated between the LD and the control group.

In sum, the Bender appears to provide useful information concerning the visual-motor functioning of "learning disabled" children, and might advantageously be included routinely in an assessment battery when a learning disability is suspected.

BENDER PERFORMANCE AND READING IMPAIRMENT

Assuming that (1) a certain degree of maturity in visual-motor perception is necessary before a child can learn to read, and (2) the perception of patterns and spatial relationships, and the organization of configurations are essential parts of the reading process, Koppitz (1964) designed a study to determine whether total Developmental Errors and/or any particular signs or deviations on the Bender were associated with problems in reading. The Ss were first and second graders with *exceptionally* high or low reading achievement scores on the Metropolitan Achievement Test. Chi squares computed for high and low achievers and total Bender scores above and below the normative score for the respective age levels were significant, as were similar analyses for 22 of the 30 individual Bender scoring items.

However, since this study examined high and low achievers —but not average achievers—the results are subject to question in terms of their utility in identifying children with reading impairments in the general population.

Thweatt (1963) also designed a study to determine the validity of the Koppitz scoring system in differentiating good and poor readers. Two separate groups of first grade children were administered the Bender, and a composite score was computed for each S. It was assumed that children falling below each group's mean composite score (8.6 and 9.1 respectively) would experience no reading problems, while those who had scores above the mean would experience reading problems. The criterion measures (the Reading Vocabulary and Reading Comprehension subtests of the Durrell Analysis of Reading Difficulty) were administered to each S two years later, in the third grade. A S was considered to have a reading problem if either his vocabulary or comprehension score (or both) was five months or more below his grade placement.

In both groups all of the Ss scoring below the group's Bender mean were reading on grade level while 10 of 13 and five of nine scoring above their respective group's Bender mean had reading problems. Furthermore, individual correlations of Bender composite scores and reading vocabulary and comprehension were high and statistically significant.

Nielsen and Ringe (1969) compared the visual-perception and visual-motor performance of 20 reading disabled children selected from remedial reading classes and 20 regular class children on a test battery consisting of the Bender, the Frostig Test of Visual Perception, and the Draw-A-Person test. The 40 nine- to ten-year-old children were matched by pairs with respect to age, IQ, sex, and socioeconomic background.

The authors operationalized reading retardation as a "failure to reach a reading achievement level proper to age, intelligence, and years of instruction, necessitating transfer to a remedial reading class."

The Benders were scored by the Koppitz (1964) method. Seven of the 20 disabled readers received a score of four errors or more as opposed to only one of 20 in the normal group (this one individual was later found to be retarded in reading and placed in a remedial reading class).

The authors performed a chi square analysis on trichotomized Bender scores (0-1, 2-3, and 4-7) and reading groups. They reported that a significantly greater number of children in the remedial reading group had Bender scores of four or more.

Similar analyses for specific types of errors (e.g., rotation, distortion, angulation) showed that only rotation differentiated significantly between the groups. Eleven children in the reading disabled group, as opposed to only four in the normal group, made rotations in their Bender reproductions.

Black (1973) also compared Bender rotation errors in 100 normal and 100 mildly to moderately retarded readers matched for age, grade, and WISC Full Scale IQ. The mean age of the retarded group was 8.15 and the normal group was 8.26. Bender rotation incidence was 50 percent for normal readers and 47 percent for retarded readers. This difference was not statistically significant.

Significant correlations, however, were obtained between Bender rotation errors and the following variables: (1) WRAT reading, (2) WRAT spelling, (3) age, (4) letter reversals, and (5) word reversals.

Hunter and Johnson (1971) compared the Bender performance of 20 readers and 20 nonreaders matched for age, sex (all males), and grade level. The group of nonreaders ($\overline{X}$ age = 9-9) averaged 2.4 years below age-grade expectancy. The control group ($\overline{X}$ age = 9-11) was actually accelerated in reading by almost two years. Using Koppitz's (1964) *Developmental Scoring System*, the nonreaders were shown to have a significantly greater number of errors than the readers ($\overline{X}$s = 3.0 and 1.8, respectively).

A further classification of Ss according to good (three or fewer errors) and poor (four or more errors) revealed a significantly greater number of poor Benders in the nonreading group. No significant differences were noted between the groups for distortion, rotation, or perseveration errors, but nonreaders made significantly more integration errors.

The authors found a number of other differences between the readers and nonreaders. The readers had significantly higher WISC Verbal IQs (but not Performance of Full Scale IQs), as well as higher Information, Vocabulary, Digit Span, Arithmetic, Similarities, and Coding subtest scores. They also differed significantly in such factors as familial incidence of dyslexia, laterality (higher percentage of left-handedness in nonreaders), and birth order (nonreaders tended to be born later).

Lingren (1969) compared 20 disabled and 20 normal readers (matched for intelligence, sex, and age) on the Bender, the Auditory Discrimination Test, and a visual matching task. The mean age of the group was 10.5 years (range was 8-14 years).

Fifty percent of the reading disabled group and 20 percent of the normal readers obtained *Developmental Error Scores* of three or greater. On the Auditory Discrimination Test 40 percent of the disabled readers exceeded the cut-off score of three errors, but none of the normal readers did so. The former difference was not significant but the latter was. The groups did not differ significantly in visual-motor matching speed.

The author interpreted the results in line with Benton's (1962) conclusion that older dyslexic children do not exhibit differences in form perception to the same degree as younger children. While this is probably true to some extent, it is not possible to conclude that older dyslexic children do not exhibit visual-motor integration difficulties. In fact, 50 percent do. It would have been interesting to determine the percent of normals and dyslexic children exhibiting both visual and auditory difficulties.

Conner (1968) compared the Bender performance of 30 good and 30 poor second grade readers (upper and lower 27% on the California Reading Test) with average or above average intelligence, matched for CA, IQ and sex. Bender protocols were scored by the Koppitz system.

Separate analyses of variance were computed for the total score, as well as distortion, integration, perseveration, and rotation errors. Significant differences were found between the two groups on both the composite score and distortion errors.

Silberberg and Feldt (1968) examined the incidence of six distinct diagnostic patterns in 146 first, second, and third graders referred for psychological evaluation.

(1) The "concrete" group had WISC Verbal IQ scores significantly lower than Performance IQ (13 points) and the lowest Verbal scaled score on the Similarities subtest.

(2) The "nonvisual" group had Bender Developmental Error Scores one or more standard deviations above the expected mean for their chronological age.

(3) The "Performance-Bender" group had Performance IQs significantly greater than Verbal IQs and Bender scores one or more standard deviations above the mean for their age-groups.

(4) The "High Performance" group had Performance IQs significantly higher than Verbal IQs.

(5) The "Similarities" group had the Similarities subtest as the lowest WISC score.

(6) The "Other" group did not meet the criteria for inclusion in any of the groups identified above.

Ninety-four of the Ss were adequate readers and 52 were non-readers.

The authors found no significant relationships between test performance and reading ability. Furthermore, Koppitz's (1964) *Error Scores* were not correlated significantly with reading discrepancy scores (difference between expected and actual performance in reading).

Ackerman, Peters, and Dykman (1971), previously cited, examined the relationship between Gray Oral Reading Test performance and Bender error scores of 82 LD children. The median Gray reading quotient (grade equivalent/grade level × 100) was 60 for those with adequate Benders (based on Koppitz scores) and 56 for those with poor Benders (not statistically significant).

When the Gray protocols were analyzed "clinically" three groups were identified: those with serious reading disabilities, those with mild reading disabilities, and those who were adequate readers but had other learning disabilities. Sixty-eight percent of those Ss with severe reading disabilities, 60 percent with mild disabilities, and 76 percent of the adequate readers had *poor* Benders. The authors concluded, therefore, that the Bender was of little value in predicting reading achievement in the age range studied.

In sum, the research findings concerning the relationship between Bender performance and reading impairment have been inconsistent. However, there appear to be several variables that may influence the predictive power of the Bender. For example, the severity and precise nature of the reading disability are important considerations. Similarly, age-related factors seem to play a large role in determining the relative success or failure of the Bender in predicting reading impairment. Reading, as Spache and Spache (1973) indicated, is a multifaceted process that changes its nature from one developmental stage to the next. During the earlier stages, the major functions may be visual discrimination among forms and words, and the learning of sufficient common words to enable the reader to begin reading. Later, the process may shift to one involving more complex thought processes—recalling, interpreting, judging, and evaluating. Even if the child possesses sufficient skill in all of these areas, he still must integrate them into a unified process in order to avoid fumbling over a reading passage.

A study, which is consistent with this notion, was conducted by Satz, Rardin, and Ross (1972). This study was designed to test a theory to account for the pattern of deficit in developmental dyslexia—"the disorder is not a unitary syndrome, but rather reflects a lag in the maturation of the CNS which delays the acquisition of those skills which are in ascendancy at different developmental ages." More specifically, the authors postulated that skills which develop ontogenetically earlier (e.g. visual-motor) would be more delayed in younger dyslexic children (ages 7-8), while skills which develop later (e.g. language and formal operations) would be more delayed in older dyslexic children (ages 11-12).

The Ss in this study were selected on the basis of teacher recommendations and the following criteria:

(1) a severe reading problem (teacher judgment)
(2) no gross physical, sensory, or neurological handicaps (teacher judgment)
(3) Caucasian males of normal intelligence
(4) ages seven to eight and younger, or 11 to 12 and older.

Final selection was based on average to above average scores on the Performance scale of the WISC. There were 20 Ss, of whom 10 fell in the younger and 10 in the older group.

Twenty additional children were selected as control Ss, matched with the disabled readers on all variables except for their reading at grade level or above. All forty Ss attended a middle-class school.

Six criterion measures were administerd to the Ss. The Bender and two other nonlanguage tests (the *Recognition-Discrimination test* and the *Auditory-Visual test*) were postulated to represent skills which develop ontogenetically earlier than those represented in the three language tests (the WISC Verbal scale, the Verbal Fluency test and the Dichotic Listening test).

Unfortunately, the authors did not adequately describe the Bender scoring criteria utilized in the study. They simply stated that "the protocols were independently rated by four examiners on the basis of poor score (score = 1), medium (score = 2), and good (score = 3)." They also failed to mention the experience level of the judges.

The results, for the Bender at least, confirmed the hypotheses in that visual-motor integration performance differentiated between dyslexic and normal *young* children but not older children. In contrast, the language task differentiated the groups of older children but not the younger children.

Because of the ambiguity in the report of the scoring procedure for the Bender and the fact that this test fails to discriminate well at the higher age levels, there is some question about the validity of the obtained results. Nevertheless, the hypotheses are interesting and merit further investigation.

Koppitz (1975a) designed a study to explore the relationship of reading and performance on the Bender and the *Visual Aural Digit Span Test* in eight- and nine-year-old children. The Ss were two groups of 23 special class pupils with learning disabilities and a control group ($N = 30$) of normally functioning public school pupils. The learning disabled groups were matched for age and IQ. However, one group included only Ss with severe learning disabilities who had little or no reading skills as measured by the WRAT. The second group of Ss was able to read, but possessed serious difficulties in other academic (e.g. mathematics) and personal/social areas. The control group was comparable to the LD groups in age and IQ.

Koppitz (1975a) reported mean Error Scores of 5.2 for the

reading disabled group, 4.3 for the LD group and 2.3 for the control group. Chi square analyses based on scores above and below the total group mean on the Bender revealed that the controls were significantly better than either the reading disabled or learning disabled groups, but the latter two groups did not differ significantly from one another.

The VADS measure was found to be more closely related to reading disability and significantly differentiated the reading disabled group from the learning disabled and control groups. The latter two groups, both with good reading skills, did not differ in VADS performance.

Koppitz concluded, therefore, that while the Bender "is primarily a visual-motor integration test and relates to children's mental maturity and overall school functioning, the VADS Test seems to reflect mainly children's visual-aural integration, sequencing, and recall, and it seems to be specifically related to reading."

Binkley, Maggart, and Vandever (1974) designed a study to determine if the inconsistencies in the research on Bender performance and reading were due to *severity* of the reading problem. Forty-two children were selected randomly from several seventh grade corrective reading classes. All were reading at least two years below grade placement as measured by the Metropolitan Achievement Test, had scores of 75 or above on the *Otis Quick Scoring Mental Ability Test,* and came from low income families.

Sixteen Ss (eight boys and eight girls) were found to have adequate Benders (fewer than four errors) as determined by Koppitz's (1964) system. Twenty-six (15 boys and 11 girls) had inadequate Benders (four or more errors). The two groups were comparable in both IQ and age.

The criterion measures were: (1) the *California Test of Personality,* (2) the *Gates Reading Survey,* and (3) the *Gates Basic Reading Test.*

A discriminant analysis was conducted to determine whether differences existed between Ss in the two groups on the three criterion measures. The multivariate F indicated a significant overall difference between the groups. More specific analyses revealed significant differences between the Bender groups (in favor of the adequate Bender group) on both of the reading tests, but not the personality test, although the latter approached significance.

Broadhurst and Phillips (1969) compared the Bender and reading achievement of a representative group of eleven-year-old British schoolchildren. The children were compared on the basis of Koppitz's (1964) errors (three and fewer versus four or more) and their level of reading ability. Chi square analyses revealed the following: (1) all Ss with a reading age less than seven years made four or more errors, but many Ss who made four or more errors had reading ages above seven years, and (2) all Ss with reading level at 13 years and higher made fewer than four errors.

On the whole, it appears that the Bender may be useful in the diagnosis of reading impairment. Nevertheless, as Keogh and Becker (1973) suggested, caution *must* be taken when making predictions about a particular child. In a similar vein, Barrett (1965) contends that visual perception plays a part during the early stages of reading but becomes far less important later when cognitive and linguistic competencies move into the foreground. In the final analysis, visual perception does not contribute enough to bear the entire burden of prediction. Furthermore, Koppitz (1970) noted that reading problems can be diagnosed with the Bender *only if they derive (at least in part) from difficulties in visual-motor perception,* but not if they are caused primarily by other factors, such as language disabilities or specific memory deficits. Finally, reading disorders, according to Jansky and deHirsch (1972), are always related to constellations of dysfunctions and environmental factors. These authors agree with Lambert (1967) that investigations of academic effectiveness—or in this case lack of it—should emphasize a multivariate rather than a single-variable design.

MULTIVARIATE STUDIES

There have been two extensive multivariate studies involving the Bender on the prediction of reading disorders. deHirsch, Jansky, and Langford (1966) designed a study with a threefold purpose in mind:

(1) to determine to what extent certain tests administered in kindergarten would predict reading achievement at the end of the second grade,

(2) to identify those tests which are most effective in predicting reading disorders, and

(3) to combine the best predictors into an instrument that could be used for the identification of "high risk" children.

First a large battery of tests was administered to a group of 53 kindergarten children. These tests were selected on the assumption that a child's perceptual-motor and linguistic functioning in kindergarten forecasts later performance on such highly integrated tasks as reading, writing, and spelling. Those tests that were the best predictors of children experiencing academic problems in second grade were retained in the *Predictive Index*. The *Predictive Index* included the following tests: (1) The Bender-Gestalt Test, (2) Pencil Use, (3) Categories, (4) *Gates Word Matching Subtest*, (5) *Horst Reversals Test*, (6) *Wepman Auditory Discrimination Test*, (7) Number of words used in a story, and (8) Word Recognition I, II, and III. The criterion measure was second-grade performance on a combination of the *Gates Advanced Primary* and the *Gray Oral Reading* tests.

The *Predictive Index* score (failure on seven or more of the tests) was found to be effective in identifying 91 percent of the failing readers and produced a false positive rate of 10 percent.

A child's *Predictive Index* score was determined from the number of tests on which he or she scored at or above the critical score level (the level on each test that best discriminated between failing readers and the rest of the children). For example, the critical score for the Bender was 1, indicating that the child could copy at least five of the six designs correctly.

In a refinement of their earlier work Jansky and deHirsch (1972) identified several problems with their Predictive Index which seemed so responsive to teachers' needs. Among the inadequacies of the Index were the following:

(1) the sample size on which it was based was too small

(2) the IQ range was restricted to the 90-116 range

(3) the socioeconomic status of the Ss was more homogeneous than desirable

(4) the statistical procedures used did not allow differential weighting of predictive indicators according to the extent of their contribution to the prediction

(5) the administration of the ten-test battery was too time-consuming

(6) the battery had to be administered by highly trained professionals.

In addition to addressing these sampling and statistical concerns, the subsequent study was designed to develop a shorter, more practical, predictive instrument that could be administered by paraprofessionals and teachers. They also simplified the scoring system for the Bender.

The new sample consisted of 341 kindergarten children who were representative of the general population in terms of IQ range, and ethnic and socioeconomic characteristics.

The predictive screening battery was drawn from those tests that were considered to be potential predictors, based on their prognostic usefulness in clinical practice as well as their predictive efficiency in previous research.

The following aspects of development were considered: (1) perceptual motor organization, (2) linguistic competence in receptive and expressive areas, and (3) readiness to cope with printed symbols.

The *Sceening Index* was derived from stepwise multiple regression procedures. The tests selected, in order of contribution to subsequent reading ability were: (1) Letter Naming, (2) Picture Naming, (3) Gates Word Matching, (4) Bender-Gestalt, (5) *Binet Sentence Memory,* and (6) Word Recognition (this test was later eliminated from the Screening Battery).

This new battery identified 77 percent (96/117) of the children who failed in reading (based on a grade score of 2.2 or lower on the Gates Advanced Primary or the Gates-MacGinite Paragraph Reading Test, Primary B) at the end of second grade and erroneously selected only 19 percent (42/230) who passed the reading test (false positives).

The multiple correlation coefficient between these tests and second grade silent paragraph reading achievement was .69, accounting for 47 percent of the total variance.

Administration time for the Screening Battery is relatively short (15-20 minutes). Furthermore, supervised paraprofessionals could easily be trained to administer the battery.

OTHER APPROACHES FOR IDENTIFYING
READING IMPAIRMENTS

Background Interference

One approach for determining reading disabilities that unfortunately has not gained much attention is the Background Interference Procedure developed by Canter (1963). Although this technique has demonstrated promise in clinical diagnosis, there has been no research done on reading performance. However, Sabatino and Ysseldyke (1972) investigated the extent to which the method of presentation of Bender stimuli differentiated between readers and nonreaders.

The Ss were selected from children referred for psychological evaluation. Three hundred forty-two children, ranging in age from six years, seven months, to 11 years, eight months, were diagnosed as learning disabled based on the following criteria:

(1) WISC Full Scale IQ of 90 or better
(2) at least one year disparity between perceptual age scores earned on the Developmental Test of Visual-Motor Integration (Beery and Buktenica, 1967) and mean language age (WISC Verbal IQ)
(3) no chronic health problems, acute physical symptoms, or overt social-personal maladjustments
(4) vision and hearing within normal limits.

The Ss were divided into two groups based on their composite reading comprehension and word-recognition scores earned on the reading comprehension subtest of the Gates-MacGinitie Reading Test and the Word Recognition subtest of the Wide Range Achievement Test. There were 143 nonreaders and 199 readers.

Each child was administered four tests: (1) the Bender

(memory), (2) the Bender (standard), (3) the Bender with background stimuli (an embedded meaningless background), (4) the Bender with background stimuli (a photographic negative of the standard stimulus design cards with the most crucial portion of each design obscured). All four tests were scored according to the Koppitz (1964) scoring system, and separate $2 \times 2 \times 4$ analyses of variance (sex, readers vs. nonreaders, and age, i.e. six to seven, eight, nine, and 10).

Although readers and nonreaders did not differ significantly on either the standard or memory administration of the Bender, significant *decreases* in the performance of nonreaders were found under both background interference conditions.

Miscellaneous Studies on Learning Disabilities and Reading Impairments

Larsen, Rogers, and Sowell (1976) administered the Auditory and Visual Sequential Memory and Sound Blending subtests of the ITPA, the Wepman Auditory Discrimination Test, and the Bender-Gestalt Test to 30 normal and 59 learning disabled children, matched by age and sex. The Ss ranged in age from eight years, five months to 10 years, six months. The learning disabled Ss were classified on the basis of the following criteria:

(1) formally diagnosed and labeled as learning disabled according to the State of Texas guidelines
(2) beginning the fourth grade
(3) normal intelligence on the WISC.

This LD sample was divided into two groups: 35 Ss who were reading one grade level below their expected rate, and 24 Ss who were reading two grade levels below their expected rate. All LD Ss were receiving remedial instruction through special education programs.

The Bender was the only test to differentiate between the normal and the LD groups. However, the difference between the two LD groups was not statistically significant.

There are two difficulties with this study. First, the authors did not report how the Bender was scored. Secondly, they noted

IQ differences between the normal Ss ($\overline{X}$ = 101.23) and the LD groups ($\overline{X}$s = 96.65 and 95.12) but did not report whether this difference was significant statistically.

In a somewhat different approach to the detection and differential diagnosis of reading deficits, Stavrianos (1971) examined the predictive potential of the Bender and selected projective tests, i.e. the H-T-P and the Rorschach. She examined the test data for 325 socioeconomically advantaged boys, ages six years to 11 years, six months, of average to superior verbal intelligence. Essentially, however, this group was subdivided into four subgroups:

(1) Criterion group (N = 67) consisted of problem-free good readers who were performing well academically.

(2) Emotionally based reading deficit group (N = 78) having a history, and current evidence of, emotional and/or behavior problems sufficient to warrant referral for counseling or psychotherapy. These Ss had no perceptual-motor or neurological problems.

(3) Perceptual-motor deficit group (N = 90) having perceptual-motor immaturity and/or dysfunction indicated in developmental history and test performance. These Ss had no discernible neurological impairment.

(4) Neurological specific deficit group (N = 90) having perceptual-motor dysfunction associated with minor brain damage and/or dysfunction suggested by history, test data, and EEG.

Each group was further divided into two levels based on age (six years to eight years, six months and eight years, six months to 11 years, six months), and equated for age, grade placement, and WISC Verbal IQ. The Bender measures included the Koppitz (1964) Developmental Error Score, Organic Score, and Emotional Score.

The H-T-P drawings were scored for organic, normal, withdrawn, constricted, dependent, and impulsive characteristics as described by Jolles (1964). Rorschach protocols were scored essentially according to Klopfer (Klopfer, Ainsworth, Klopfer, and Holt, 1964), and Friedman (1953). Six patterns were distinguished:

(1) normal—balanced distribution
(2) outer restriction—adequate use of movement and form but color restricted to one FC or CF response or no color used
(3) inner restriction—adequate use of color and form but two or fewer M or FM responses
(4) constriction—both movement and color restricted and high F percent
(5) acting out—high FM, high sum C, crude C and low F percent
(6) perseveration—one or two similar responses given to all blots.

In regard to the Bender, Stavrianos (1971) reported the following findings:

(1) In general, poor readers, at both age levels, had higher Developmental Error, Organic, and Emotional Scores
(2) *Developmental Error* and Organic Scores differentiated significantly between the emotional and the specific deficit groups. At the younger age level, deficient readers with emotional problems were characterized by expansive, uncontrolled patterns, reflected in *overworked* Bender reproductions
(3) In comparison with the perceptual-motor group, boys with emotional problems obtained higher Bender Emotional Scores and showed more impulsive, expansive signs
(4) Comparison of the emotionally disturbed group and the neurologically impaired group showed that both had high Emotional scores.

In addition, the author tried to determine which measures *in combination* provided the best discrimination among the four groups. Employing a stepwise multiple discriminant analysis for each age level, with the twelve main scores as variables, the best combined variables in order of their power to discriminate at the six year to eight year, six-month level were H-T-P organic, H-T-P constricted, and Rorschach perseveration score. At the eight year, six-month to 11 year, six-month level the best discriminating variables were Bender organic, H-T-P organic, Bender emotional, and H-T-P constricted scores.

The author concluded that "Correct diagnosis of reading deficit and discrimination between emotionally based and specific reading deficit should be possible for approximately 80 to 85 percent of a comparable group" (p. 91). However, differentiation between cases involving perceptual-motor deficits and organicity on the basis of these measures alone would be highly inaccurate, especially for children under age eight years, six months.

Summary

Although several studies have examined the Bender performance of "learning disabled" children the majority of the research has focused on reading-impaired children. Generally, LD children and reading-impaired children perform more poorly on the Bender than do normal children regardless of the type of Bender analysis employed. However, since the relationship between Bender performance and reading is not consistently high, considerable caution must be exercised when making predictions about a particular child. Multivariate studies seem to hold considerably more promise, especially for the prediction of reading impairment in young children.

CHAPTER 9

NEW SCORING SYSTEMS

In a major position paper Lauretta Bender (1970) objected strenuously to all Bender-Gestalt Test scoring systems that use discrete items. She asserted that such scoring systems are inappropriate and fail to do justice to the richness of the test. Bender argued that the processes comprising integrated perceptual and motor experiences and maturational aspects cannot be adequately reduced into discrete part functions. Moreover, she contended that the major task is *not* to reproduce the test figures perfectly but to express a "living, unique perceptual-motor experience." Even the popular Koppitz (1964) objective scoring system for evaluating intelligence and school achievement and for identifying emotional, organic, and mental retardation problems was severely criticized by Bender as an oversimplification of the processes involved.

Despite Bender's vehement opposition to scoring systems, they continue to flourish with a number of new systems being added to the psychologist's repertoire over the last 16 years.

Pauker's (1976) Quick-Scoring System, which takes about 20 seconds to apply, assigns a score of 0 to reproductions approximating the original figure, a score of 2 to reproductions that deviate considerably from the original, and a score of 4 to reproductions that reveal severe distortions. Specific criteria for each of these scoring points are presented. Each of the designs is scored accordingly with questionable decisions warranting the assignment of scores of 1 or 3. Satisfactory levels of reliability and validity have been achieved with this method.

Thweatt, Obrzut, and Taylor (1972) developed a Soft-Sign scoring system to explore mild or "soft" manifestations of disturbance in visual-motor-perceptual performance. The system focuses primarily on the directional orientation to the perceptual task, such as drawing the circle first followed by the square on Design A. The Soft-Sign system consists of 33 items, each scored 0 (correct performance) or 1 (incorrect performance). The system shows high inter-scorer reliability (rank-order correlation = .96) and validity for predicting reading achievement in children. Although this method was applied only to child Ss, it may prove to be useful also with adults.

Plenk (1967) devised a scoring system for children of preschool age. The system was based on the Koppitz (1964) scoring categories, but scoring focused on "correct" aspects of the children's reproductions rather than on errors. Plenk (1967) reported adequate inter-scorer and test-retest reliabilities. Unfortunately, there has been little research on the concurrent or predictive validity of this system.

In the only study we were able to locate using this scoring system, Watkins and Watkins (1975) compared normal and emotionally disturbed children (age five to 10 years) on the Plenk (1967) scoring of the Bender. Emotionally disturbed children (selected from learning adjustment classes in public school or from those in outpatient treatment in mental health agencies) scored significantly lower on the Bender than normal control subjects. In addition, an inspection of means for the various age groupings indicated consistent improvement with age.

Jansky and deHirsch (1972) utilized a modified Bender procedure involving six of the nine designs, namely, A, 1, 2, 4, 6, and 8, and a scoring system based on Bender's (1938; 1967) method of interpretation. The score is the number of designs, ranging from none to six, in which the child fails to reproduce the essential features of the Gestalt. Although some scoring guidelines were provided by the authors, no reliability data were reported. Nevertheless, Bender scores obtained at the kindergarten level correlated significantly with second grade reading ($r = .41$) and spelling ($r = .44$) achievement. It should also be noted that the Bender was incorporated into a battery of diagnostic measures which yielded a "Predictive Index" in order to identify potential reading difficulties.

Bolton (1972) developed an objective Bender-Gestalt scoring procedure that would have particular application to deaf individuals. The scales call for global judgments and do not require attention to smaller details in the performance, require ratings in each case on a 5-point continuum, and limit the judgments to descriptions rather than requiring interpretations to be made. The eight scales were modeled after some existing scales and include the following dimensions: Pressure—heavy/light; Pressure—consistent/variable; Reproduction—exact copies/minimum resemblance; Closure—good/poor; Rotation—25°/0°; Size—expanded/reduced; Arrangement—orderly/chaotic; and Arrangement—crowded/scattered.

The estimated reliability coefficients of these scales ranged from .51 to .90. Factor analysis resulted in the identification of five personality variables which were found to be independent of nonpersonality variables. However, the variables were not significantly correlated with criterion ratings or outcome measures. Equally disappointing results were obtained with new samples of deaf clients (Bolton, Donoghue, and Langbauer 1973), casting doubt on the value of the system.

Bilu and Weiss (1974) cited some of the major inadequacies of conventional scoring systems in a rather penetrating analysis of their limitations. For one thing, the systems fail to differentiate between "essential" deviations, which presumably reflect the degree of disturbance of the individual, and the individual's own personalized style, i.e. the "stylistic" deviations. Secondly, some of the systems sample too limited a number of parameters, leading to biased conclusions. Thirdly, except for some systems, such as the Pascal and Suttell (1951) and Hain (1964) methods, the scoring procedures generally fail to assign differential weights appropriate to the severity of disturbance to the deviations. Fourthly, most scoring systems fail to specify the point at which a borderline deviation should or should not be scored. Fifthly, most systems provide only a single overall score, reflecting the total deviations observed, so that insights related to specific patternings of performance are lost. Sixthly, some of the objective scoring systems are not based on a system of adequately defined variables, leaving much to the individual rater's subjective judgment. The seventh criticism made by Bilu and Weiss (1974) pertains to the low level of theoretical sophistication, devoid of conceptual integration of the observed deviations, that allegedly characterizes most systems. Finally, they object to the lack of consideration of the possibility that different stimuli have different degrees of susceptibility to specific kinds of deviations.

In an attempt to rectify some of these presumed difficulties inherent in many scoring systems, Bilu and Weiss (1974) performed a configurational analysis of the test which resulted in the identification of seven variables that comprise a complete profile. Change of size, Contact difficulties, Rotation, Perseveration, Partial execution, Disproportion, and Distortion were the identified "essential" variables. Each of these variables was graded for severity on a continuum.

When 81 psychiatric inpatients, matched in age, intelligence, sex, and education, were compared in their Bender-Gestalt reproductions with 81 psychiatric outpatients significant differentiation, using this system, was obtained. Such differentiation was possible, however, only when moderate combined with severe deviations, or when severe deviations alone were used. The method produced very few false positives although it yielded a relatively large number of false negatives.

Size deviations, when severe, proved to be a particularly sensitive indicator for group discrimination. The frequency of occurrence of each of these variables was far less critical for differentiation among psychiatric patients than the degree of deviation produced as quantified in the Bilu-Weiss system.

In keeping with Bender's (Tolor and Schulberg, 1963) comment that psychologists have generally failed to take into account the Bender-Gestalt Test's underlying theory and that they have applied the test to areas other than the developmental sphere in the absence of an appropriate rationale, Rimmer and Weiss (1972) attempted to conceptualize the Bender-Gestalt Test within the developmental theoretical framework propounded by Piaget (1952; 1956; 1960). The test was reinterpreted as a cognitive task, and Piaget's views on arithmetical and geometrical conceptual development served as the theoretical base. A rather complex scoring system, consisting of 76 elements, was developed, leading to a profile for each protocol. Rimmer and Weiss (1972) concluded that when this scoring system, based on theoretical considerations of conceptual development, is applied to children, it is as useful as empirically based scoring systems. The authors acknowledged that not all of the Bender-Gestalt Test variance was accounted for by Piaget's theory, and that the motor-expressive component was not considered at all.

Summary

In his survey of the literature of various inspection and scoring systems, Billingslea (1963) concluded that both inspection and objective scoring procedures were capable of separating the protocols of groups with major disturbances from the protocols of groups who were normally adjusted. However, neither interpretive approach adequately treated individual diagnosis. Therefore, he advocated the discriminatory evaluation of mental processes, such as perception, problem-solving, and attitudes. The review of the current literature, as can be seen from a scanning of other sections in this volume, indicates that the most widely accepted and presently flourishing scoring systems are those of Pascal and Suttell (1951) and Koppitz (1958, 1964). These are the procedures most often cited in the literature. Other scoring systems, previously fashionable, seem to have fallen into a state of relative neglect. On the other hand, new scoring systems have evolved despite Lauretta Bender's admonition against their use. Some of these aim for greater simplification in scoring whereas others, in sharp contrast, aim for greater complexity and sophistication. The survival rate of these newer scoring systems remains to be established, although it is our expectation that they will not be widely accepted or find much practical application.

CHAPTER 10

VALIDITY AND RELIABILITY OF THE BENDER-GESTALT TEST

VALIDITY

A RATHER EXTENSIVE coverage of the literature on the validity of the Bender-Gestalt Test for the assessment of brain damage appears in the chapter that is devoted to *The Bender-Gestalt Test and Organicity*. To save space and for the convenience of the reader, no attempt will be made here to recapitulate this discussion of the literature. However, it is noted with interest that the bulk of the test's validation work relates to the diagnosis of organic pathology, which is not surprising in view of the fact that the Bender-Gestalt Test is employed by practicing clinicians much more often for organic diagnosis than for any other purpose (Schulberg and Tolor 1961).

One of several approaches to the assessment of the validity of the Bender-Gestalt Test for diverse purposes is the assessment of the degree to which artistic skill or drawing ability *per se* contributes to the caliber of the designs that are reproduced. In other words, if a significant relationship existed between drawing ability and Bender drawing accuracy, then drawing ability might be a variable that would need to be controlled in establishing the test's validity. With respect to a different graphomotor projective test, namely, the human figure drawing test, this possibility that drawing skill may be a contaminant has in fact received considerable attention. Reviews of research with the human figure drawing technique by Swenson (1957, 1968) and by Roback (1968) concluded that there is much uncertainty about the role of artistic ability in relation to clinical judgments of personality. Unfortunately, Tolor and Schulberg (1963) could not identify even a single study in the Bender literature that addressed this issue specifically. Such research neglect becomes all the more regrettable in the face of evidence (Tolor and Schulberg 1963) that the level of training generally in the field of psychology or specifically in the interpretation of Bender protocols appears to be unrelated to the degree of accuracy achieved in making an organic diagnosis. Is it possible that diagnostic judgments based on the Bender-Gestalt Test are largely a function of the drawing ability of the respondent?

With this possibility in mind we noted with interest the study by Peoples and Moll (1962) published since the previous review of the Bender-Gestalt Test. Fifty students at an institute of technology served as Ss in the first experiment. Group I consisted of 30 students who had received ratings of "A" in an engineering drawing course and Group II consisted of 20 students who had received ratings of "C." The two groups differed significantly in Bender performance as scored by the Pascal-Suttell (1951) system, supporting the possibility that drawing ability contributed to Bender performance. However, when 16 Ss in Group I were matched with Group II Ss for overall grade point average, no significant difference in Bender test performance remained.

In order to clarify which factor, overall academic ability, drawing ability, or intelligence, accounted for differences in Bender test performance found initially, a second experiment was conducted. For a new group of 89 students a correlation of .62 was obtained between grade point average and Bender performance, scored without knowledge of students' grades. An insignificant correlation of −.14 was found between the *American College Entrance Test* scores, considered a measure of intelligence, and the Bender. Peoples and Moll (1962) concluded that the relationship that had been originally observed between Bender-Gestalt performance and drawing skill was probably a function of the relationship between academic achievement and Bender reproduction accuracy; and that intelligence played little, if any, role in determining the accuracy of the Bender figures.

It would have been preferable if this important question regarding validity were treated in a more appropriate statistical manner, for example, through an analysis of variance design or by means of partial correlations. The findings as reported leave much doubt about whether drawing ability is to be implicated in the consideration of the Bender's validity.

Also bearing on the validity of the Bender-Gestalt Test is the possible effect of examiner differences on performance. Pacella (1962) hypothesized that there would be no significant examiner effect on the drawings of the designs as scored objectively or qualitatively. The study had one examiner administering the test under hostile and critical conditions and three examiners administering the test under ordinary conditions. Each of nine normal female Ss was given the Bender-Gestalt Test by the four examiners in random order during a 4-hour period. Thus, there were four protocols elicited from each S. The results indicated that neither on objective scoring of the protocols by Pascal-Suttell's (1951) method nor when the three judges were asked to select protocols associated with the hostile condition of administration were significant differences obtained. Incidental findings were that a practice effect was operative, with maximum improvement at the third trial, and that there was no delayed Bender reaction to the hostile, critical examiner.

The study might be criticized on the basis of the unknown effectiveness of the hostile-critical role assumed by one examiner, the lack of more salient examiner differences in this experimental design, the small number of Ss and Es, and the absence of contrasting (e.g. angry vs. supportive) examiner conditions. It might also be contended that other examiner variables, such as sex, ethnicity, and age, could produce interaction effects with Ss having similar or dissimilar characteristics. None of these variables was investigated in this study.

The paucity of studies comparing the relative validities of various psychological tests, including the Bender-Gestalt Test, had been noted previously by Tolor and Schulberg (1963). Wildman and Wildman (1975) undertook the task of investigating the diagnostic validity of several combinations of commonly used diagnostic techniques. The relative accuracy of different combinations of tests was determined by requesting that judges, who were six clinical psychologists with at least five years of clinical experience, sort 20 different protocols into two equal piles, one for patients and one for student nurses. The protocols were based on the test results produced by 10 student nurses and 10 female hospitalized psychiatric patients who were approximately comparable in age and education. The tests included the Bender-Gestalt, House-Tree-Person, MMPI, Thematic Apperception Test, and Rorschach.

The Bender-Gestalt Test yielded a 62 percent correct identification rate, which was significantly better than chance, and in combination with the House-Tree-Person Test, a 53 percent correct identification rate, which was not significantly better than chance expectations. Moreover, the Bender-Gestalt was found to be second in accuracy of diagnostic judgment among the four projective instruments employed, next in order after the Rorschach Inkblot Test whose use resulted in a 65 percent average accuracy rate for the six judges. However, the MMPI, an objective personality measure, yielded the greatest number of correct placements into the patient or normal categories, namely 88 percent. Despite the statistically significant findings obtained with the use of the Bender-Gestalt and Rorschach tests, the authors expressed much reservation concerning the clinical utility of these two tests for individual diagnosis.

We might add that in clinical practice neither the Bender-Gestalt Test nor the Rorschach blots are generally employed for purposes of differentiating grossly normal from heterogeneous patient populations. In addition, this study provides no information on the nature of the diagnostic problems represented in this patient group nor on the adjustment level of the students who represented the normal group.

Wagner and Murray (1969) found that five independent diagnosticians were able to differentiate significantly between the Bender protocols of 32 pairs of organic and nonorganic children. However, in a critique of this study, Mordock (1969b) identified two major weaknesses: (a) the selection of a control group composed of "good" students as opposed to one composed of children having difficulty in school, but with no evidence of neurological disorders (e.g. emotionally disturbed children), and (b) the establishment of the criterion group based on criteria (e.g. EEG) of questionable validity.

Stone (1966) used correlation and cluster analysis to evaluate the responses to the various Bender-Gestalt designs. The protocols of 50 hospitalized male psychiatric patients, mostly psychotics, were scored independently by two raters using the Pascal-Suttell (1951) system. Product-moment correlations were then computed between each of eight (sic) Bender-Gestalt designs. These correlations ranged from .34 to .78, with a median r of .63. A cluster analysis revealed that only two designs fell outside the cluster, leading to the conclusion that the Bender-Gestalt designs elicit a rather unidimensional response. The author went beyond this finding to suggest that if pressed for time, clinicians could administer solely Design 8 since it had the highest correlation (.67) with the other designs. Another suggestion made was that a short version of the Bender, consisting of Designs 1, 2, and 8, be used. In our opinion much would be lost if one focused principally on the fact that there is an overall response tendency to do fairly well or to do fairly poorly on the Bender designs generally and discounted the differences often observed in the performance on the individual designs. The total time consumed in administering all of the designs is so modest that the advantages of an abbreviated version elude us.

Also relating to the issue of validity is Gilbert's (1971) reported use of the Bender-Gestalt Test, along with several other psychological measures, to determine changes in insight associated with counseling in psychiatric patients. There is no indication of how the Bender-Gestalt Test was used in this research to test the hypothesis that insight-inducing counseling is more efficacious than either reassurance or no counseling and no reassurance. Insight was operationally defined in terms of the number of items endorsed on the *Mooney Problem Check List* that refer to internal or motivational factors in relation to items dealing with environmental circumstances. Even this procedure is questionable since an individual's problems may in fact be situationally determined and therefore endorsing such test items does not automatically indicate lack of insight. Additionally, there is no diagnostic information provided about the patient sample. In sum, the conclusion that these patients probably had insufficient potential for acquiring insight seems totally unwarranted. The study, therefore, offers no adequate test of the validity of the Bender-Gestalt Test even though it appeared that it might be helpful in this regard.

Although an extensive report on the literature on the validity of the Bender-Gestalt Test for the prediction of children's academic performance appears in the chapters devoted to *The Bender-Gestalt Test and School Performance* and *The Bender-Gestalt Test and Learning Disabilities,* there have been several additional studies which focused on the ability of the Bender in aiding the differential diagnosis of adolescents with learning difficulties. For example, Mordock, Terrill, and Novik (1968) found that both the Hain (1964) and the Koppitz (1964) systems could differentiate Ss with CNS impairment from those without such impairment. CNS damage was established by physicians on the basis of positive evidence of encephalopathy. The group differences, however, were not great enough, and there were so many false negatives, using both systems, that the authors concluded that the Bender-Gestalt Test has little utility for individual prediction. However, the organic group consisted of such diverse abnormalities, including psychomotor epilepsy, metabolic disorders, impaired cerebellar function, and Rh factor, that it is amazing that the Bender was able to achieve any degree of significant concurrent validity.

Another study of concurrent validity with an adolescent population was done by Oliver and Kronenberger (1971). The performance of 12 brain-damaged, 12 emotionally disturbed, and 12 normal male adolescents, between the ages of 11 years and 15 years, 11 months, matched for intelligence and age, was scored by the Koppitz Scoring System (Koppitz 1964). Each protocol was scored separately on the *Developmental Scoring System,* measuring maturation in visual-motor perception, the Brain-Damaged System, measuring brain-damage, and the Emotional Scoring System, measuring emotional disturbance and problems.

Significant overall group differences were found on each of these scales. For example, there was a significantly greater number of developmental indicators for the brain-damaged as compared with the emotionally disturbed and normal groups.

The emotionally disturbed group also differed significantly in developmental indicators from the normal group. The emotional indicators, while capable of differentiating emotionally disturbed and brain-damaged youth from normals, did not separate brain-damaged from emotionally disturbed youth. Finally, the indicators of brain-damage revealed significant differences for every group compared with every other group, with normals receiving the lowest mean score and the organics the highest mean score.

The findings of this study lend further support to the concurrent validity of the Bender-Gestalt Test for adolescent males.

Several studies have demonstrated the relationship between visual perceptual maturation and Bender performance. In one of the earliest studies, Allen (1968b) provided evidence that in moderately to mildly retarded adolescents, with a mean age of 14, there is a definite relationship between level of visual perceptual maturation, as measured by the Developmental Test of Visual Perception (Frostig, Lefever, and Whittlesey 1964), and the quality of the Bender designs drawn, as determined by the Keogh-Smith (1961) five-point rating scale. Similar results were obtained in a second study (Allen 1969).

Culbertson and Gunn (1966) reported a significant correlation of .52 between Bender Developmental Errors (Koppitz 1964) and scores on the Frostig Developmental Test of Visual Perception in a clinical population composed of children diagnosed as emotionally disturbed, schizophrenic, retarded, and brain-damaged. More specific analyses revealed that Bender scores were significantly correlated to Subtests I (Eye-motor Coordination) and V (Spatial Relations) of the Frostig Test, but not to Subtests II (Figure Ground), III (Form Constancy), and IV (Position in Space).

Bauman and St. John (1971) reported low but statistically significant correlations between the Bender-Gestalt Test (using Koppitz's 1964 norms) and Frostig Subtest III, and scores on the Minnesota Percepto-Diagnostic Test in low achieving school children ranging in age from 6 years, 5 months to 10 years, 11 months (median = eight years, six months) and of average intelligence.

Wedell and Horne (1969), in a comparison of the 20 highest and 20 lowest scoring children on the Bender (based on the

Keogh and Smith, 1961, scoring system), found significant relationships with several other perceptual-motor tasks, including a multiple choice matching task, a tracing task, a plasticine copying task, as well as handwriting, spelling, and vocabulary.

Sabatino and Becker (1969) reported low to moderate, but statistically significant correlations between the Bender Developmental Error Scores (for both copy and recall phases of the test) and performance on a test of auditory-visual perceptual integration in four separate samples (5-, 6-, 7-, and 8-year-old children).

Krauft and Krauft (1972) reported statistically significant correlations between the Bender performance of educable retarded children ($N = 24$) and scores on the Developmental Test of Visual-motor Integration (Beery & Buktenica 1967). The correlations between Beery and Buktenica's (1967) test and Bender scores, based on Bender's (1938) system and Koppitz's (1964) system, were .82 and .63 respectively. Significant relationships were also found between the two scoring systems, on the one hand, and age and Verbal IQ, on the other hand.

Simensen (1974a) reported significant correlations between Bender *Developmental Error Scores* and WISC Block Design scores ($r = .23$) and Memory-for-Designs scores ($r = .46$) in a group of 87 boys and girls randomly selected from grades three, four, and five in an urban public school system.

RELIABILITY

Turning now to the question of the reliability of the Bender-Gestalt Test, there is considerable evidence both of satisfactory inter-scorer and satisfactory test-retest reliability for this instrument. For example, two groups of scorers, namely, four clinically trained psychologists and four untrained students, were requested by Morsbach, DelPriori, and Furnell (1975) to score 40 children's protocols by means of the Koppitz (1964) revised scoring system. The same protocols were then scored after a six-month interval. The average inter-scorer reliability for the two groups of raters combined was .94, with the clinical raters achieving a coefficient of .91 and the untrained raters achieving a coefficient of .96. An analysis of the inter-scorer reliability for the subcategories "Distortion," "Rotation," "Integration," and "Perseveration" revealed no systematic variation in reliability. Test-retest correlations were found to be high for the Total Score and for the individual categories for both groups of raters. Moreover, no significant differences were obtained in mean scores over the time interval investigated.

This study, therefore, supports both the inter-rater and the test-retest reliability of the Bender-Gestalt Test.

Further evidence of the high degree of agreement among scorers who use the Koppitz scoring system derives from Hustak, Dinning, and Andert's (1976) work with retarded adults. Three graduate students, trained near the doctoral level in clinical psychology, scored the protocols of 102 inpatient retardates. Their inter-rater correlations ranged from .92 to .95. The Hustak et al. (1976) study also produced a test-retest reliability coefficient of .80 over an interval of eight to 146 months (Mean interval = 59.6 months). Change scores from first to second testing were not significantly related to duration of time interval, once more supporting the test's stability over time. These reliability estimates are comparable to those obtained with children and other types of adult populations (Becker and Sabatino 1971; Egeland, Rice, and Penny 1967; Goff and Parker 1969; Kaspar and Lampel 1972; Matranga, Jensen, and Prandoni 1972; Miller, Lowenfeld, Linder and Turner 1963; Ruckhaber 1964; Ryckman, Rentfrow, Fargo, and McCartin 1972; Snyder and Kalil 1968; Wallbrown, Wallbrown, and Engin 1976).

However, there have been some inconsistent findings in the research on inter-scorer reliability. For example, Morsbach, DelPriori, and Furnell (1975) reported that there were no significant differences in mean scores assigned by naive raters, but experienced raters tended to deviate from each other often to a significant degree. Similarly, Egeland, Rice, and Penny (1967) noted significant variability in the mean absolute scores for the *Developmental Error Score* and two of the specific error types (rotation and perseveration) for each of the scorers. This suggests that there may be a "subjective" factor involved in scoring Bender protocols, even when an "objective" scoring system is utilized.

Further inconsistencies were noted by Wallbrown, Wallbrown, and Engin (1976), who investigated the test-retest (9- to 14-day intervals) reliabilities of the total Developmental Error Score as well as the four major error types: distortion, rotation, integration, and perseveration. Although, the reliability estimates for the total error scores, distortion errors, and rotation errors were satisfactory, those for integration and perseveration errors were *very* low. Comparable results were obtained in a second study by Engin and Wallbrown (1976). Therefore, although specific errors may vary when a child produces the same designs on different occasions the total score tends to remain the same. In fact, Koppitz (1975b) cautioned that ". . . protocols should always be evaluated by means of the total Developmental Bender score and not on the basis of individual scoring points" (p. 15). However, even greater caution should be used in interpreting emotional and organic signs. Goff and Parker (1969) reported that the test-retest (2-week intervals) reliability for the total Development Error Score was satisfactory but emotional and organic indicators were found to be far less consistent.

Snyder and Kalil (1968), in an extensive study involving 654 first grade Bender protocols, addressed several important questions concerning the reliability of the Koppitz (1964) scoring system. In addition to reporting satisfactory inter-scorer reliability, they noted the following findings:

(1) The mean Developmental Error Scores and (*SDs*) for the three raters were strikingly similar for this sample.

(2) Generally, there was high agreement among the raters for individual scoring items, but there were definite "problem" items (numbers 1a, 12a, 13, 14, 18a, 21a, 21b, and 22).

(3) Items presenting scoring problems occurred on those designs that are more difficult for children to reproduce.

Based on their findings, the authors presented several suggestions for improving scoring precision.

(1) Since beginning examiners tend to "overscore," caution should be exercised not to violate Koppitz's suggestion to the effect, "When in doubt, do not score."

(2) Care should be taken not to misunderstand the instructions in the manual. The scoring of Design 6 (angulation and perseveration) is a prime example of scoring difficulties involving both instructional confusion and human error.

(3) Since examiner errors on Designs 1 and 2 (perseveration) are frequently due to lack of care or simply not counting dots or columns, special attention should be paid to these factors.

(4) Since examiners have difficulty deciding whether a mark is a dot or a circle, especially in the reproductions of young children, care must be exercised in making these determinations.

(5) Examiners should use a "checklist" since some errors (e.g. 18b on Design 6) and even complete designs are overlooked.

(6) Examiners should pay close attention to the child's behavior, since otherwise they may increase the likelihood of scoring errors due to interpretation of faint lines, overlapping designs, erasures, and paper orientation.

Based on these observations, Koppitz (1975b) revised her scoring manual for the *Developmental Bender Test Scoring System*. At this time, there has been no research on the reliability of this "revision."

There has been some discussion over the use of standard scores (Furr 1970; Hartlage and Lucas 1971; Holroyd 1971), item analysis (Lambert 1971), factor analysis (Hofmann 1976), and curve fitting procedures (Choynowski 1970) to enhance the utility of Koppitz's (1964) *Developmental Scoring System*. Also, Holroyd (1966) developed a guide "to aid in the mechanics of scoring the test and in the integration and interpretation of results" (p. 440). These studies, however, have had little impact on the clinical applications of Koppitz's system.

MISCELLANEOUS STUDIES ON RELIABILITY

Teachers of the learning disabled, when appropriately trained in the Bender-Gestalt Test and its scoring by the Koppitz (1964) method, achieved a high degree of inter-rater reliability among teachers ($r = .89$) and between teachers and psychologists ($r = .915$) (Foster, Boeck, and Reese 1976).

Pauker (1976) developed a simple and rapid scoring system, the Quick-Scoring System, for the Bender-Gestalt Test which yielded a correlation of .98 between two independent raters. In addition, a trainee's ratings correlated .95 with each of the experienced raters.

Summary

In this chapter we have explored the validity and reliability of the Bender-Gestalt Test. While we have not repeated the fairly extensive literature on the validity of the instrument for the identification of organic pathology, we submit that not much of the more current literature has addressed other problems associated with validity. For example, the role of artistic skill or drawing ability as a contaminant in establishing the test's validity is still uncertain. With regard to possible examiner effects, much remains to be researched. Another area in which our knowledge is far from complete is that of the comparative validity of the Bender-Gestalt Test in relation to other instruments. The scanty data available, however, suggest that the Bender is modestly valid and certainly as valid as the Rorschach for limited purposes. The research also suggests that the test has validity for adolescents with learning disabilities, for adolescents with either emotional or organic problems, and for adolescents who are retarded. Some of the research on validity leaves much to be desired from a methodological perspective, and some of it continues to be downright poor.

The research on reliability without exception demonstrates that satisfactory inter-rater and test-retest reliabilities are obtained with objective scoring systems and for raters having varying degrees of clinical sophistication. However, the research also suggests that one should rely on "total" errors rather than "specific" items or error types when interpreting an individual's protocol.

CHAPTER 11

INTERPRETATION OF SELECTED BENDER PROTOCOLS

IN THIS CHAPTER we will offer some comments about the Bender-Gestalt Test based on research findings and our clinical experience with this device.

As Murstein (1968) stated so well, ". . . it makes a big difference who administers the test. There is really no such thing as technique validity—only technique-tester validity." The Bender-Gestalt test is merely a series of designs until the examiner gives it life. Therefore, we will present several protocols to provide the reader with some flavor of the clinical interpretive processes involved in formulating tentative hypotheses about the personality functioning of several individuals whose Bender-Gestalt Test protocols are reproduced here. It is obvious that by presenting only the patient's test productions derived from a single test an incomplete picture of the patient will emerge. All of these patients were actually administered an entire battery of tests. It is equally true that there are many features even on the Bender-Gestalt Test about which we are not commenting. Our intent, however, is not to strive for a comprehensive personality profile based on the Bender-Gestalt drawings, but simply to illustrate some types of information that might be gleaned from the test material, and, even within this more limited goal, to highlight only those features that seem to be most salient. We are also, for the purposes stated, deliberately avoiding the use of any of the quantitative scoring systems that might be employed to good advantage. These interpretations are being made without the benefit of descriptions of the test approach and other observational notations, which would play an important role in the interpretive process.

Case 1—MM

This is a 15-year, 10 month-old male whose therapist referred him to help gain a better understanding of his personality dynamics.

First is the observation that this protocol is characterized by very large design drawings dispersed over a great deal of space. Since the instructions in the administration included reference to nine geometric designs that were to be reproduced and the patient fit only six on one side of the paper, there is considerable support for the interpretive hypothesis that he lacks an appreciation of realistic boundaries, that he is likely to have an impulse control problem involving an inappropriate intrusion upon the rights of others, and that his planning and foresight abilities are considerably impaired. Moreover, the large size of the renditions suggests an overcompensatory striving to mask feelings of underlying personal inadequacy.

Secondly, since the designs were made with very heavy line pressure, with some exceptions, such as the circle of Design A and most of Design 6, a hostile, antisocial, possibly even violently aggressive, tendency would be postulated. In this connection we also note that the square of Design A impinges upon the circle, and that pointed sections on Designs 7 and 8 are greatly exaggerated.

A certain carelessness characterizes much of the patient's performance. He appears to be relatively unconcerned about the impression that he creates on others. Evidence for this hypothesis derives also from the heavily reinforced lines being left in an uncorrected state of disarray (see Designs A, 4, 7 and 8).

The dots of Design 1 become progressively larger and darker, and there is an increased separation of the circles of Design 2 as the patient proceeds from left to right, suggesting that his performance deteriorates when he is involved in routine tasks requiring perseverance, that his frustration tolerance is quickly exhausted, and that he has little patience for performing exacting tasks.

The evidence for strong regressive trends is adduced from the patient's performance on Designs 3 and 5 where he produces loops instead of dots. An uneven, poorly modulated affective expression is suggested by the marked variation in the curvature on Design 6.

The patient's recall performance is interpreted as reflecting a relatively high degree of intelligence, based on the recall of eight figures. More speculatively, a tendency to become self-protective because of his perceived sexual vulnerability in relation to females, based on his closing the open "male" component of Design 4, is suggested.

In sum, this protocol is consistent with an impulse control problem in an intelligent youth who is likely to be socially injudicious and quite hostile, especially toward females.

Case 2—ML

This protocol was produced by a 21-year-old female who had been referred because her psychiatrist suspected the presence of a schizophrenic disorder.

The associations to the designs probably were the most revealing aspect of the entire protocol, since they reflected an idiosyncratic thought pattern. The associations indicate an unusual preoccupation with reproductive processes. Unless such test behavior could be accounted for on the basis of prolonged experience in uncovering psychotherapy, or possibly on the basis of the "regression in the service of the ego" that distinguishes the highly creative person, both of which possibilities could be excluded in this case, it would likely reflect the failure of the defense system and the eruption of primary process ideation. The initial association, "fertilization," on Design A and the later "man and woman" response on Design 4 seem to illustrate the initial crumbling of repressive defenses in this woman.

Additionally, her references to abstract forces, i.e. "electricity" and "tension or pulling . . . sort of pulling and releasing," not only might have sexual significance but also are entirely consistent with the patient's experiencing an intense inner conflict and ambivalence. Abstract concepts might also serve as a defense against focusing on distressing feeling states. The ambivalence toward male sexuality is also hinted at by the reference to

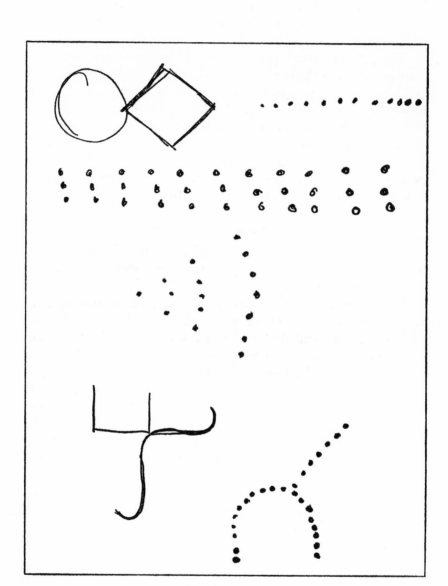

Patient MM.

Patient MM.

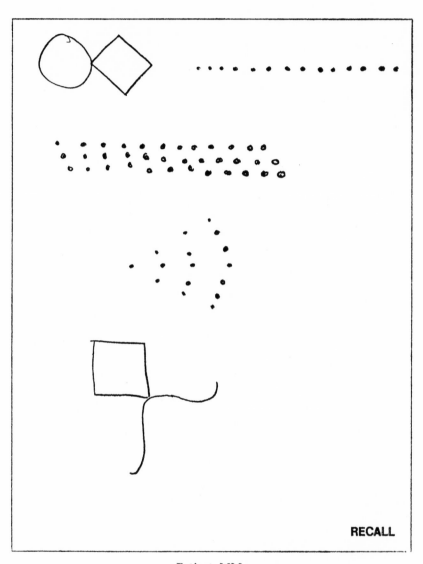

RECALL

Patient MM.

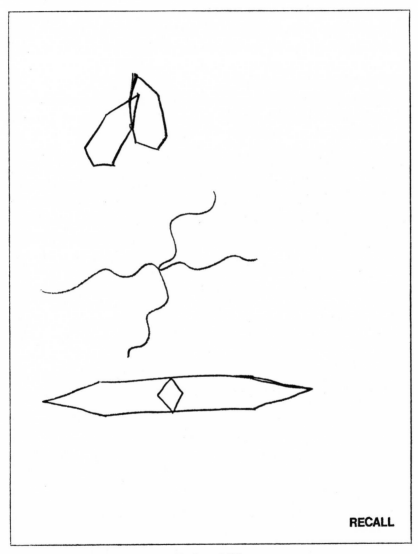

RECALL

Patient MM.

"something very beautiful" in response to the male symbol on Design 8 combined with the reference to anger on Design 7 (which may symbolize phallic sexuality).

Continuing with the patient's associations, a tentative interpretation of the tunnel response on Figure 5 might revolve around strong withdrawal tendencies or perhaps a desire to overcome a withdrawn adjustment style.

The actual drawings suggest that thoughts of sexual relations are replete with conflict for this patient (note the size disparities on Designs 4 and 5 and the distortions on Designs 7 and 8). The difficulties expressed in making an adequately rounded component on Designs 4 and 5, as is seen by the false starts and erasures of the less abundant female symbols, could very well speak for a sense of profound feminine inadequacy. The darkened dots on Design 5 and the aborted, but not erased, rendition of Design 1, suggest that this patient is both angry, a feeling which her association to Design 7 suggests tends to be projected onto others, and that she possesses some awareness of her inadequate functioning but is able to make only partial correction for it.

Her recall of eight figures suggests that she has retained well-developed intellectual skills, but her performance also shows considerable impairment in mentation.

Overall, the patient's Bender-Gestalt Test protocol reveals some of the features that could very well be associated with an incipient schizophrenic development.

Case 3—JS

This 34-year-old lady was referred for purposes of assisting in the establishment of a diagnosis and for delineating the personality dynamics.

The most striking feature in this protocol is the patient's need to separate all of her designs in small compartments. Even before making the actual designs, she prepares for the institution of isolation and compartmentalization defenses by drawing the confining compartments. She appears to be warding off the threat of loss of control, and, possibly, massive confusion, by relying on extraordinarily rigid defenses. That this effort at defense is

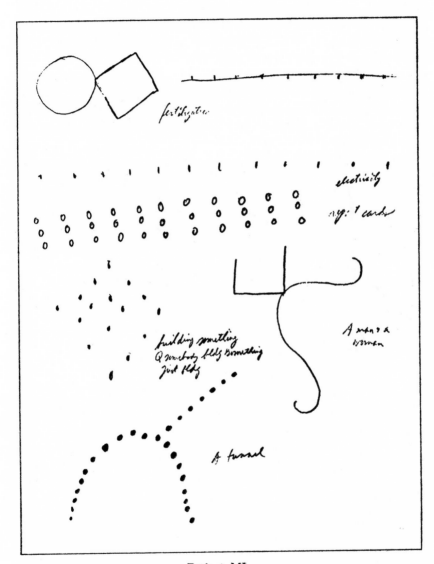

Patient ML.

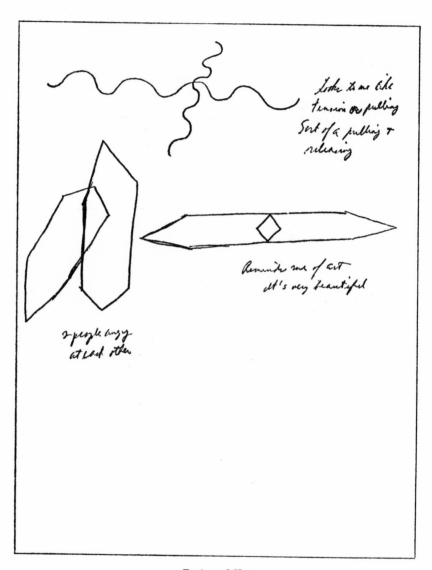

Patient ML.

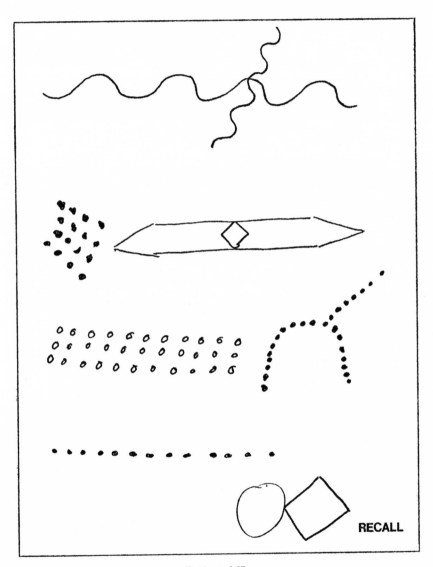

Patient ML.

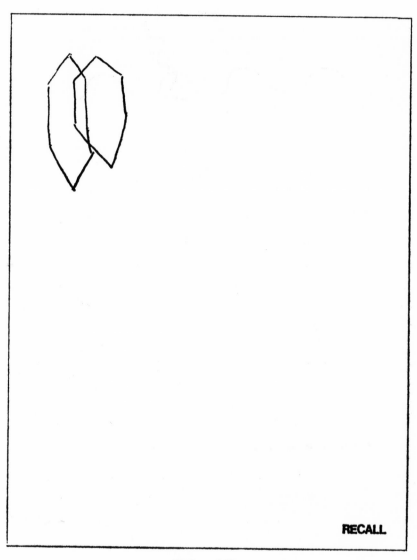

RECALL

Patient ML.

not very efficiently applied and that it is not particularly effective is suggested by the fact that at least one figure, namely Design 2, remains uncontained. Supporting this contention is the observation that the walls of the compartments are unevenly drawn and made with varying dimensions.

The effort to utilize this mode of control is carried into the recall situation as well but this time with even less success, if one takes note of the simplifications of the figures.

The delicate line quality betrays a lack of self-confidence as does the diminutive size of the configurations themselves.

The foreshortened Designs 7 and 8 suggest that this lady has invested much energy to curb hostile and sexual impulses at the expense of greater efficiency and spontaneity in functioning.

It did not come as any great surprise after inspection of this Bender, therefore, that the other tests in the psychological test battery revealed a hysterical personality struggling against decompensating to a more regressed state.

Case 4—JG

This 57-year-old woman was referred for psychological assessment to determine possibly organically based impairment and to evaluate personality dynamics.

A strong case for organicity can be made on the basis of this woman's extremely poor recall performance. However, there are other indications of organic pathology found in the copy phase of the Bender-Gestalt Test. For example, the protocol is characterized by inconsistent perceptual-motor functioning as evidenced by the uneven figure sizes and expansive tendencies, as well as the shaky, unsteady line quality of the reproductions.

It appears that this woman fears loss of stability and is expending a considerable amount of energy in her attempts to maintain control (note how she fills circles to make dots on Designs 1, 3, and 5). While these attempts at control are obviously not totally successful, the amount of energy expended is likely to leave her generally unproductive.

Although she craves attention (note the wide fluctuations on Design 6) and strives to be assertive and to present a socially

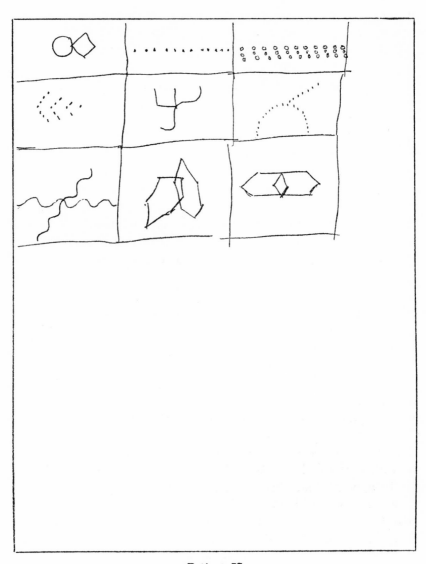

Patient JS.

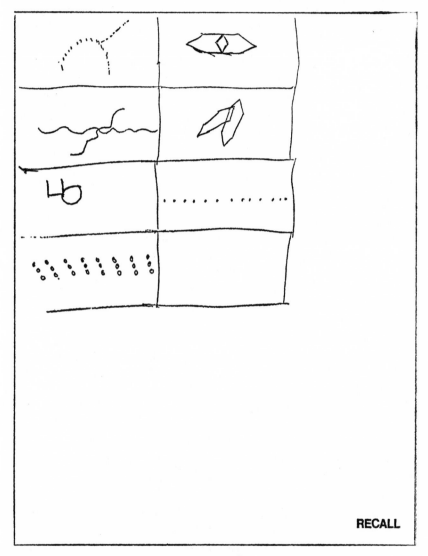

RECALL

Patient JS.

acceptable facade (angulation on Design 3) possibly to cover up feelings of inadequacy in her feminine role, it is likely that she will have difficulty coping with environmental demands due to her instability (e.g., use of paper edge for baseline in Design 5), as well as her strong need for affection and nurturance as evidenced by the expanded curved—or female—portions (symbolizing oral dependency) of Designs 4 and 5.

Overall, this woman exhibits significant problems maintaining physical, cognitive, and emotional control. It was not surprising that further testing showed average intelligence, while her history indicated chronic alcohol problems.

Case 5—AB

This 13-year, 11-month-old girl was referred for psychological evaluation of her personality dynamics.

The most striking feature of this protocol is her attempt to protect herself from a world which she perceives to be hostile and threatening. This hypothesis is based on several aspects of her "elaborations," such as her passive, ineffectual turning inward on Designs 3 and 5, the low self-esteem in the small size of the figures and the downward slanting of Design 2, and the withdrawal or isolation associated with "closing off" Designs 1 and 4. There is also an obvious concern over losing control which is most notable on Design 1 (copy phase). Here she had difficulty making dots, became expansive as she neared the end of the paper and finally completed the remaining dots (in this case circles) underneath the original row. This highly idiosyncratic way of dealing with anxiety was at least partially successful as evidenced by her improved performance on Designs 2 and 3. Nevertheless, it indicates a regressive tendency and confusion under stress.

Another noteworthy aspect of the testing concerns her conflicts surrounding interpersonal relations. While this is evident in her tension (shaky and overworked line quality) in reproducing those figures associated with interpersonal contact (Designs 4, 6, 7, and 8), this tendency is accentuated in her elaborations.

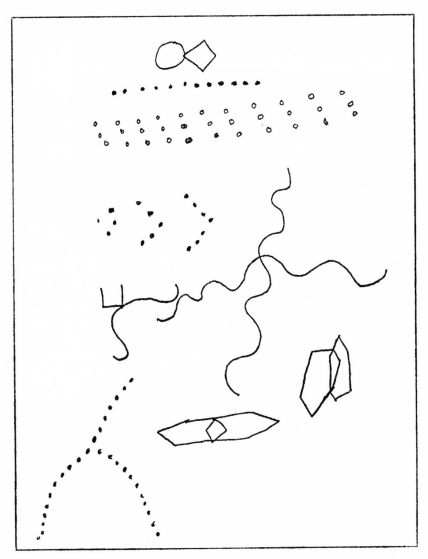

Patient JG.

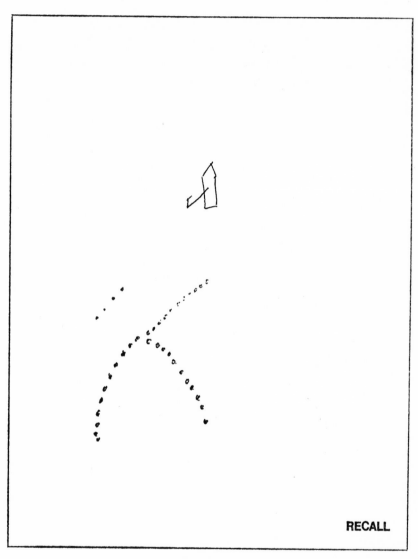

RECALL

Patient JG.

Here she does not deal with relationships, but separates the dynamic aspects of these figures (e.g. Designs 6 and 7).

A third feature of the drawings is her anxiety over her sexual identity and the development and acceptance of the feminine role. This concern is most obvious in her attempt to obscure the male and female components of Design A (elaboration phase), but is also evident in her ineffectual attempt to identify with the female role (Design 4, elaboration phase), and her withdrawal from the sexual aspects of Designs 7 and 8.

In sum, this girl is likely to isolate herself from a threatening world because she is unprepared to deal with it.

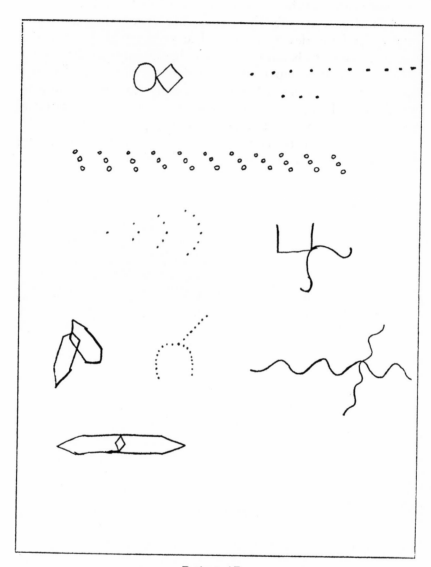

Patient AB.

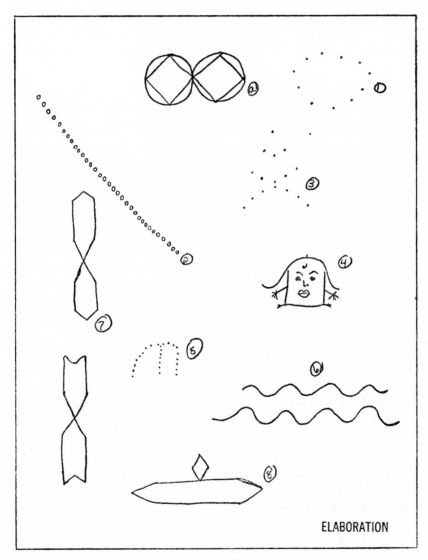

Patient AB.

CHAPTER 12

CONCLUSIONS

In undertaking the arduous task of evaluating the current scientific status of the Bender-Gestalt Test we have endeavored not only to summarize and synthesize the relevant research findings, but we have also indicated approaches which are subject to criticism, developments that are laudable, and methods by which some of the research could be improved. At this time we do not intend to recapitulate the major results derived from the literature analysis for each topic covered by the various chapters, but instead we wish to highlight several global impressions which have evolved from our search of the Bender-Gestalt Test literature. These impressions, which we wish to share with the reader, are partially based on a "feel" for the work done with this psychological method.

First, we are particularly impressed with the sheer amount of research productivity with the Bender-Gestalt Test over the past 16 years. The several hundreds of published reports appearing in the English-language literature reveal an undiminished interest in this instrument despite the general decline in the value assigned by many mental health professionals to the diagnostic process. Moreover, although there is great unevenness in the quality of the Bender research done, ranging from the simplistic to the most sophisticated, in general the caliber of the research has improved appreciably over the period covered by this review. Consequently, our understanding of this frequently used instrument has benefited.

Second, one notes with great interest the changing patterns of topics that have been investigated. While the Bender-Gestalt Test continues to be studied most commonly for its value in diagnosing organic pathology, it seems to be increasingly researched for applications to a variety of problems affecting children. It would appear that school psychologists and others have discovered the potential utility of this instrument as a predictor of, and sensitive screening device for, a variety of learning problems and as a measure of performance in relation to specific subject areas. Other topics which previously captured the interest of psychologists to a much greater extent, such as the relationship between age and Bender performance, or intelligence and Bender performance, seem to have receded in importance. The same applies to studies in which neurotic or character and behavior disorder patients are used as subjects. This type of study has become nearly extinct.

Third, while there is much support for the view that Bender-Gestalt performance fairly accurately portrays visual-motor integrative maturation between the ages of four and 11, there is a continuing need for carefully conceived research on the specific functions tapped by the Bender-Gestalt Test. We need to know more precisely what this test measures and exactly how it does so. In other words, even though some work has been done to elucidate the processes involved, there is much more that needs to be done.

Fourth, we are still in need of research on several pivotal issues associated with the validity of the Bender-Gestalt Test. Among these urgent needs are the specification of the role of artistic skill or drawing ability, the possible examiner effects on performance, and the comparative validity of the Bender in relation to other psychological methods for specific assessment purposes. Moreover, predictive studies employing the Bender are quite scarce indeed.

Fifth, there has been further proliferation of methods for Bender administration and interpretation. Thus, for example, we now have multiple-choice forms, abbreviated versions, and group procedures as well as methods employing background interference with either the stimuli themselves or with the response. Of all the newer techniques of administration, Canter's (1963) Background Interference Procedure clearly stands out in terms of generating exciting new research of a systematic type and aiding in the diagnostic process.

Sixth, as for the newly developed scoring systems, they have also flourished. While some of these scoring systems seem to aim for greater simplification in scoring, others endeavor to achieve greater complexity and increased informational yield. It is our judgment that most of these newer systems will not be widely accepted and will not survive the test of time.

Seventh, there is mounting evidence for the sensitivity of the Bender-Gestalt Test as a diagnostic measure of organic pathology when group differentiations are made. Furthermore, the Bender appears to accomplish this task as successfully as most other psychological and physical measures with which it has been compared.

Eighth, it is encouraging to note the interesting newer work done in the area of personality study employing the Bender-Gestalt Test. We are particularly impressed with the revival of the projective use of the Bender. We would very much like to see even more research on projective applications of this test with close collaboration between psychologists who are capable of devising scientifically sound designs and psychologists who are clinically experienced. Furthermore, there is a need for more systematic research focusing on clearly conceptualized hypotheses concerning the relationship between Bender performance and personality dynamics.

Finally, regarding children's academic performance, the univariate studies have been rather disappointing, and the utility of the Bender, when used in conjunction with other instruments, as a predictor of achievement, requires more research. Those studies that have undertaken multivariate analyses indicate that the Bender-Gestalt Test can be a valuable aid in predicting early school achievement as well as specific deficiencies, such as reading disabilities in young children.

On an overall basis, we find that the Bender-Gestalt Test research indicates that the importance assigned by psychologists to this instrument as a significant component in the test battery is largely justified. As our understanding of the assessment process in general, and the Bender-Gestalt Test, in particular, increases, we will be able to delineate even more precisely the appropriate uses of this test. With further research geared to the specific theoretical and applied issues outlined in this chapter, we trust this goal will be more nearly achieved.

BIBLIOGRAPHY

Abrams, S. The upper weight level premature child. *Diseases of the Nervous System*, 1969, *30*, 414-417.

Ackerman, P. T., Peters, J. E., & Dykman, R. A. Children with specific learning disabilities: Bender Gestalt test findings and other signs. *Journal of Learning Disabilities*, 1971, *4*, 437-446.

Adams, J. Canter Background Interference Procedure applied to the diagnosis of brain damage in mentally retarded children. *American Journal of Mental Deficiency*, 1970, *75*, 57-64.

Adams, J. Comparison of task-central and task-peripheral forms of the Canter BIP in diagnosing brain damage in adults. *Perceptual and Motor Skills*, 1971, *33*, 1259-1267.

Adams, J., & Canter, A. Performance characteristics of school children on the BIP Bender test. *Journal of Consulting and Clinical Psychology*, 1969, *33*, 508.

Adams, J., Hayden, B., & Canter, A. The relationship between the Canter Background Interference Procedure and the hyperkinetic behavior syndrome. *Journal of Learning Disabilities*, 1974, *7*, 110-115.

Adams, J., Kenny, T. J., & Canter, A. The efficacy of the Canter Background Interference Procedure in identifying children with cerebral dysfunction. *Journal of Consulting and Clinical Psychology*, 1973, *40*, 498.

Adams, J., & Lieb, J. J. Canter BIP and Draw-A-Person test performance of Negro and Caucasian children. *Psychology in the Schools*, 1973, *10*, 299-304.

Adams, J., Peterson, R. A., Kenny, T. J., & Canter, A. Age effects and revised scoring of the Canter BIP for identifying children with cerebral dysfunction. *Journal of Consulting and Clinical Psychology*, 1975, *43*, 117-118.

Albott, W. L., & Gunn, H. E. Bender-Gestalt performance by culturally disadvantaged first graders. *Perceptual and Motor Skills*, 1971, *33*, 247-250.

Allen, R. M. Experimental variation of the mode of reproduction of the Bender-Gestalt stimuli by mental retardates. *Journal of Clinical Psychology*, 1968, *24*, 199-202. (a)

Allen, R. M. Visual perceptual maturation and the Bender Gestalt Test quality. *Training School Bulletin*, 1968, *64*, 131-133. (b)

Allen, R. M. The Developmental Test of Visual Perception and the Bender Gestalt Test achievement of educable mental retardates. *Training School Bulletin*, 1969, *66*, 80-85.

Allen, R. M., & Adamo, C. A study of the Bender-Gestalt figures and visual perception. *Acta Psychologica*, 1969, *31*, 394-396.

Allen, R. M., Adamo, C., Alker, L. N., & Levine, M. N. A study of recognition and reproduction of Bender-Gestalt figures by children of average and below intelligence. *Journal of Genetic Psychology*, 1971, *119*, 75-78.

Allen, R. M., & Frank, G. H. Experimental variation of the mode of reproduction of the Bender-Gestalt stimuli. *Journal of Clinical Psychology*, 1963, *19*, 212-214.

Allen, R. M., Haupt, T. D., & Jones, R. W. Visual perceptual abilities and intelligence in mental retardates. *American Journal of Clinical Psychology*, 1965, *21*, 299-300.

Ames, L. B. Calibration of aging. *Journal of Personality Assessment*, 1974, *38*, 505-529.

Ammons, R. B., & Ammons, C. H. *The Quick Test (QT)*. Missoula, MT: Psychological Test Specialists, 1962.

Andert, J. N., Dinning, W. D., & Hustak, T. L. Koppitz errors on the Bender-Gestalt for adult retardates: Normative data. *Perceptual and Motor Skills*, 1976, *42*, 451-454.

Andert, J. N., Hustak, T. L., & Dinning, W. D. Bender-Gestalt reproduction times for retarded adults. *Journal of Clinical Psychology*, 1978, *34*, 927-929.

Anglin, R., Pullen, M., & Games, P. Comparison of two tests of brain damage. *Perceptual and Motor Skills*, 1965, *20*, 977-980.

Arbit, J., & Zager, R. Psychometrics of a neuropsychological test battery. *Journal of Clinical Psychology*, 1978, *34*, 460-465.

Armentrout, J. A. Bender Gestalt recall: Memory measure or intelligence estimate? *Journal of Clinical Psychology*, 1976, *32*, 832-834.

Armstrong, R. G. Recall patterns on the Bender Gestalt. *Journal of Projective Techniques and Personality Assessment*, 1963, *27*, 418-422.

Armstrong, R. G. A reevaluation of copied and recalled Bender-Gestalt reproductions. *Journal of Projective Techniques and Personality Assessment*, 1965, *29*, 134-139.

Arnold, L. E., Huestis, R. D., Wemmer, D., & Smeltzer, D. J. Differential effect of amphetamine optical isomers on Bender Gestalt performance of the minimally brain dysfunctioned. *Journal of Learning Disabilities*, 1978, *11*, 127-132.

Ascough, J. C., & Dana, R. H. Concurrent validities of the Mosaic and Bender-Gestalt tests. *Journal of Consulting Psychology*, 1962, *26*, 430-434.

Aylaian, A., & Meltzer, M. L. The Bender-Gestalt Test and intelligence. *Journal of Consulting Psychology,* 1962, *26,* 483.

Baer, D. J., & Gale, R. H. Intelligence and Bender Gestalt Test performance of institutionalized and noninstitutionalized school children. *Journal of Genetic Psychology,* 1967, *111,* 119-124.

Baker, E. H., & Thurber, S. Bender Gestalt test performance and the word recognition skills of disadvantaged children. *Journal of School Psychology,* 1976, *14,* 64-66.

Barrett, T. C. Visual discrimination tasks as predictors of first grade reading achievement. *Reading Teacher,* 1965, *18,* 276-282.

Barron, F. An ego strength scale which predicts response to psychotherapy. *Journal of Consulting Psychology,* 1953, *17,* 327-335.

Bauman, E., & St. John, J. The clinical usefulness of some tests of visual perception. *Psychology in the Schools,* 1971, *8,* 247-249.

Becker, J. T., & Sabatino, D. A. Reliability of individual tests of perception administered utilizing group techniques. *Journal of Clinical Psychology,* 1971, *27,* 86-88.

Beery, K. E., & Buktenica, N. A. *Developmental Test of Visual-Motor Integration.* Chicago: Follett Educational Corp., 1967.

Bender, L. *A Visual Motor Gestalt Test and Its Clinical Use.* American Orthopsychiatric Association, Research Monographs, 1938. No. 3.

Bender, L. On the proper use of the Bender-Gestalt test. *Perceptual and Motor Skills,* 1965, *20,* 189-190.

Bender, L. The Visual Motor Gestalt function in 6- and 7-year-old normal and schizophrenic children. In G. A. Jervis and J. Zubin (Eds)., *Psychopathology of Mental Development.* New York: Grune & Stratton, 1967.

Bender, L. Use of the Visual Motor Gestalt Test in the diagnosis of learning disabilities. *Journal of Special Education,* 1970, *4,* 29-39.

Benton, A. L. A visual retention test for clinical use. *Archives of Neurology and Psychiatry,* 1945, *54,* 212-216.

Benton, A. L. *The Revised Visual Retention Test: Clinical and Experimental Applications.* New York: Psychological Corporation, 1955.

Benton, A. L. Dyslexia in relation to form perception and directional sense. In J. Money (Ed.), *Reading Disability: Progress and Research Needs in Dyslexia.* Baltimore: Johns Hopkins Press, 1962.

Bernstein, I. H. A comparison of schizophrenics and nonschizophrenics on two methods of administration of the Bender-Gestalt Test. *Perceptual and Motor Skills,* 1963, *16,* 757-763.

Beyel, V., Fracchia, J., Sheppard, C., & Merlis, S. Relationships among Raven Progressive Matrices avoidable and atypical errors and Bender Gestalt errors. *Perceptual and Motor Skills,* 1971, *33,* 1269-1270.

Billingslea, F. Y. The Bender-Gestalt: A review and a perspective. *Psychological Bulletin,* 1963, *60,* 233-251.

Bilu, U., & Weiss, A. A. A configurational analysis of the Bender-Gestalt Test. *Israel Annals of Psychiatry and Related Disciplines*, 1974, *12*, 37-52.

Binkley, M. E., Maggart, W., & Vandever, T. R. Reading retardation and Bender Gestalt performance. *Psychology in the Schools*, 1974, *11*, 400-402.

Black, F. W. Reversal and rotation errors by normal and retarded readers. *Perceptual and Motor Skills*, 1973, *36*, 895-898.

Blatt, S. J. Review of E. Aronow and M. Reznikoff "Rorschach content interpretation." New York: Grune & Stratton, 1976. In *Contemporary Psychology*, 1978, *23*, 251-253.

Bolton, B. Quantification of two projective tests for deaf clients. *Journal of Clinical Psychology*, 1972, *28*, 554-556.

Bolton, B., Donoghue, R., & Langbauer, W. Quantification of two projective tests for deaf clients: A large sample validation study. *Journal of Clinical Psychology*, 1973, *29*, 249-250.

Brannigan, G. G., Barone, R. J., & Margolis, H. Bender Gestalt signs as indicants of conceptual impulsivity. *Journal of Personality Assessment*, 1978, *42*, 233-237.

Brannigan, G. G., & Benowitz, M. L. Bender Gestalt signs and antisocial acting tendencies in adolescents. *Psychology in the Schools*, 1975, *12*, 15-17.

Brilliant, P. J., & Gynther, M. D. Relationships between performance on three tests for organicity and selected patient variables. *Journal of Consulting Psychology*, 1963, *27*, 474-479.

Broadhurst, A., & Phillips, C. J. Reliability and validity of the Bender-Gestalt Test in a sample of British school children. *British Journal of Social and Clinical Psychology*, 1969, *8*, 253-262.

Brown, F. The Bender Gestalt and acting out. In L. E. Abt and S. L. Weissman (Eds.), *Acting Out: Theoretical and Clinical Aspects*. New York: Grune & Stratton, 1965.

Brown, W. R., & McGuire, J. M. Current assessment practices. *Professional Psychology*, 1976, 7, 475-484.

Bruck, M. A note on modified instruction for Bender-Gestalt elaborations and associations. *Journal of Projective Techniques*, 1962, *26*, 277.

Bruell, J. H., & Albee, G. W. Higher intellectual functions in a patient with hemispherectomy for tumors. *Journal of Consulting Psychology*, 1962, *26*, 90-98.

Bruhn, A. R., & Reed, M. R. Simulation of brain damage on the Bender-Gestalt Test by college subjects. *Journal of Personality Assessment*, 1975, *39*, 244-255.

Butler, O. T., Coursey, R. D., & Gatz, M. Comparison of the Bender Gestalt test for both black and white brain-damaged patients using two scoring systems. *Journal of Consulting and Clinical Psychology*, 1976, *44*, 280-285.

Byrd, E. The clinical validity of the Bender-Gestalt Test with children: A developmental comparison of children in need of psychotherapy and children judged well-adjusted. *Journal of Projective Techniques*, 1956, *20*, 127-136.

Canter, A. A background interference procedure for graphomotor tests in the study of deficit. *Perceptual and Motor Skills*, 1963, *16*, 914.

Canter, A. A background interference procedure to increase sensitivity of the Bender-Gestalt Test to organic brain disorder. *Journal of Consulting Psychology*, 1966, *30*, 91-97.

Canter, A. BIP Bender test for the detection of organic brain disorder: Modified scoring and replication. *Journal of Consulting and Clinical Psychology*, 1968, *32*, 522-526.

Canter, A. A comparison of the background interference procedure effect in schizophrenic, nonschizophrenic, and organic patients. *Journal of Clinical Psychology*, 1971, *27*, 473-474.

Canter, A. *The Canter Background Interference Procedure for the Bender Gestalt Test: Manual for Administration, Scoring, and Interpretation.* Nashville, Tenn.: Counselor Recordings and Tests, 1976.

Canter, A., & Straumanis, J. J. Performance of senile and healthy aged persons on the BIP Bender Test. *Perceptual and Motor Skills*, 1969, *28*, 695-698.

Carlson, L. D. A comparison of Negro and Caucasian performance on the Bender-Gestalt test. *Journal of Clinical Psychology*, 1966, *22*, 96-98.

Carter, C. H. *Handbook of Mental Retardation Syndromes.* Springfield: Charles C Thomas, Publisher, 1966.

Carter, D. E., Spero, A. J., & Walsh, J. A. A comparison of the visual aural digit span and the Bender Gestalt as discriminators of low achievement in the primary grades. *Psychology in the Schools*, 1978, *15*, 194-198.

Caskey, W. E., Jr., & Larson, G. L. Two modes of administration of the Bender Visual-Motor Gestalt Test to kindergarten children. *Perceptual and Motor Skills*, 1977, *45*, 1003-1006.

Cattell, R. B. *16 Personality Factor Questionnaire.* Champaign, Ill.: Institute for Personality and Ability Testing, 1962.

Cellura, A. R., & Butterfield, E. C. Intelligence, the Bender Gestalt Test and reading achievement. *American Journal of Mental Deficiency*, 1966, *71*, 60-63.

Cerbus, G., & Oziel, I. J. Correlation of the Bender Gestalt and WISC for Negro children. *Perceptual and Motor Skills*, 1971, *32*, 276.

Chang, T. M., & Chang, U. A. Relation of visual-motor skills and reading achievement in primary grade pupils of superior ability. *Perceptual and Motor Skills*, 1967, *24*, 51-53.

Choynowski, M. Curve fitting as a method of statistical correction of developmental norms, shown on the example of the Bender-Koppitz Test. *Journal of Clinical Psychology*, 1970, *26*, 135-141.

Clarke, B. R., & Leslie, P. T. Visual-motor and reading ability of deaf children. *Perceptual and Motor Skills,* 1971, *33,* 263-268.

Clawson, A. The Bender Visual Motor Gestalt Test as an index of emotional disturbance in children. *Journal of Projective Techniques,* 1959, *23,* 198-206.

Colarusso, R., & Hammill, D. *The Motor Free Test of Visual Perception.* San Rafael, California: Academic Therapy Publications, 1972.

Condell, J. The Bender Gestalt test with mentally retarded children using the Koppitz revised scoring system. *Journal of Clinical Psychology,* 1963, *19,* 430-431.

Connor, J. P. Bender Gestalt Test performance as a predictor of differential reading performance. *Journal of School Psychology,* 1968, 7, 41-44.

Cooper, J. R., & Barnes, E. J. Technique for measuring reproductions of visual stimuli: II. Adult reproductions of the Bender-Gestalt. *Perceptual and Motor Skills,* 1966, *23,* 1135-1138.

Cooper, J. R., Dwarshuis, L., & Blechman, G. Technique for measuring reproductions of visual stimuli: III. Bender Gestalt and severity of neurological deficit. *Perceptual and Motor Skills,* 1967, *25,* 506-508.

Corotto, L. V., & Curnutt, R. H. Ego--strength: A function of the measurement instrument. *Journal of Projective Techniques,* 1962, *26,* 228-230.

Coy, M. N. The Bender Visual-Motor Gestalt Test as a predictor of academic achievement. *Journal of Learning Disabilities,* 1974, 7, 317-319.

Crenshaw, D., Bohn, S., Hoffman, M. M., Mattheus, J., & Offenbach, S. The use of projective methods in research. *Journal of Projective Techniques and Personality Assessment,* 1968, *32,* 3-9.

Culbertson, F. M., & Gunn, R. C. Comparison of the Bender Gestalt Test and the Frostig Test in several clinic groups of children. *Journal of Clinical Psychology,* 1966, *22,* 439.

Curnutt, R. H., & Lewis, W. B. The relationship between 2 scores on the Bender Gestalt and F+% on the Rorschach. *Journal of Clinical Psychology,* 1954, *10,* 96-97.

Davis, L. J., Jr., & Swenson, W. M. Factor analysis of the Wechsler Memory Scale. *Journal of Consulting and Clinical Psychology,* 1970, *35,* 430.

de Cato, C. M., & Wicks, R. J. *Case Studies of the Clinical Interpretation of the Bender Gestalt Test.* Springfield: Charles C Thomas, Publisher, 1976.

deHirsch, K., Jansky, J., & Langford, W. S. *Predicting Reading Failure.* New York: Harper & Row, Publisher, 1966.

Deich, R. F. Reproduction and recognition as indices of perceptual impairment. *American Journal of Mental Deficiency,* 1968, *73,* 9-12.

De Levie, A. Bender-Gestalt distortion on recall associated with recent physical trauma. *Proceedings of the Annual Convention of the American Psychological Association*, 1970, 5, 711-712.

Dibner, A. S., & Korn, E. J. Group administration of the Bender Gestalt test to predict early school performance. *Journal of Clinical Psychology*, 1969, 25, 265-268.

Dierks, D., & Cushna, B. Sex differences in the Bender Gestalt performance of children. *Perceptual and Motor Skills*, 1969, 28, 19-22.

Diller, L., & Weinberg, J. Bender Gestalt Test distortions in hemiplegia. *Perceptual and Motor Skills*, 1965, 20, 1313-1323.

Donnelly, E. F., & Murphy, D. L. Primary affective disorder: Bender-Gestalt sequence of placement as an indicator of impulse control. *Perceptual and Motor Skills*, 1974, 38, 1079-1082.

Doubras, S. G., & Mascarenhas, J. Relations among Wechsler Full Scale scores, organicity-sensitive subtest scores and Bender Gestalt error scores. *Perceptual and Motor Skills*, 1969, 29, 719-732.

Dykman, R. A., Peters, J. E., & Ackerman, P. T. Experimental approaches to the study of minimal brain dysfunction: A follow-up study. *Annals of New York Academy of Sciences*, 1973, 205, 93-108.

Egeland, B., Rice, J., & Penny, S. Inter-scorer reliability on the Bender Gestalt Test and the revised Visual Retention Test. *American Journal of Mental Deficiency*, 1967, 72, 96-99.

Eichler, M., & Norman, J. Repeated use of the Bender-Gestalt Test in a study of an induced toxic state. *Perceptual and Motor Skills*, 1965, 20, 1033-1036.

Engin, A. W., & Wallbrown, F. H. The stability of four kinds of perceptual errors on the Bender Gestalt. *Journal of Psychology*, 1976, 94, 123-126.

Erwin, E. F., & Hampe, W. Assessment of perceptual-motor changes following electroshock treatment. *Perceptual and Motor Skills*, 1966, 22, 770.

Fanibanda, D. K. Cultural influence on Hutt's adaptation of Bender Gestalt test: A pilot study. *Journal of Personality Assessment*, 1973, 37, 531-536.

Farmer, R. H. Functional changes during early weeks of abstinence, measured by Bender-Gestalt. *Quarterly Journal of Studies on Alcohol*, 1973, 34, 786-796.

Fiedler, M. G., & Schmidt, E. P. Sex differences in Bender-Gestalt drawings of seven-year old children. *Perceptual and Motor Skills*, 1969, 29, 753-754.

Fitts, W. H. *Manual for the Tennessee Self-Concept Scale*. Nashville, Tenn.: Counselor Recordings and Tests, 1965.

Flick, G. L., & Duncan, C. Perceptual-motor dysfunction in children with sickle-cell trait. *Perceptual and Motor Skills*, 1973, 36, 324.

Foster, G. G., & Boeck, D. G., & Reese, J. A comparison of special education teacher and psychologist scoring of the Bender Visual Motor
Gestalt Test. *Psychology in the Schools,* 1976, *13,* 146-148.

Freed, E. X. Frequencies of rotations on group and individual administrations of the Bender-Gestalt test. *Journal of Clinical Psychology,* 1964,
20, 120-121.

Freed, E. X. Incidence of Bender-Gestalt figure rotations among mentally
defective psychiatric patients. *American Journal of Mental Deficiency,*
1965, *69,* 514.

Freed, E. X. Comparison on admission and discharge of Bender-Gestalt
test performance by hospitalized psychiatric patients. *Perceptual and
Motor Skills,* 1966, *23,* 919-922. (a)

Freed, E. X. Susceptibility of individual Bender-Gestalt test designs to
rotation by psychiatric patients. *Journal of Clinical Psychology,* 1966,
22, 98-99. (b)

Freed, E. X. Actuarial data on Bender-Gestalt Test rotations by psychiatric patients. *Journal of Clinical Psychology,* 1969, *25,* 252-255.

Freed, E. X., & Hastings, K. C. A further note on the stimulus factor in
Bender-Gestalt test rotations. *Journal of Clinical Psychology,* 1965, *21,*
64.

Friedman, A. F., Wakefield, J. A., Sasek, J., & Schroeder, D. A new scoring
system for the Spraings Multiple Choice Bender Gestalt Test. *Journal
of Clinical Psychology,* 1977, *33,* 205-207.

Friedman, H. Perceptual regression in schizophrenia. *Journal of Projective
Techniques,* 1953, *17,* 171-185.

Friedman, J., Strochak, R. D., Gitlin, S., & Gottsagen, M. L. Koppitz
Bender scoring system and brain injury in children. *Journal of Clinical
Psychology,* 1967, *23,* 179-182.

Frostig, M., Le Fever, D. W., & Whittlesey, J. R. B. *Administration and
Scoring Manual: Developmental Test of Visual Perception.* Palo Alto,
Calif.: Consulting Psychologists Press, 1964.

Fuller, G. B. A further study on rotations: Cross-validation. *Journal of
Clinical Psychology,* 1963, *19,* 127-128.

Fuller, G. B., & Chagnon, G. Factors influencing rotation in the Bender
Gestalt performance of children. *Journal of Projective Techniques,* 1962,
26, 36-46.

Fuller, G. B., & Laird, J. T. The Minnesota percepto-diagnostic test.
Journal of Clinical Psychology, 1963, *19,* 3-24. (Monograph Supple-
ment No. 16) (a)

Fuller, G. B., & Laird, J. T. Comments and findings about rotations. *Perceptual and Motor Skills,* 1963, *16,* 673-679. (b)

Furr, K. D. Standard scores for the Koppitz Developmental Scoring System.
Journal of Clinical Psychology, 1970, *26,* 78-79.

Garron, D. C., & Cheifetz, D. I. Comment on "Bender Gestalt discernment of organic pathology." *Psychological Bulletin,* 1965, *63,* 197-200.

Garron, D. C., & Cheifetz, D. I. Electroshock therapy and Bender-Gestalt performance. *Perceptual and Motor Skills,* 1968, *26,* 9-10.

Gavales, D., & Millon, T. Comparison of reproduction and recall size deviations in the Bender-Gestalt as measures of anxiety. *Journal of Clinical Psychology,* 1960, *16,* 278-280.

Gibson, E. J., Gibson, J. J., Pick, A. D., & Osser, H. A developmental study of the discrimination of letter-like forms. *Journal of Comparative and Physiological Psychology,* 1962, *55,* 987-996.

Giebink, J. W., & Birch, R. The Bender Gestalt Test as an ineffective predictor of reading achievement. *Journal of Clinical Psychology,* 1970, *26,* 484-486.

Gilbert, J. Insight acquisition and counseling with group test data: A negative outcome with some wry reflections on certain imperatives of research in the clinical area. *Psychology,* 1971, *8,* 9-14.

Gilbert, J. *Interpreting Psychological Test Data.* New York: Van Nostrand: Reinhold, 1978.

Gilbert, J. C., & Levee, R. F. Performances of deaf and normally hearing children on the Bender Gestalt and the Archimedes Spiral Test. *Perceptual and Motor Skills,* 1967, *24,* 1059-1066.

Gilmore, G., Chandy, J., & Anderson, T. The Bender-Gestalt and the Mexican-American student: A report. *Psychology in the Schools,* 1975, *12,* 172-175.

Goff, A. F., & Parker, A. Reliability of the Koppitz scoring system for the Bender Gestalt test. *Journal of Clinical Psychology,* 1969, *25,* 407-409.

Goldfried, M. R., & Ingling, J. H. The connotative and symbolic meaning of the Bender-Gestalt. *Journal of Projective Techniques and Personality Assessment,* 1964, *28,* 185-191.

Goldman, H., Gomer, F. E., & Templer, D. I. Long-term effects of electroconvulsive therapy upon memory and perceptual motor performance. *Journal of Clinical Psychology,* 1972, *28,* 32-34.

Graham, F. K., & Kendall, B. S. Performance of brain-damaged cases on a Memory-for-Designs Test. *Journal of Abnormal and Social Psychology,* 1946, *41,* 303-314.

Graham, F. K., & Kendall, B. S. Memory-for-Designs Test: Revised general manual. *Perceptual and Motor Skills,* 1960, *11,* 147-188.

Gravitz, H. L., & Handler, L. Effects of different modes of administration on the Bender Visual Motor Gestalt Test. *Journal of Consulting and Clinical Psychology,* 1968, *32,* 276-279.

Gregory, M. K. Emotional indicators on the Bender-Gestalt and the Devereux Child Behavior Rating Scale. *Psychology in the Schools,* 1977, *14,* 433-437.

Griffith, R. M., & Taylor, V. H. Bender-Gestalt figure rotations: A stimulus factor. *Journal of Consulting Psychology,* 1961, *25,* 89-90.

Guertin, W. H., & Davis, H. C. Similarities of meaning of elements and figures of the Bender-Gestalt. *Journal of Projective Techniques,* 1963, *27,* 68-72.

Guilford, J. P., & Zimmerman, W. S. *The Guilford-Zimmerman Aptitude Survey.* Part V. *Spatial Orientation.* Beverly Hills, Calif.: Sheridan Supply, 1947.

Guilford, J. P., & Zimmerman, W. S. *The Guilford-Zimmerman Aptitude Survey.* Part VI. *Spatial Visualization.* Beverly Hills, Calif.: Sheridan Supply, 1953.

Hain, J. D. The Bender-Gestalt Test: A scoring method for identifying brain damage. *Journal of Consulting Psychology,* 1964, *28,* 34-40.

Hammer, E. Acting out and its prediction by projective drawing assessment. In L. E. Abt and S. L. Weissman (Eds.), *Acting Out: Theoretical and Clinical Aspects.* New York: Grune & Stratton, 1965.

Handler, L., & McIntosh, J. Predicting aggression and withdrawal in children with the Draw-A-Person and Bender Gestalt. *Journal of Personality Assessment,* 1971, *35,* 331-337.

Hartlage, L. C. Differential diagnosis of dyslexia, minimal brain damage and emotional disturbances in children. *Psychology in the Schools,* 1970, *7,* 403-406.

Hartlage, L. C., & Lucas, D. G. Scaled score transformations of Bender Gestalt expectancy levels for young children. *Psychology in the Schools,* 1971, *8,* 76-78.

Hartlage, L. C., & Lucas, T. L. Differential correlates of Bender-Gestalt and Beery Visual Motor Integration test for black and for white children. *Perceptual and Motor Skills,* 1976, *43,* 1039-1042.

Hasazi, J. E., Allen, R. M., & Wohlford, P. Effects of mode of administration on Bender-Gestalt Test performance of familial retardates. *Journal of Clinical Psychology,* 1971, *27,* 360-362.

Hauer, A. L., & Armentrout, J. A. Failure of the Bender-Gestalt and Wechsler tests to differentiate children with and without seizure disorders. *Perceptual and Motor Skills,* 1978, *47,* 199-202.

Hayden, B. S., Talmadge, M., Hall, M., & Schiff, D. Diagnosing minimal brain damage in children: A comparison of two scoring systems. *Merrill-Palmer Quarterly of Behavior and Development,* 1970, *16,* 278-285.

Haynes, J. R. Factor-analytic study of performance on the Bender-Gestalt. *Journal of Consulting and Clinical Psychology,* 1970, *34,* 345-347.

Haynes, J. R., & Sells, S. B. Assessment of organic brain damage by psychological tests. *Psychological Bulletin,* 1963, *60,* 316-325.

Henderson, N. B., Butler, B. U., & Gaffeney, B. Effectiveness of the WISC and Bender Gestalt test in predicting arithmetic and reading achievement of white and nonwhite children. *Journal of Clinical Psychology,* 1969, *25,* 268-271.

Hirschenfang, S., Berman, D., & Benton, J. G. Follow-up study of Bender-

Gestalt reproductions by right and left hemiplegic patients. *Perceptual and Motor Skills*, 1967, *25*, 339-340.

Hirschenfang, S., Schulman, L., & Benton, J. G. Psychosocial factors influencing the rehabilitation of the hemiplegic patient. *Diseases of the Nervous System*, 1968, *29*, 373-379.

Hirschenfang, S., Silber, M., & Benton, J. G. Comparison of Bender-Gestalt reproductions by patients with peripheral neuropathy. *Perceptual and Motor Skills*, 1967, *24*, 1317-1318.

Hofmann, R. J. A common factor structure of Bender Gestalt protocols of young children. *Perceptual and Motor Skills*, 1976, *42*, 1039-1048.

Holland, T. R., & Wadsworth, H. M. Comparison and contribution of recall and Background Interference Procedures for the Bender-Gestalt Test with brain-damaged and schizophrenic patients. *Journal of Personality Assessment*, 1979, *43*, 123-127.

Holroyd, J. Cross validation of the Koppitz Bender-Gestalt signs of cerebral dysfunctioning. *Journal of Clinical Psychology*, 1966, *22*, 200.

Holroyd, R. G. On the translation of Koppitz' normative data into standard scores: A response to Furr. *Journal of Clinical Psychology*, 1971, *27*, 88.

Horine, L. C., & Fulkerson, S. C. Utility of the Canter Background Interference Procedure of differentiating among the schizophrenias. *Journal of Personality Assessment*, 1973, *37*, 48-52.

Howard, J. The group Bender Gestalt test as a screening procedure for the identification of children with lag in visual perceptual development. *Journal of School Psychology*, 1970, *8*, 64-65.

Hunter, E. J., & Johnson, L. C. Developmental and psychological differences between readers and nonreaders. *Journal of Learning Disabilities*, 1971, *4*, 572-577.

Hustak, T. L., Dinning, W. D., & Andert, J. N. Reliability of the Koppitz scoring system of the Bender Gestalt test. *Journal of Clinical Psychology*, 1976, *32*, 468-469.

Hutt, M. L. *A Tentative Guide for the Administration and Interpretation of the Bender-Gestalt Test.* U.S. Army Adjutant General's School. (Restricted) 1945.

Hutt, M. L. The projective use of the Bender-Gestalt test. In A. L. Rabin (Ed.), *Projective Techniques in Personality Assessment.* New York: Springer, 1968.

Hutt, M. L. *The Hutt Adaptation of the Bender-Gestalt Test.* (2nd ed.) New York: Grune & Stratton, 1969.

Hutt, M. L. *The Hutt Adaptation of the Bender-Gestalt Test.* (3rd ed.) New York: Grune & Stratton, 1977.

Hutt, M. L. The Hutt Adaptation of the Bender-Gestalt Test: Diagnostic and therapeutic implications. In B. B. Wolman (Ed.). *Clinical Diagnosis of Mental Disorders.* New York: Plenum, 1978.

Hutt, M. L. Adience-abience. In R. H. Woddy (Ed.), *Encyclopedia of Clinical Assessment*. San Francisco: Jossey-Bass, in press.

Hutt, M. L., & Briskin, G. J. *The Clinical Use of the Revised Bender Gestalt Test*. New York: Grune & Stratton, 1960.

Hutt, M. L., & Dates, B. G. Reliabilities and interrelationships of two HABGT scales in a male delinquent population. *Journal of Personality Assessment*, 1977, *41*, 353-357.

Hutt, M. L., Dates, B. G., & Reid, D. M. The predictive ability of HABGT scales for a male delinquent population. *Journal of Personality Assessment*, 1977, *41*, 492-496.

Hutt, M. L., & Gibby, R. G. *An Atlas for the Hutt Adaptation of the Bender-Gestalt Test*. New York: Grune & Stratton, 1970.

Hutt, M. L., & Miller, L. J. Further studies of a measure of adience-abience: Reliability. *Journal of Personality Assessment*, 1975, *39*, 123-128.

Hutt, M. L., & Miller, L. J. Interrelationships of psychopathology and adience-abience on the HABGT. *Journal of Personality Assessment*, 1976, *40*, 135-139.

Hutton, J. B. Bender recall of children as related to age and intelligence. *Perceptual and Motor Skills*, 1966, *23*, 34.

Isaac, B. Perceptual-motor development of first graders related to class, race, intelligence, visual discrimination and motivation. *Journal of School Psychology*, 1973, *11*, 47-55.

Jacobs, E. A., Winter, P. M., Alvis, H. J., & Small S. M. Hyperoxygenation effect on cognitive functioning in the aged. *New England Journal of Medicine*, 1969, *281*, 753-757.

Jacobs, J. C. Group administration of the Bender Gestalt Test. *Psychology in the Schools*, 1971, *8*, 345-346.

Jansky, J., & deHirsch, K. *Preventing Reading Failure*. New York: Harper & Row, Publishers, 1972.

Jernigan, A. J. Large scale assessment of state mental patients. *Journal of Clinical Psychology*, 1967, *23*, 504-506. (a)

Jernigan, A. J. Rotation style on the Bender Gestalt Test. *Journal of Clinical Psychology*, 1967, *23*, 176-179. (b)

Johnson, J. E., Hellkamp, D. J., & Lottman, T. J. The relationship between intelligence, brain damage, and Hutt-Briskin errors on the Bender-Gestalt. *Journal of Clinical Psychology*, 1971, *27*, 84-85.

Johnson, J. H. Bender-Gestalt constriction as an indicator of depression in psychiatric patients. *Journal of Personality Assessment*, 1973, *37*, 53-55.

Jolles, I. *A Catalogue for the Qualitative Interpretation of the House-Tree-Person*. Beverly Hills, Calif.: Western Psychological Services, 1964.

Kagan, J. Impulsive and reflective children: Significance of conceptual tempo. In J. D. Krumboltz (Ed.), *Learning and the Educational Process.* Chicago: Rand McNally, 1965.

Kaspar, J. C., & Lampell, A. K. Interrater reliability for scoring the Bender Gestalt using the Koppitz method. *Perceptual and Motor Skills,* 1972, *34,* 765-766.

Keim, R. P. Visual-motor training, readiness, and intelligence of kindergarten children. *Journal of Learning Disabilities,* 1970, *3,* 256-259.

Kelly, T. J., & Amble, B. R. I.Q. and perceptual motor scores as predictors of achievement among retarded children. *Journal of School Psychology,* 1970, *8,* 99-103.

Kennedy, W. A. Cultural deprivation: Its role in central nervous system functioning. In J. L. Khanna, (Ed.) *Brain Damage and Mental Retardation: A Psychological Evaluation.* Springfield: Charles C Thomas, Publisher, 1968.

Kenny, T. J. Background Interference Procedure: A means of assessing neurologic dysfunction in school-age children. *Journal of Consulting and Clinical Psychology,* 1971, *37,* 44-46.

Kent, G. H. Emergency battery of one-minute tests. *Journal of Psychology,* 1942, *13,* 141-164.

Keogh, B. K. The Bender Gestalt as a predictive and diagnostic test of reading performance. *Journal of Consulting Psychology,* 1965, *29,* 83-84. (a)

Keogh, B. K. School achievement associated with successful performance on the Bender Gestalt Test. *Journal of School Psychology,* 1965, *3,* 37-40. (b)

Keogh, B. K. The copying ability of young children. *New Research in Education,* 1968, *11,* 43-47.

Keogh, B. K., & Becker, L. D. Early detection of learning problems: Questions, cautions and guidelines. *Exceptional Children,* 1973, *40,* 5-12.

Keogh, B. K., & Smith, C. E. Group techniques and proposed scoring system for the Bender Gestalt Test with children. *Journal of Clinical Psychology,* 1961, *17,* 172-175.

Keogh, B. K., & Smith, C. E. Visual-motor ability for school prediction: A seven year study. *Perceptual and Motor Skills,* 1967, *25,* 101-110. (a)

Keogh, B. K., & Smith, C. E. Changes in copying ability of young children. *Perceptual and Motor Skills,* 1968, *26,* 773-774. (b)

Keogh, B. K., Vernon, M., & Smith, C. E. Deafness and visual-motor function. *Journal of Special Education,* 1970, *4,* 41-47.

Keogh, B. K., & Vormeland, O. Performance of Norwegian children on the Bender Gestalt and Draw-A-Person tests. *Scandinavian Journal of Education,* 1970, *14,* 105-111.

Kerekjarto, M. von. Untersuchung über die Diskriminationskraft dreier Tests zur Erfassung Zerebraler Schaden. Bericht über den 23. Kongress Deutscher Gestalt für Psychologie, Göttingen, 1962.

Kerr, A. S. Determinants of performance of the Bender Gestalt Test and Raven's Progressive Matrices (1947) Test. *Journal of Learning Disabilities,* 1972, *5,* 219-221.

Klatskin, E. H., McNamara, N. E., Shaffer, D., & Pincus, J. Minimal organicity in children of normal intelligence: Correspondence between psychological test results and neurological findings. *Journal of Learning Disabilities,* 1972, *5,* 213-218.

Klopfer, B., Ainsworth, D., Klopfer, W. G., & Holt, R. R. *Developments in the Rorschach Technique.* Vol. I. New York: Harcourt, Brace & World, 1954.

Ko, Y. The frequency of eye-movement on the Bender Gestalt Test as a measure of attention breadth. *Acta Psychologica Taiwanica,* 1971, *13,* 67-74.

Ko, Y. The Bender-Gestalt Test as a test for visual-verbal coordination. *Acta Psychologica Taiwanica,* 1972, *14,* 52-66.

Koppitz, E. M. The Bender-Gestalt Test and learning disturbance in young children. *Journal of Clinical Psychology,* 1958, *14,* 292-295.

Koppitz, E. M. The Bender-Gestalt Test for children: A normative study. *Journal of Clinical Psychology,* 1960, *16,* 432-435.

Koppitz, E. M. Diagnosing brain damage in young children with the Bender Gestalt Test. *Journal of Consulting Psychology,* 1962, *26,* 541-546.

Koppitz, E. M. *The Bender-Gestalt Test for Young Children.* New York: Grune & Stratton, 1964.

Koppitz, E. M. Emotional indicators on human figure drawings of shy and aggressive children. *Journal of Clinical Psychology,* 1966, *22,* 466-469.

Koppitz, E. M. Brain damage, reading disability, and the Bender Gestalt Test. *Journal of Learning Disabilities,* 1970, *3,* 420-433.

Koppitz, E. M. *Children with Learning Disabilities: A Five-year Follow-up Study.* New York: Grune & Stratton, 1971.

Koppitz, E. M. Bender Gestalt Test performance and school achievement: A nine year study. *Psychology in the Schools,* 1973, *10,* 280-284.

Koppitz, E. M. The Bender Gestalt test and Visual Aural Digit Span Test and reading achievement. *Journal of Learning Disabilities,* 1975, *8,* 154-157. (a)

Koppitz, E. M. *The Bender Gestalt Test for Young Children.* (Vol. 2). New York: Grune & Stratton, 1975. (b)

Koppitz, E. M., Mardis, V., & Stephens, T. A note on screening school beginners with the Bender Gestalt Test. *Journal of Educational Psychology,* 1961, *52,* 80-81.

Koppitz, E. M., Sullivan, J., Blyth, D. D., & Shelton, J. Prediction of first grade achievement with the Bender-Gestalt Test and human figure drawings. *Journal of Clinical Psychology,* 1959, *15,* 164-168.

Korin, H. Comparison of psychometric measures in psychiatric patients using heroin and other drugs. *Journal of Abnormal Psychology,* 1974, *83,* 208-212.

Korman, M., & Blumberg, S. Comparative efficiency of some tests of cerebral damage. *Journal of Consulting Psychology,* 1963, *27,* 303-309.

Korner, I. N. Test report evaluation. *Journal of Clinical Psychology,* 1962, *28,* 194-197.

Kramer, E., & Fenwick, J. Differential diagnosis with the Bender Gestalt Test. *Journal of Projective Techniques and Personality Assessment,* 1966, *30,* 59-61.

Krauft, V. B., & Krauft, C. C. Structured vs. unstructured visual-motor tests for educable retarded children. *Perceptual and Motor Skills,* 1972, *34,* 691-694.

Krop, H. D., & Smith, C. R. Effects of special education on Bender-Gestalt performance of the mentally retarded. *American Journal of Mental Deficiency,* 1969, *73,* 693-699.

Kwawer, J. S. Male homosexual psychodynamics and the Rorschach test. *Journal of Personality Assessment,* 1977, *41,* 10-18.

Labrentz, E., Linkenhoker, F., & Aaron, P. G. Recognition and reproduction of Bender Gestalt figures: A developmental study of the lag between perception and performance. *Psychology in the Schools,* 1976, *13,* 128-133.

Lachmann, F. M., Bailey, M. A., & Berrick, M. E. The relationship between manifest anxiety and the clinician's evaluations of projective test responses. *Journal of Clinical Psychology,* 1961, *17,* 11-13.

Lacks, P. B., Colbert, J., Harrow, M., & Levine, J. Further evidence concerning the diagnostic accuracy of the Halstead organic test battery. *Journal of Clinical Psychology,* 1970, *26,* 480-481.

Lambert, N. M. Predicting and evaluating the effectiveness of children in school. In E. M. Bower and W. G. Hollister (Eds.), *Behavioral Science Frontiers in Education.* New York: Wiley, 1967.

Lambert, N. M. An evaluation of scoring categories applicable to children's performance on the Bender Visual Motor Gestalt Test. *Psychology in the Schools,* 1970, *7,* 275-287.

Lambert, N. M. An item analysis and validity investigation of Bender Visual Motor Gestalt Test score items. *Psychology in the Schools,* 1971, *8,* 78-85.

Landis, B., Baxter, J., Patterson, R. H., & Tauber, C. E. Bender-Gestalt evaluation of brain dysfunction following open-heart surgery. *Journal of Personality Assessment,* 1974, *38,* 556-562.

Lapointe, R. E. The use of psychological tests by Ontario psychologists. *Ontario Psychologist,* 1974, *6,* 75-82.

Larsen, S. C., Rogers, D., & Sowell, V. The use of selected perceptual tests in differentiating between normal and learning disabled children. *Journal of Learning Disabilities*, 1976, 9, 85-90.

Leonard, C. V. Bender-Gestalt as an indicator of suicidal potential. *Psychological Reports*, 1973, 32, 665-666.

Lerner, E. A. *The Projective Use of the Bender-Gestalt Test*. Springfield: Charles C Thomas, Publisher, 1972.

Lessler, K., & Bridges, J. S. The prediction of learning problems in a rural setting: Can we improve on readiness tests? *Journal of Learning Disabilities*, 1973, 6, 90-94.

Lessler, K. M., Schoeniger, D. W., & Bridges, J. S. Prediction of first grade performance. *Perceptual and Motor Skills*, 1970, 31, 751-756.

Levine, J., & Feirstein, A. Differences in test performance between brain-damaged, schizophrenic, and medical patients. *Journal of Consulting and Clinical Psychology*, 1972, 39, 508-511.

Levy, M. R., & Fox, H. M. Psychological testing is alive and well. *Professional Psychology*, 1975, 6, 420-434.

Lieberman, L. R. Drawing norms for the Bender-Gestalt figures. *Journal of Clinical Psychology*, 1968, 24, 458-463.

Lifshitz, M. Bender-Gestalt Test and social interaction of kindergarten children: Effects of socialization practices. *Psychology in the Schools*, 1978, 15, 180-188.

Lingren, R. H. Performance of disabled and normal readers on Bender-Gestalt, Auditory Discrimination Test and visual-motor matching. *Perceptual and Motor Skills*, 1969, 29, 152-154.

Locher, J., & Worms, F. Visual scanning strategies of neurologically impaired, perceptually impaired, and normal children viewing the Bender-Gestalt designs. *Psychology in the Schools*, 1970, 14, 147-157.

Lowenfeld, M. *The Lowenfeld Mosaic Test*. London: Newman Neame, 1954.

Lubin, B., Wallis, R. R., & Paine, C. Patterns of psychological test usage in the United States: 1935-1969. *Professional Psychology*, 1971, 2, 70-74.

Lyle, O. E., & Gottesman, I. I. Premorbid psychometric indicators of the gene for Huntington's Disease. *Journal of Consulting and Clinical Psychology*, 1977, 45, 1011-1022.

Lyle, O., & Quast, W. The Bender Gestalt: Use of clinical judgment versus recall scores in prediction of Huntington's Disease. *Journal of Consulting and Clinical Psychology*, 1976, 44, 229-232.

Maloney, M. P., & Ward, M. P. Bender-Gestalt Test performance of "organic" and "functional" mentally retarded subjects. *Perceptual and Motor Skills*, 1970, 31, 860.

Marmorale, A. M., & Brown, F. Comparison of Bender Gestalt and WISC correlations for Puerto Rican, white, and Negro children. *Journal of Clinical Psychology*, 1975, 31, 465-468.

Marmorale, A. M., & Brown, F. Bender-Gestalt performance of Puerto Rican, white, and Negro children. *Journal of Clinical Psychology*, 1977, *33*, 224-228.

Marsh, G. G. Impaired visual-motor ability of children with Duchenne muscular dystrophy. *Perceptual and Motor Skills*, 1972, *35*, 504-506.

Matranga, J. T., Jensen, D. E., & Prandoni, J. R. Bender-Gestalt protocols of adult Negro male offenders: Normative data. *Perceptual and Motor Skills*, 1972, *35*, 101-102.

McCarthy, D. P. The feasibility of a group Bender-Gestalt Test for pre-school and primary school-aged children. *Journal of School Psychology*, 1975, *13*, 134-141.

McConnell, O. L. Koppitz' Bender-Gestalt scores in relation to organic and emotional problems in children. *Journal of Clinical Psychology*, 1967, *23*, 370-374.

McGuire, F. L. A comparison of the Bender-Gestalt and flicker fusion as indicators of central nervous system involvement. *Journal of Clinical Psychology*, 1960, *16*, 276-278.

McHugh, A. Children's figure drawings in neurotic and conduct disturbances. *Journal of Clinical Psychology*, 1966, *22*, 219-221.

McNamara, J. R., Porterfield, C. L., & Miller, L. E. The relationship of the Wechsler Preschool and Primary Scale of Intelligence with the Colored Progressive Matrices (1956) and Bender Gestalt Test. *Journal of Clinical Psychology* 1969, *25*, 65-68.

Michel, W. *Personality and Assessment.* New York: Wiley, 1968.

Miller, L. C., Lowenfeld, R., Linder, R., & Turner J. Reliability of Koppitz' scoring system for the Bender Gestalt. *Journal of Clinical Psychology*, 1963, *19*, 211.

Miller, L. J., & Hutt, M. L. Psychopathology scale of the Hutt adaptation of the Bender-Gestalt Test: Reliability. *Journal of Personality Assessment*, 1975, *39*, 129-131.

Mills, H. D. The research use of projective techniques: A seventeen year survey. *Journal of Projective Techniques and Personality Assessment*, 1965, *29*, 513-515.

Mlodnosky, L. B. The Bender Gestalt and the Frostig as predictors of first grade reading achievement among economically deprived children. *Psychology in the Schools*, 1972, *9*, 25-30.

Money, J., & Nurcombe, B. Ability tests and cultural heritage: The Draw-A-Person and Bender tests in Aboriginal Australia. *Journal of Learning Disabilities*, 1974, *7*, 297-303.

Mordock, J. B. Effect of stress on perceptual-motor functioning of adolescents with learning difficulties. *Perceptual and Motor Skills*, 1969, *29*, 883-886. (a)

Mordock, J. B. A procedural critique of "Bender Gestalts of organic children: Accuracy of clinical judgement." *Journal of Projective Techniques and Personality Assessment*, 1969, *33*, 489-491. (b)

Mordock, J. B., Terrill, P. A., & Novik, E. The Bender-Gestalt Test in differential diagnosis of adolescents with learning difficulties. *Journal of School Psychology,* 1968, *7,* 11-14.

Morgenstern, M., & McIvor, W. The relationship between Bender Gestalt performance and achievement among retardates. *Training School Bulletin,* 1973, *70,* 84-87.

Morsbach, G., Del Priori, C., & Furnell, J. Two aspects of scorer reliability in the Bender-Gestalt Test. *Journal of Clinical Psychology,* 1975, *31,* 90-93.

Mosher, D. L., & Smith, J. P. The usefulness of two scoring systems for the Bender Gestalt Test for identifying brain damage. *Journal of Consulting Psychology,* 1965, *29,* 530-536.

Munz, A., & Tolor, A. Psychological effects of major cerebral excision: Intellectual and emotional changes following hemispherectomy. *Journal of Nervous and Mental Disease,* 1955, *121,* 438-443.

Murphy, G. M. Visual-motor coordination and perception at the beginning of the first grade. *New England Guidance Research Digest,* 1964, *5,* 9.

Murstein, B. I. Discussion for current status of some projective techniques. *Journal of Projective Techniques and Personality Assessment,* 1968, *32,* 229-232.

Nahas, A. D. The prediction of perceptual motor abnormalities in paranoid schizophrenia. *Research Communications in Psychology, Psychiatry and Behavior,* 1976, *1,* 167-181.

Nawas, M. M., & Worth, J. W. Suicidal configurations in the Bender-Gestalt. *Journal of Projective Techniques and Personality Assessment,* 1968, *32,* 392-394.

Nemec, R. E. Effects of controlled background interference on test performance by right and left hemiplegics. *Journal of Consulting and Clinical Psychology,* 1978, *46,* 294-297.

Newcomer, P., & Hammill, D. Visual perception of motor impaired children: Implications for assessment. *Exceptional Children,* 1973, *39,* 335-337.

Nielson, H. H., & Ringe, K. Visuo-perceptive and visuo-motor performance of children with reading disabilities. *Scandinavian Journal of Psychology,* 1969, *10,* 225-231.

Norfleet, M. A. The Bender Gestalt as a group screening instrument for first grade reading potential. *Journal of Learning Disabilities,* 1973, *6,* 384-388.

Norton, J. C. The Trail Making Test and Bender Background Interference Procedure as screening devices. *Journal of Clinical Psychology,* 1978, *34,* 916-922.

Oberleder, M. Adapting current psychological techniques for use in testing the aging. *Gerontologist,* 1967, *7,* 188-191.

Obrzut, J. E., Taylor, H. D., & Thweatt, R. C. Re-examination of Koppitz' Developmental Bender Scoring System. *Perceptual and Motor Skills,* 1972, *34,* 279-282.

Oliver, R. A., & Kronenberger, E. J. Testing the applicability of Koppitz's Bender-Gestalt scores to brain-damaged, emotionally disturbed and normal adolescents. *Psychology in the Schools,* 1971, *8,* 250-253.

Pacella, J. J. Inter-examiner effects on the Bender-Gestalt. *Journal of Clinical Psychology,* 1962, *18,* 23-26.

Pacella, M. J. The performance of brain damaged mental retardates on successive trials of the Bender-Gestalt. *American Journal of Mental Deficiency,* 1965, *69,* 723-728.

Palkes, H., & Stewart, M. Intellectual ability and performance of hyperactive children. *American Journal of Orthopsychiatry,* 1972, *42,* 35-39.

Pardue, A. M. Bender-Gestalt test and background interference procedure in discernment of organic brain damage. *Perceptual and Motor Skills,* 1975, *40,* 103-109.

Pascal, G. R., & Suttell, B. J. *The Bender-Gestalt Test.* New York: Grune & Stratton, 1951.

Pascal, G. R., & Thoroughman, J. C. Relationship between Bender-Gestalt test scores and the response of patients with intractable duodenal ulcer to surgery. *Psychosomatic Medicine,* 1964, *26,* 625-627.

Patel, S., & Bharucha, E. P. The Bender Gestalt Test as a measure of perceptual and visuo-motor defects in cerebral palsied children. *Developmental Medicine and Child Neurology,* 1972, *14,* 156-160.

Pauker, J. D. A quick-scoring system for the Bender-Gestalt: Interrater reliability and scoring validity. *Journal of Clinical Psychology,* 1976, *32,* 86-89.

Peek, R. M., & Quast, W. A. *A Scoring System for the Bender Gestalt Test.* Minneapolis, Minn.: Authors, 1951.

Peoples, C., & Moll, R. P. Bender Gestalt performance as a function of drawing ability, school performance, and intelligence. *Journal of Clinical Psychology,* 1962, *18,* 106-107.

Phelps, W. R. Further evidence on the Hain scoring method of the Bender-Gestalt Test. *Journal of Learning Disabilities,* 1968, *1,* 358-360.

Piaget, J. *The Child's Conception of Number.* London: Routledge & Kegan Paul, 1952.

Piaget, J. *The Child's Conception of Space.* London: Routledge & Kegan Paul, 1956.

Piaget, J. *The Child's Conception of Geometry,* London: Routledge & Kegan Paul, 1960.

Plenk, A. M. Development of a scoring system for the Bender Gestalt Test for children of preschool age. Unpublished doctoral dissertation, University of Utah, 1968.

Plenk, A. M., & Jones, J. An examination of the Bender Gestalt performance of three and four year olds and its relationship to Koppitz scoring system. *Journal of Clinical Psychology*, 1967, *23*, 367-370.

Pope, P., & Snyder, R. T. Modification of selected Bender designs and interpretations of the first graders' visual-perception maturation with implications for Gestalt theory. *Perceptual and Motor Skills*, 1970, *30*, 263-267.

Prado, W. M., Peyman, D. A., & Lacey, O. L. A validation study of measures of flattened affect on the Bender-Gestalt Test. *Journal of Clinical Psychology*, 1960, *16*, 435-438.

Psychological Research and Development Corporation. *Spiral Aftereffect Manual*. Tampa, Fla.: Author, 1958.

Quattlebaum, L. F. A brief note on the relationship between two psychomotor tests. *Journal of Clinical Psychology*, 1968, *24*, 198-199.

Quattlebaum, L. F., & White, W. F. Relationships among the Quick Test, two measures of psychomotor functioning, and age. *Perceptual and Motor Skills*, 1969, *29*, 824-826.

Raskin, L. M., Bloom, A. S., Klee, S. H., & Reese, A. The assessment of developmentally disabled children with the WISC-R, Binet and other tests. *Journal of Clinical Psychology*, 1978, *34*, 111-114.

Reinehr, R. C., & Golightly, C. The relationship between the Bender Gestalt and the Organic Integrity Test. *Journal of Clinical Psychology*, 1968, *24*, 203-204.

Reitan, R. M. *Trail Making Test: Manual for Administration, Scoring, and Interpretation*. Indianapolis, Ind.: 1956 (Mimeo).

Reitman, E. E., & Cleveland, S. E. Changes in body image following sensory deprivation in schizophrenic and control groups. *Journal of Abnormal and Social Psychology*, 1964, *68*, 168-176.

Reznikoff, M., & Olin, T. D. Recall of the Bender Gestalt designs by organic and schizophrenic patients: A comparative study. *Journal of Clinical Psychology*, 1957, *8*, 183-186.

Rice, J. A. Feasibility of perceptual-motor training for Head-start children: An empirical test. *Perceptual and Motor Skills*, 1972, *34*, 909-910.

Richardson, W., & Rubino, C. The Purdue Perceptual Motor Survey and the Bender Gestalt as measures of perceptual motor abilities in children. *Ontario Psychologist*, 1971, *3*, 243-247.

Rimmer, A., & Weiss, A. A. A model of conceptual development for the Bender-Gestalt Test. *Israel Annals of Psychiatry and Related Disciplines*. 1972, *10*, 188-196.

Roback, H. B. Human figure drawings: Their utility in the clinical psychologist's armamentarium for personality assessment. *Psychological Bulletin*, 1968, *70*, 1-19.

Rockland, L. H., & Pollin, W. Quantification of psychiatric mental status. *Archives of General Psychiatry*, 1965, *12*, 23-28.

Rogers, D. L., & Swenson, W. M. Bender-Gestalt recall as a measure of memory versus distractibility. *Perceptual and Motor Skills*, 1975, *40*, 919-922.

Roos, P. Performance of psychiatric patients on two measures of ego strength. *Journal of Clinical Psychology*, 1962, *28*, 48-50.

Rosecrans, C. J., & Schaffer, H. B. Bender-Gestalt time and score differences between matched groups of hospitalized psychiatric and brain damaged patients. *Journal of Clinical Psychology*, 1969, *25*, 409-410.

Roseman, M. F., & Albergottie, G. J. Personality scales of the Bender-Gestalt Test. *Catalog of Selected Documents in Psychology*, 1973, *3*, 10.

Rosenberg, L. A., & Rosenberg, A. M. The effect of tachistoscopic presentation on the Hutt-Briskin Bender-Gestalt scoring system. *Journal of Clinical Psychology*, 1965, *21*, 314-316.

Royer, F. L., & Holland, T. R. Rotations of visual designs in psychopathological groups. *Journal of Consulting and Clinical Psychology*, 1975, *43*, 546-556.

Ruckhaber, C. J. A technique for group administration of the Bender Gestalt Test. *Psychology in the Schools*, 1964, *1*, 53-56.

Russell, E. W. The Bender-Gestalt and the Halstead-Reitan battery: A case study. *Journal of Clinical Psychology*, 1976, *32*, 355-361.

Ryckman, D. B., Rentfrow, R., Fargo, G., & McCartin, R. Reliabilities of three tests of form-copying. *Perceptual and Motor Skills*, 1972, *34*, 917-918.

Sabatino, D. A., & Becker, J. T. Relations among five basic tests of behavior. *Perceptual and Motor Skills*, 1969, *29*, 487-490.

Sabatino, D. A., & Cramblett, H. G. Behavioral sequelae of California encephalitis virus infection in children. *Developmental Medicine and Child Neurology*, 1968, *10*, 331-337.

Sabatino, D. A., & Ysseldyke, J. E. Effect of extraneous "background" on visual-perceptual performance of readers and non-readers. *Perceptual and Motor Skills*, 1972, *35*, 323-328.

Safrin, R. K. Differences in visual perception and in visual-motor functioning between psychotic and nonpsychotic children. *Journal of Consulting Psychology*, 1964, *28*, 41-45.

Sahay, M., & Singh, M. V. Time factor as a prognostic indicator on the Bender-Gestalt test. *Journal of Clinical Psychology*, 1975, *31*, 720-722.

Salzman, L. F., & Harway, N. I. Size of Bender-Gestalt drawings in psychotic depression. *Perceptual and Motor Skills*, 1965, *20*, 1235-1236.

Salzman, L. F., & Harway, N. I. Size of figure drawings of psychotically depressed patients. *Journal of Abnormal Psychology*, 1967, *72*, 205-207.

Satz, P., Rardin, D., & Ross, J. An evaluation of a theory of specific developmental dyslexia. *Child Development*, 1971, *42*, 2009-2021.

Schulberg, H. C., & Tolor, A. The use of the Bender-Gestalt in clinical practice. *Journal of Projective Techniques,* 1961, *25,* 347-351.

Schulberg, H. C., & Tolor, A. The "meaning" of the Bender-Gestalt Test designs to mental patients. *Journal of Projective Techniques,* 1962, *26,* 455-461.

Schwartz, M. L., & Dennerll, R. D. Immediate visual memory as a function of epileptic seizure type. *Cortex,* 1969, *5,* 69-74.

Schwartz, M. L., & Dennerll, R. D. Neuropsychological assessment of children with, without, and with questionable epileptogenic dysfunction. *Perceptual and Motor Skills,* 1970, *30,* 111-121.

Shapiro, E., Shapiro, A. K., & Clarkin, J. Clinical psychology testing in Tourette's syndrome. *Journal of Personality Assessment,* 1974, *38,* 464-478.

Shemberg, K., & Keeley, S. Psychodiagnostic training in the academic setting: Past and present. *Journal of Consulting and Clinical Psychology,* 1970, *34,* 205-211.

Silber, M., Hirschenfang, S., & Benton, J. G. Psychological factors and prognosis in peripheral neuropathy. *Diseases of the Nervous System,* 1968, *29,* 688-692.

Silberberg, N., & Feldt, L. Intellectual and perceptual correlates of reading difficulties. *Journal of School Psychology,* 1968, *6,* 237-245.

Silverstein, A. B. Psychological testing practices in state institutions for the mentally retarded. *American Journal of Mental Deficiency,* 1963, *68,* 440-445.

Silverstein, A. B., & Mohan, P. J. Bender-Gestalt figure rotations in the mentally retarded. *Journal of Consulting Psychology,* 1962, *26,* 386-388.

Simensen, R. J. Correlations among Bender-Gestalt, WISC block design, Memory-For-Designs, and Pupil Rating Scale. *Perceptual and Motor Skills,* 1974, *38,* 1249-1250. (a)

Simensen, R. J. Bender-Gestalt correlates among normal and retarded students: CA, IQ, and pursuit rotor performance. *Journal of Clinical Psychology,* 1974, *30,* 172-175. (b)

Singh, B. The Bender-Gestalt Test as a group test. *Ontario Journal of Educational Research,* 1965, *8,* 35-45.

Smith, A. Ambiguities in concepts and studies of "brain damage" and "organicity." *Journal of Nervous and Mental Disease,* 1962, *135,* 311-326.

Smith, C. E., & Keogh, B. K. The group Bender-Gestalt as a reading readiness screening instrument. *Perceptual and Motor Skills,* 1962, *15,* 639-645.

Smith, C. E., & Keogh, B. K. Developmental changes on the Bender Gestalt Test. *Perceptual and Motor Skills,* 1963, *17,* 465-466.

Smith, D. C., & Martin, R. A. Use of learning cues with the Bender Visual Motor Gestalt Test in screening children for neurological impairment. *Journal of Consulting Psychology,* 1967, *31,* 205-209.

Snortum, J. R. Performance of different diagnostic groups on the tachistoscopic and copy phases of the Bender-Gestalt. *Journal of Consulting Psychology,* 1965, *29,* 345-351.

Snyder, R. T., & Freud, S. L. Reading readiness and its relation to maturational unreadiness as measured by the spiral after-effect and other visual-perceptual techniques. *Perceptual and Motor Skills,* 1967, *25,* 841-854.

Snyder, R. T., Holowenzak, S. P., & Hoffman, N. A cross-cultural item-analysis of Bender-Gestalt protocols administered to ghetto and suburban children. *Perceptual and Motor Skills,* 1971, *33,* 791-796.

Snyder, R. T., & Kalil, J. Item analysis, inter-examiner reliability and scoring problems for Koppitz scoring on the Bender Gestalt for six-year olds. *Perceptual and Motor Skills,* 1968, *27,* 1351-1358.

Snyder, R. T., & Snyder, P. P. Maturational changes in visual-motor perception: An item analysis of Bender-Gestalt errors from ages 6 to 11. *Perceptual and Motor Skills,* 1974, *38,* 51-59.

Song, A. Y., & Song, R. H. The Bender-Gestalt Test with the Background Interference Procedure in mental retardates. *Journal of Clinical Psychology,* 1969, *25,* 69-71.

Spache, G. D., & Spache, E. B. *Reading in the Elementary School.* Boston: Allyn and Bacon, Inc., 1973.

Spivack, G., & Spotts, J. *Devereux Child Behavior (DCB) Rating Scale Manual.* Devon, Penn.: The Devereux Press, 1966.

Spraings, V. *The Spraings Multiple Choice Bender Gestalt Test.* Olympia, Wash.: Sherwood Press, 1966.

Spreen, O., & Benton, A. L. Comparative studies of some psychological tests for cerebral damage. *Journal of Nervous and Mental Disease,* 1965, *140,* 323-333.

Stavrianos, B. K. Can projective measures aid in the detection and differential diagnosis of reading deficits? *Journal of Projective Techniques and Personality Assessment,* 1971, *35,* 80-91.

Steinman, W. M. The use of ambiguous stimuli to predict general competence. *Journal of the Scientific Laboratories of Denison University,* 1967, *48,* 7-14.

Sternberg, D., & Levine, A. An indicator of suicidal ideation on the Bender Visual-Motor Gestalt Test. *Journal of Projective Techniques and Personality Assessment,* 1965, *29,* 377-379.

Sternlicht, M., Pustel, G., & Siegel, L. Comparison of organic and cultural-familial retardates on two visual-motor tasks. *American Journal of Mental Deficiency,* 1968, *72,* 887-889.

Stoer, L., Corotto, L. V., & Curnutt, R. H. The role of visual perception in the reproduction of Bender-Gestalt designs. *Journal of Projective Techniques and Personality Assessment,* 1965, *29,* 473-478.

Stone, L. A. A cluster analysis of the Bender Gestalt test designs. *Journal of Clinical Psychology,* 1966, *22,* 94-96.

Sundberg, N. D. The practice of psychological testing in clinical services in the United States. *American Psychologist*, 1961, *16*, 79-83.

Suszek, R. F., & Klopfer, W. G. Interpretation of the Bender-Gestalt Test: The associative value of the figures. *American Journal of Orthopsychiatry*, 1952, *22*, 62-75.

Swenson, C. H. Empirical evaluations of human figure drawings. *Psychological Bulletin*, 1957, *54*, 431-461.

Swenson, C. H. Empirical evaluations of human figure drawings. *Psychological Bulletin*, 1968, *70*, 20-44.

Tamkin, A. S. An evaluation of the construct validity of Barron's ego-strength scale. *Journal of Clinical Psychology*, 1957, *13*, 156-158.

Taylor, H. D., & Thweatt, R. C. Cross-cultural developmental performance of Navajo children on the Bender Gestalt Test. *Perceptual and Motor Skills*, 1972, *35*, 307-309.

Taylor, J. B. The Bender-Gestalt as a measure of intelligence and adjustment in the lower intellectual range. *Journal of Consulting Psychology*, 1965, *29*, 595.

Telegdy, G. A. The effectiveness of four readiness tests as predictors of first grade achievement. *Psychology in the Schools*, 1975, *12*, 4-11.

Temmer, H. W. Wechsler Intelligence scores and Bender-Gestalt performance in adult male mental defectives. *American Journal of Mental Deficiency*, 1965, *70*, 142-147.

Thelen, M. H., & Ewing, D. R. Roles, functions, and training in clinical psychology: A survey of academic clinicians. *American Psychologist*, 1970, *25*, 550-554.

Throne, F. M., Kaspar, J. C., & Schulman, J. L. Performance time and brain damage ratings. *American Journal of Mental Deficiency*, 1964, *68*, 656-659.

Thweatt, R. C. Prediction of school learning disability through the use of the Bender Gestalt Test: A validation study of Koppitz' scoring technique. *Journal of Clinical Psychology*, 1963, *19*, 216-217.

Thweatt, R. C., Obrzut, J. F., & Taylor, H. D. The development and validation of a soft-sign scoring system for the Bender Gestalt. *Psychology in the Schools*, 1972, *9*, 170-174.

Tien, H. C. Organic Integrity Test (OIT). *Archives of General Psychiatry*, 1960, *3*, 43-52.

Tolor, A. Structural properties of the Bender-Gestalt Test associations. *Journal of Clinical Psychology*, 1957, *13*, 176-178.

Tolor, A. The "meaning'" of the Bender-Gestalt designs: A study in the use of the semantic differential. *Journal of Projective Techniques*, 1960, *24*, 433-438.

Tolor, A. Diagnosing the state of the diagnostic function: An analysis of the literature. *Journal of Clinical Psychology*, 1973, *29*, 338-342.

Tolor, A., & Schulberg, H. C. *An Evaluation of the Bender-Gestalt Test.* Springfield: Charles C Thomas, Publisher, 1963.

Tuddenham, R. D. Review of *An Evaluation of the Bender-Gestalt Test* by A. Tolor & H. C. Schulberg. Buros, O. K. (Ed.) *The Sixth Mental Measurements Yearbook.* Highland Park, N.J.: Gryphen Press, 1965.

Uyeno, E. Differentiating psychotics from organics on the Minnesota Percepto-Diagnostic Test. *Journal of Consulting Psychology,* 1963, 27, 462.

Vega, M., & Powell, A. The effects of practice on Bender-Gestalt performance of culturally disadvantaged children. *Florida Journal of Educational Research,* 1970, 12, 45-49.

Verma, S. K. Some perceptuo-motor disturbances on the Bender-Gestalt Test as effected by change in the orientation of paper. *Indian Journal of Clinical Psychology,* 1974, 1, 61-63.

Verma, S. K., Wig, N. N., & Shah, D. K. Validity of Bender Gestalt Test in Indian psychiatric patients. *Indian Journal of Applied Psychology,* 1972, 9, 65-67.

Vormeland, O. The Bender Gestalt Test as group test with young children. *Pedagogisk Forskning: Scandinavian Journal of Educational Research,* 1968, 1, 21-38.

Wade, T. C., & Baker, T. B. Opinions and use of psychological tests: A survey of clinical psychologists. *American Psychologist,* 1977, 32, 874-882.

Wade, T. C., Baker, T. B., Morton, T. L., & Baker, L. J. The status of psychological testing in clinical psychology: Relationships between test use and professional activities and orientations. *Journal of Personality Assessment,* 1978, 42, 3-10.

Wagner, E. E., & Evans, K. A. A brief note on the comparison of two graphomotor techniques in diagnosing brain damage. *Journal of Projective Techniques and Personality Assessment,* 1965, 30, 54.

Wagner, E. E., Klein, I., & Walter, T. Differentiation of brain damage among low IQ subjects with three projective techniques. *Journal of Personality Assessment,* 1978, 42, 49-55.

Wagner, E. E., & Murray, A. Bender-Gestalts of organic children: Accuracy of clinical judgment. *Journal of Projective Techniques and Personality Assessment,* 1969, 33, 240-242.

Wagner, E. E., & Schaff, J. E. Design reproduction with motor performance held constant. *Journal of Projective Techniques and Personality Assessment,* 1968, 32, 395-396.

Walker, M. N., & Streff, J. J. A perceptual program for classroom teachers: Some results. *Genetic Psychology Monographs,* 1973, 87, 253-288.

Wallbrown, F. H., Wallbrown, J. D., & Engin, A. E. The test-retest reliability of the Bender-Gestalt for first-grade children. *Perceptual and Motor Skills,* 1976, 42, 743-746.

Wallbrown, F. H., Wirth, E., & Engin, A. W. Some evidence relevant to Kagan's comments on the clinical interpretation of the Bender-Gestalt. *Journal of Clinical Psychology,* 1975, 37, 345-347.

Wallbrown, J. D., Engin, A. W., Wallbrown, F. H., & Blaha, J. The prediction of first grade achievement with selected perceptual-cognitive tests. *Psychology in the Schools*, 1975, *12*, 140-149.

Wallbrown, J. D., & Wallbrown, F. H. Further evidence concerning the validity of Kagan's comments on the clinical interpretations of the Bender-Gestalt. *Perceptual and Motor Skills*. 1975, *41*, 51-54.

Wallbrown, J. D., Wallbrown, F. H., & Engin, A. W. The validity of two clinical tests of visual-motor perception. *Journal of Clinical Psychology*, 1977, *33*, 491-495.

Watkins, J. M., & Watkins, D. A. Comparison of normal and emotionally disturbed children by the Plenk scoring system for the Bender-Gestalt. *Journal of Clinical Psychology*, 1975, *31*, 71-74.

Watson, C. G. The separation of NP hospital organics from schizophrenics with three visual motor screening tests. *Journal of Clinical Psychology*, 1968, *24*, 412-414.

Wechsler, D. A standardized memory scale for clinical use. *Journal of Psychology*, 1945, *19*, 87-95.

Wedell, K., & Horne, I. E. Some aspects of perceptuo-motor disability in five and a half year old children. *British Journal of Educational Psychology*, 1969, *39*, 174-182.

Weinstein, S., & Johnson, L. The Bender-Gestalt Test in differential diagnosis of temporal lobectomy and schizophrenia. *Perceptual and Motor Skills*, 1964, *18*, 813-820.

Weiss, A. A. Bender-Gestalt performance and concept formation. *Israel Annals of Psychiatry and Related Disciplines*, 1969, *7*, 76-81. (a)

Weiss, A. A. Directionality in four Bender-Gestalt figures. *Perceptual and Motor Skills*, 1969, *29*, 59-62. (b)

Weiss, A. A. Reproduction from memory and frequency of recall of Bender-Gestalt figures in non-clinical subjects of different ages. *Israel Annals of Psychiatry and Related Disciplines*, 1970, *8*, 143-145.

Weiss, A. A. Directionality in four Bender-Gestalt figures: II. *Perceptual and Motor Skills*, 1971, *32*, 412-414. (a)

Weiss, A. A. Incidence of rotations of Bender-Gestalt figures in three age groups of normal Israeli school children. *Perceptual and Motor Skills*, 1971, *32*, 691-694. (b)

Weiss, A. A. The influence of sheet positions on placements of Bender-Gestalt figures. *Israel Annals of Psychiatry and Related Disciplines*, 1971, *9*, 63-67. (c)

Weiss, A. A. Long-term psychodiagnostic follow-up: An avenue to validation of psychological tools. *Israel Annals of Psychiatry and Related Disciplines*, 1977, *15*, 33-40.

Werner, E. E., Simonian, K., & Smith, R. S. Reading achievement, language functioning and perceptual-motor development of ten and eleven year olds. *Perceptual and Motor Skills*, 1967, *25*, 409-420.

West, P. A., Hill, S. Y., & Robins, L. N. The Canter Background Interference Procedure (BIP): Effects of demographic variables on diagnosis. *Journal of Clinical Psychology*, 1977, *33*, 765-771.

White, R. B. Variations of Bender-Gestalt constructions and depression in adult psychiatric patients. *Perceptual and Motor Skills*, 1976, *42*, 221-222.

White, R. B., Jr., & McGraw, R. K. Note on the relationship between downward slant of Bender figures 1 & 2 and depression in adult psychiatric patients. *Perceptual and Motor Skills*, 1975, *40*, 152.

Wiener, G. The Bender Gestalt as a predictor of minimal neurological deficit in children eight to ten years old. *Journal of Nervous and Mental Diseases*, 1966, *143*, 275-280.

Wiener, G., Rider, U. R., Fischer, L. K., & Harper, P. A. Correlates of low birth weight: Psychological status at six to seven years of age. *Pediatrics*, 1965, *35*, 434-444.

Wiener, G., Rider, U. R., Oppel, W. C., & Harper, P. A. Correlates of low birth weight: Psychological status at eight to ten years of age. *Pediatric Research* 1968, *2*, 110-118.

Wikler, A., Dixon, J. F., & Parker, J. B. Brain function in problem children and controls: Psychometric, neurological, and electroencephalographic comparisons. *American Journal of Psychiatry*, 1970, *127*, 634-645.

Wildman, R. W., & Wildman, R. W. II. An investigation into the comparative validity of several diagnostic tests and test batteries. *Journal of Clinical Psychology*, 1975, *31*, 455-458.

Wise, J. H. Stick copying of designs by preschool and young school-age children. *Perceptual and Motor Skills*, 1968, *37*, 1159-1168.

Wohlford, P., & Flick, G. L. Sex-of-rater bias in clinical diagnosis of organic brain damage using the Bender-Gestalt and Memory-for-Designs tests. *Perceptual and Motor Skills*, 1969, *29*, 107-114.

Yulis, S. The relationship between the Canter Background Interference Procedure (BIP) and intelligence. *Journal of Clinical Psychology*, 1969, *25*, 405-406.

Yulis, S. Performance of normal and organic brain-damaged subjects on the Canter Background Interference Test as a function of drive. *Journal of Consulting and Clinical Psychology*, 1970, *34*, 184-188.

Zach, L., & Kaufman, J. The effect of verbal labeling on visual motor performance. *Journal of Learning Disabilities*, 1969, *2*, 218-222.

Zach, L., & Kaufman, J. How adequate is the concept of perceptual deficit for education? *Journal of Learning Disabilities*, 1972, *5*, 351-356.

Zuelzer, M. B., Stedman, J. M., & Adams, R. Koppitz Bender Gestalt scores in first grade children as related to ethnocultural background, socioeconomic class, and sex factors. *Journal of Consulting and Clinical Psychology*, 1976, *44*, 875-876.

AUTHOR INDEX

231

SUBJECT INDEX

A

Abience, 35, 36
Aboriginals, 26
Acting Out, 45, 51, 57, 58, 63
Adience, 35, 36
Adience-Abience Scale, 35, 36, 37, 38, 61
  and brain damage, 35
  meaning of, 35
  and psychopathology, 37
  and psychotherapy, 36
  rationale for, 35
  and reliability, 36, 38
  and schizophrenia, 36
  and sex, 37
  test factors, 35
  validity of, 38
Adolescence, 51, 52, 58, 172-173
  acting out, 51
  anxiety, 52
Adjustment, 32, 36, 48-53, 54, 56, 57, 58-61, 63
Age, *see* Maturation, 21-23, 34
Aged, and recall ability, 83-84, 123
  see also Organicity
Aggression, 56, 180
  see also Anti-social behavior, Hostility
Aging, 83-84, 113
Alcoholics, viii, 13, 78, 79, 194
  personality in, 59, 63, 79, 194
American College Entrance Test, 168
Ammons Full-Range Picture Vocabulary Test, 118
Anti-social behavior, 58, 180
Anxiety, viii, 46, 52-53, 57, 63, 194, 195
  reaction, 60, 116, 194, 195
  size of designs, 46, 194
Aphasia, 144

Aphasia Screening Test, 74
Arteriogram, 70
Association Phase: 61
Auditory-Visual Test, 152

B

Background Interference, 16-19, 53, 65-69, 80, 103-104, 112, 157, 201
Barron's Ego-Strength Scale, 50
Bean Bucket Game, 141
Bender-Gestalt Designs, Administration of, 7, 10-20
  association, 15, 181, 186
  elaboration, 15, 194, 195
  group, 16, 19, 201
  memory reproduction, 13, 19, 23, 39, 45, 46, 80-81, 99-100, 118-119, 158
  multiple choice, 10, 11, 30, 78, 140, 201
  oral descriptions, 15
  position of cards or paper, 11, 12, 14, 16, 97
  repeatedly copying designs, 53
  simplified designs, 29
  successive presentations, 15-16, 99
  tachistoscopic, viii, 12-13, 14, 45, 78
Bender-Gestalt, designs
  Design A, 40, 66, 85, 88, 94, 130, 138, 180, 181, 197
  Design 1, 40, 46, 85, 130, 138, 171, 177, 180, 186, 191, 194
  Design 2, 39, 40, 46, 52, 85, 130, 138, 171, 177, 180, 191, 194
  Design 3, 29, 39, 40, 41, 42, 80, 85, 88, 94, 180, 191, 194
  Design 4, 25, 38, 40, 41, 42, 80, 85, 94, 130, 138, 180, 181, 186, 194, 197

239